Leading for Change Through Whole-School Social-Emotional Learning

Strategies to Build a Positive School Culture

Jennifer E. Rogers

FOR INFORMATION:

CORWIN
A SAGE Company
2455 Teller Road
Thousand Oaks, California 91320
(800) 233-9936
www.corwin.com

SAGE Publications Ltd.
1 Oliver's Yard
55 City Road
London EC1Y 1SP
United Kingdom

SAGE Publications India Pvt. Ltd.
B 1/I 1 Mohan Cooperative Industrial Area
Mathura Road, New Delhi 110 044
India

SAGE Publications Asia-Pacific Pte. Ltd.
18 Cross Street #10-10/11/12
China Square Central
Singapore 048423

Program Director: Jessica Allan
Content Development Editor: Lucas Schleicher
Senior Editorial Assistant: Mia Rodriguez
Production Editor: Amy Schroller
Copy Editor: Cate Huisman
Typesetter: Hurix Digital
Proofreader: Lawrence W. Baker
Indexer: Sheila Bodell
Cover Designer: Candice Harman
Marketing Manager: Deena Meyer

Printed in the United States of America

Names: Rogers, Jennifer E., author.

Title: Leading for change through whole-school social-emotional learning : strategies to build a positive school culture / Jennifer E. Rogers.

Description: First edition. | Thousand Oaks, CA : Corwin, A SAGE Company, [2019] | Includes bibliographical references and index.

Identifiers: LCCN 2018054569 | ISBN 9781544352985 (pbk. : alk. paper)

Subjects: LCSH: Affective education. | Social learning. | Emotional intelligence—Study and teaching. | School management and organization. | School improvement programs.

Classification: LCC LB1072 .R66 2019 | DDC 370.15/34—dc23 LC record available at https://lccn.loc.gov/2018054569

This book is printed on acid-free paper.

SUSTAINABLE FORESTRY INITIATIVE
Certified Chain of Custody
Promoting Sustainable Forestry
www.sfiprogram.org
SFI-01268

SFI label applies to text stock

19 20 21 22 23 10 9 8 7 6 5 4 3 2 1

Contents

Preface

*L*eading for Change Through Whole-School Social-Emotional Learning: Strategies to Build a Positive School Culture is designed for educators and stakeholders who are engaged in systems change work in their local schools and districts. Social-emotional learning (SEL) is being adopted by schools and districts across the country. Many educators understand *why* it is important to use evidence-based practices to improve the lives and educational outcomes for students. However, they struggle with *how* to introduce and integrate programs and processes into their school culture in a systemic way.

As educators, we are beginning to get a better appreciation and understanding for SEL; however, we are also confronting the difficulty of adding "one more thing" to the educational agenda. In addition, we are challenged with the increase in students who require more intervention due to a variety of factors, some of which are identified in the *Why Now?* section of this book. But these challenges give us cause for including systemic prevention for all students. As we face more complex issues in our society, we see more complex issues in our classrooms. Our teachers and staff need strategies to create an environment where students can learn despite some of the challenges they may face. Individuals, schools, and systems pay the price for confronting these difficulties day after day without having the tools to navigate them. We need to improve our school climates systemically. That begins with looking within at our individual skills and beliefs. SEL provides skills and strategies to be resilient in the face of hardship, to communicate with others when we need help, to collaborate with our staff to come up with the best action plan, and to develop self-care skills to ensure that our educators are not burning out and leaving the profession. It is crucial to include SEL in our educational systems, for all of us.

I have spent the last 20-plus years in various roles in education. I worked as a substitute teacher, in a before- and after-school care program, as a practicum student, in numerous internships at all levels (elementary, middle, high), and as a counselor, researcher, counselor educator, administrator, and consultant. I have worked with schools in four different states across the country. These experiences have taught me that we need to do more to support school personnel to create school environments that are positive and productive. We need to provide them with tools and strategies that will help them make their vision into reality: strategies that can be adopted by individuals and groups, teachers, administrators, counselors, and all other school personnel. Educators need tools to engage in a process that is unique to their school or district but is rooted in evidence and experience. This book is designed to help educators and change agents meet the challenges of implementation of SEL in their environments. The purpose is to help others learn from my experiences in development, implementation, training, coaching, and planning for systems change. I also honor my professional responsibility as a school counselor and counselor educator to advocate for systems change that will serve the students, faculty, and staff that we entrust with our children.

The purpose of this book is to help educators understand the process of integrating SEL into their curriculums, using data to inform (not overwhelm), and using a systems lens to design programming to fit their school needs. It addresses the topics that many educators struggle with when they begin to learn about and consider development and implementation of an SEL program. This book contains worksheets that are developed from my research on advocacy, SEL, implementation science, and systems change. Each chapter contains strategies from practitioners in the field, resources, and reflection questions. At the end of the book, there is an appendix that includes checklists, a rubric, and sample data sources such as exit tickets for the educators to use in their work.

This book is designed for the "change agent." (The change agent will be addressed directly in the following pages.) Because this is a personal and unique experience that the change agent will be working through, I address the change agent directly. Anyone who is involved in the educational system can be a change agent. Most likely, change agents are administrators, student or pupil support teachers and coaches, superintendents, directors, special education staff, counselors, school psychologists, and teachers. Advocates of system change are varied depending on the environment. For some schools, change happens at a grassroots level with a few teachers taking the lead. In other districts, it is the superintendent who listens to the community and wants to integrate SEL into the system. Sometimes it is the special education department that is overwhelmed by the number of students who qualify for services and is looking to add more prevention before these students require targeted interventions. It may be school counselors who understand the need for everyone to participate to attain positive outcomes. It can be a school psychologist who looks at the data and determines that implementation should be a priority, or a principal who wants an entire building to understand the strategies to engage in SEL work and forms a work group to do so. Families and community members who have heard about SEL and want to know what it can look like in a school may advocate for this work. The entry point (the who) may vary. But the goal is for change agents, whatever their titles, to find the book helpful in moving their schools forward.

Readers can use this book to provide a framework to begin their own implementation. It provides a practical context in which to place all the terminology. There is a discussion of the current research on SEL and systems change. The resource section at the end of each chapter is for the reader to discover other sources of information that might be of use when designing trainings, educating stakeholders, or embedding strategies. At the end of each chapter, there are questions for change agents and their teams to prompt reflection and to consider when implementing SEL strategies and programs. Every chapter contains multiple case examples from the field. The identifying details have been changed to maintain the confidentiality of the individuals and schools. The purpose is to share the author's real-world experience with the reader. There are also selected excerpts from other coaches, administrators, teachers, and counselors who work in schools across the country. School teams can use the information provided to design professional development. Readers can track their progress through the sample checklist. The worksheets can be used to collect evidence of the decision-making process that schools have used during implementation.

This book is designed to build the capacity of the change agent and all other stakeholders in the school system. As I have worked with and talked to educators around the country, I understand that there is not just one method for schools to be successful. We need to understand that each environment has different challenges and strengths. Schools who adopt lockstep implementation have a difficult time keeping up with the intervention, especially if they have a change in leadership. But if schools consider their specific school culture, learn from implementation science, develop their own strategies, start with prevention (Tier 1), collect data that is usable, reflect on their learning, empower their stakeholders to participate in the process, and check on the effect to the system, they can build a generation of students who benefit from strong social and emotional skills. Improving these skills will help them be successful in college and careers, relationships with their partners, employment, and eventually in raising their own children. We have the power to help, to improve, to change, to better the lives of children and youth, but we need all the best strategies to help us. This book will help you develop your strategies.

Enjoy the journey, change agent, we need you!

Acknowledgments

Corwin gratefully acknowledges the contributions of the following reviewers:

Debbie Arakaki
Curriculum Coordinator/Coach
Kalihi Uka Elementary School
Honolulu, HI

Gloria Avolio, PhD
School Counselor
Hillsborough County Public Schools
Tampa, FL

Carol Campbell
Principal
Grant High School
Portland, OR

Georgina Castilleja
Middle School Principal
Houston Independent School District
Houston, TX

Laura Schaffer Metcalfe
Education Director
Mesa Community College High School Transition Programs
Mesa, AZ

Derek R. Peil
Language Arts Teacher, K-5 Summer Program Administrator, and Coach
Fremont County School District #1
Lander, WY

Bonnie Tryon, EdD
Mentor/Coach
Cobleskill, NY

Rosemarie Young, EdD
Chair, Graduate Advanced Programs
Bellarmine University
Louisville, KY

About the Author

Jennifer E. Rogers is the founder of Rogers Training Solutions, LLC. She works with educational stakeholders on developing tools and strategies to increase positive student outcomes. Rogers Training Solutions, LLC, provides consulting, professional development, workshops, coaching, and one-on-one leadership support for individuals and organizations exploring social, emotional, and behavioral interventions in school environments.

Dr. Rogers has shown a strong commitment to children and adolescents and their families for over 20 years. She has worked with school districts across the country as a school counselor, researcher, administrator, coach trainer, and consultant. Schools benefit from her experience as a licensed professional counselor and her training as a counselor educator to create programs to meet the social, emotional, and behavioral needs for students.

She has experience with implementing and measuring the impact of interventions in counseling, prevention, and early intervention. She has advocated for, written about, researched, and implemented districtwide SEL programs. She has created interventions, trained staff, used data to support implementations, and worked to integrate SEL into curriculums; and has delivered professional presentations on childhood trauma and resiliency, mental health issues, relationship strategies, proactive classroom management, toxic stress, parenting strategies, mindfulness, and self-care.

Dr. Rogers's professional goals align with her core mission to make SEL an integral part of education for all students. To reach this goal, her belief is that we must work to support systemic change and create a common understanding among all stakeholders of the benefits of SEL to positive school culture.

This book is dedicated to the change agents who strive to work on behalf of our youth.

It is dedicated to the educators I have worked alongside.

It is dedicated to the students that I have had the privilege to know.

But most of all, this book is dedicated to my beloved family: Wally, Jackson, and Brynn. Thank you for standing by me.

Introduction

Using Social-Emotional Learning to Make Your School More Positive and Productive

> *The greatest hope for traumatized, abused, and neglected children is to receive a good education in schools where they are seen and known, where they learn to regulate themselves, and where they can develop a sense of agency. At their best, schools can function as islands of safety in a chaotic world.*
>
> **—Bessel Van Der Kolk**

Is your school an "island of safety"? Do you have days that you leave the school building so exhausted that even your hair hurts? Do you have the same level of excitement for a three-day weekend as your birthday or your best friend coming to town? Have you ever walked into a staff break room and walked right back out because you can't stand the constant complaining? Do you find yourself becoming more jaded with the thought that kids are getting worse and their parents don't care or care too much? Do you find yourself asking, Is the stress worth it?

If you have times that you feel this way, you are not alone. K–12 teachers in the United States tend to become less engaged at work after their first year, according to a Gallup poll (Lopez & Sidhu, 2013). The Gallup poll categorizes people in three ways: engaged, not engaged, or actively disengaged. Gallup defines engaged workers as those who are "deeply involved in and enthusiastic about their work and actively contributing to their organization" and actively disengaged workers as "emotionally disconnected from their work and workplace, and these workers jeopardize the performance of their teams" (Harter & Blacksmith, 2012, p. 3). These results are based on phone interviews conducted with a random sample of 151,284 adults, including 7,265 K–12 teachers, between January and December 2012. According to a report from the Robert Wood Johnson Foundation and Penn State called "Teacher Stress and Health: Effects on Teachers, Students, and Schools" (Greenberg, Brown, & Abenavoli, 2016), there are four main sources of teacher stress. The first source is the overall school organization, which includes such things as poor leadership, unhealthy school climate, and lack of support among colleagues. The second source is job demands that are increased with high-stakes testing, high-need students, and demanding parents. The third source is having minimal work resources that limit the teacher's ability to make decisions. The fourth source of stress is an inability to manage work pressures and create positive classroom environments.

One of the solutions that schools and districts can use is investing in SEL practices that result in positive student outcomes and happier and healthier teachers. SEL can be the key to not only helping improve student social and emotional competencies but also increasing teachers' job satisfaction: "These findings support other studies showing that teachers trained and supported in implementing SEL programs have lower job-related anxiety and depression, higher quality classroom interactions with students, greater teacher engagement, and greater perceived job control" (Greenberg et al., 2016, p. 8).

Investing in this type of change is not easy. It requires educators and stakeholders to think differently about some of their challenges in schools. We must learn different skills and strategies for approaching the work of implementation. The purpose of this book is to provide immediate ideas and strategies for adults to make their lives and the lives of children better. The intent is to help those who feel stuck, without a champion or someone to help them, and give them ways to work through some of their daily challenges. This book is addressed to you, the change agent. "You" can be one person in a school, a group, a leadership team, or an entire staff. The strategies I suggest are for systemic and personal change for educators and other stakeholders to improve the overall school culture as well as the social, emotional, and behavioral skills of youth in and out of the school environment.

What Does Social-Emotional Learning Have to Do With Systems Change?

If we want to have real lasting success in creating a better school environment, where social and emotional skills are demonstrated by students and adults, we must first become leaders and advocates of system change. Your experiences and thoughts about what changes need to happen are vital to create movement toward change. You have the power to work with others to help make things better at your school.

SEL is focused on developing self-awareness, self-management, social awareness, relationship skills, and responsible decision-making skills. The ultimate goal is to improve school environments, where students and staff feel safe and connected to the school and to each other. There are many benefits from this type of change. As we know,

> If students feel more secure in their belonging in school, they may approach others in the academic environment more and with more positive attitudes, building better relationships, reinforcing their feelings of belonging, and laying the groundwork for later academic success. (Yeager & Walton, 2011, p. 275)

This type of change requires a systems lens that looks at the school environment, the people, the procedures, and the culture.

Systems change takes a broader view to determine what changes can be made to impact our day-to-day lives in a positive way. Individuals who have spent time in school systems for a long time can tell you about the many different changes that they have experienced in education over the years and how those changes have made a change to the entire system, for better and for worse.

One large change that you may have experienced is the influx of new teachers. The teacher workforce is changing. In the 2011–12 school year, 45 percent of the teaching force (almost half) had 10 or fewer years of experience (Ingersoll, Merrill, & Stuckey, 2014). The odds of the teachers in your school being new or fairly new to the profession are high. That means in many school buildings you are working with people who have very little experience. They are missing experience that can be so valuable to building the networks of support for new teachers.

Maintaining consistency in a building is a challenge, as an average of 41 percent of new teachers leave the field within the first five years (Ingersoll et al., 2014) . The reason most often reported for leaving their teaching career is dissatisfaction. They report being dissatisfied with school and working conditions such as salaries, classroom resources, student misbehavior, accountability, opportunities for development, input into decision making, and school leadership (Ingersoll et al., 2014).

Recently, schools have increased their focus on equity and inclusion. School systems have been challenged by a requirement to create environments where each child has an equitable opportunity to learn (Berg, Osher, Moroney, & Yoder, 2017). Equity includes equitable opportunities to learn, access to resources that are differentiated for everyone's needs, and ensuring equitable outcomes for every student regardless of status (Berg et al., 2017). Systemic issues can impact the amount and type of services students receive. SEL interventions can address equity through whole-school prevention, where all students are encouraged to learn and practice social and emotional skills as part of their education.

Whether you are an administrator, a teacher, a parent, a counselor, or any other school professional, you must not wait to work toward making change. Becoming a force of change is a mindset. You are the owner of your experience in education. Your expertise can help your system improve. Finding out what other people in the system think is where you begin to quantify and understand the issue. It can be a messy and difficult road, because any change can be difficult. It is my hope that my struggles and hard-earned understandings may ease the path for others. It will require focus on the vision, leadership and collaboration, and ability to see a problem from multiple perspectives. Rather than dwell on the difficulty, focus instead on the mission to help make the lives of children—and the people who teach them—better.

Fair Warning: The Challenge of Systems Change

Systems change is not a new discussion for schools. Many educators, policy makers, parents, and citizens see the need for transformation in the schools. This is especially true when changing school culture to be more positive and less punitive, creating an environment that values and teaches SEL; that is inclusive of all cultural, racial, and ethnic backgrounds; and that celebrates diversity. And while there are many schools and districts that are tackling this difficult task, we are still struggling.

It requires a tremendous effort from all stakeholders to make systems change work. As educators, we hope to adopt practices that are high quality and evidence based. Thomas Kane, a Harvard economist, captured some of our issues with systems change in an article titled, "Shooting Bottle Rockets at the Moon: Overcoming the Legacy of Incremental Educational Reform" (2014). He explains that we fail to calculate the thrust needed to get these well-intentioned reforms off the ground. And while the proposals may be directionally correct, they fail. Kane posits that is because we have not provided reasonable expectations about the magnitude of the change required to meet our educational goals. "When we fail to right-size our reform efforts, we breed a sense of futility among teachers, parents, and policymakers" (Kane, 2014, p. 1). This frustration is immediately evident for those who attempt systems change. This can be termed "initiative fatigue" and comes along with direct or indirect resistance to any well-meaning change efforts. The efforts of introducing SEL can be diluted by the other programs that cover similar ground such as bullying prevention, health initiatives, violence prevention, and school safety.

Researchers have found adopting prevention interventions to be challenging for schools and districts. In 2011, Aber, Brown, Jones, Berg, and Torrente discussed five challenges that research-based prevention interventions must address if these interventions are to use research effectively to lead to improvements in the strength and scale of mental, emotional, and behavioral health of children.

1. The first challenge is in the difference between faith-based and evidence-based training and development. The beliefs and attitudes of practitioners (teachers)

and the relation of these beliefs and attitudes to teachers' well-established preferences for specific forms of helping behaviors are often obstacles to the adoption and scale-up of evidence-based approaches.

2. The second challenge is changing teachers' mindsets so they focus on "essential ingredients" rather than brands. Educators can be sold that one curriculum or packaged program can meet all their needs. But it is more important for them to focus on the components and competencies that are essential ingredients to the change process.

3. The third challenge is in translating what works under stringent research conditions to what works in the real world. This includes how we scale up or grow and sustain the intervention.

4. The fourth challenge is in moving from innovative programs to systems and policies that enable the values and political conflicts of mental health promotion and SEL to be effectively addressed.

5. And the fifth challenge is "how to emerge from a narrow, timid approach to a broader, bolder approach to transform not only practice but also the attitudes, beliefs, values, and policies that constrain the use of science to transform the lives of children." (Aber et al., 2011, pp. 418–420)

Changing and sustaining school culture can require an examination and transformation of the infrastructure, norms, and policies within school environments as well. The terms *culture* and *climate* are often used interchangeably, but there is an important distinction. A school's culture is like its personality, while the climate is more like an attitude (Gruenert, 2008). It is much easier to change one's attitude than one's personality. This makes changing culture an even larger, although necessary, challenge. To shape a new culture, change agents and school leaders must assess the climate first to determine how problematic issues became rooted in the culture (Gruenert, 2008).

This means that schools must confront their current and prevalent beliefs, norms, and procedures with a new lens. And while we have many great tools for innovations and recommendations for change, neglecting the environmental factors and complexity can make these tools ineffective despite evidence of a need to use them and the positive outcomes they have produced in other environments.

The focus must be on the context of the culture and the process of the intervention and its effects on the system. SEL adoption is dependent on the local context. One of the challenges is to determine the school's and the community's tolerance for change and the speed at which these changes are acceptable. Practitioners and experts should collaborate as they evaluate the changes that are made within the school environment. This collaboration will allow for outcomes to be scaled up and duplicated in other systems.

We need to do more to support school personnel to create school environments that are positive and productive. We need to provide them with the tools and strategies that will help them make their vision a reality. This includes strategies to embed SEL in the fabric of the school culture—strategies that can be adopted by individuals and groups, teachers, administrators, counselors, and all other school personnel. Educators need the tools to engage in a process that is unique to their school or district but is rooted in evidence and experience. This resource is designed to help educators and change agents meet the challenges of implementation of SEL in their environments.

Systems change can be challenging and demanding on the system, but it can be especially challenging for individuals. It is important for individuals involved in systems change to have a realistic sense of their personal strengths and limitations. Ratts and Chen-Hayes (2007) recommended that individuals considering being systems change agents should think through the possible positive and negative outcomes for themselves and the system. This is the only way to prepare for the ups and downs of systems change work.

Change agents should begin with an understanding of group behavior and motivations for change to promote healthy systems. The use of social, emotional, or behavioral interventions will not replace the need for traditional education reform but instead should work to augment it, so reforms are more effective and acceptable. Change agents will often look to interventions such as specific curriculums or processes to help improve the behaviors of students. But it is important to understand "how they interact with recursive processes already present in the schools, such as the quality of students' developing relationships with peers and teachers, their beliefs about their ability, and their acquisition of academic knowledge" (Yeager & Walton, 2011, p. 275).

SEL is systems change. When implementing SEL for the whole school, it will impact the system in unforeseen ways. Schools I have worked with have looked at the way their classrooms are arranged, the books they read, the way they conduct assemblies or whole-school meetings, their discipline procedure, and the way that students and adults are expected to solve problems. And beyond the school day, the way educators work with parents and the community can also be impacted by introducing SEL practices.

This book is designed for educators who are engaged in systems change work in their local schools and districts. SEL is being adopted by schools and districts across the country. This book was developed from research on advocacy, SEL, implementation science, and systems change.

In the first chapter, the book addresses the question, Why now? The mental health of our students, teacher burnout and stress, adverse childhood experiences, prevention, and outcomes are just the beginning of the discussion for why a school or district would take on SEL. Chapter 2 dives into SEL with a look at the research, evidence, and practices. The next ten chapters break down the strategies of SEL:

1. Identify your why.

2. Adopt a framework.

3. Do your detective work—data collection and data analysis.

4. Work with others to develop a vision to guide change.

5. Understand the politics of your workplace.

6. Develop an action plan for implementation.

7. Invest in your infrastructure.

8. Plan for resistance to change.

9. Assess your outcomes.

10. Fill in the gaps of your foundation.

Chapter 13 is the conclusion of the book, and at the end there are additional resources for practitioners to adopt for their own systems change work. After each chapter, there are resources, reflection questions, and a quotation from a change agent, called Practitioner's Voice.

Why Now?

Schools are challenged with students exhibiting mental health issues, adverse childhood experiences (ACEs), and escalated behavior in the classroom. Teacher burnout and stress can result from feeling hopeless in the face of some of these issues. Now is the time to focus on prevention and outcomes. There are programs created to improve student behavior and social-emotional skills that benefit teachers, staff, and systems. Here is one example of why a school or district would take on social-emotional learning (SEL).

Mental Health of Our Students

Students like Kenny are not unusual in our schools and communities. According to the National Alliance on Mental Illness (NAMI, 2016), one in five children ages 13–18 have or will have a serious mental illness. Attention deficit hyperactivity disorder (ADHD)

"That Student"

A Case Study

Kenny was a fifth-grade boy who looked like he belonged in ninth grade. He was the tallest and biggest boy in the school. He arrived at the end of his fourth-grade year and immediately got the attention of the principal, counselor, and dean. His fifth-grade teacher, Ms. Abrams, had difficulty managing her class with his constant disruptions. Kenny would try to get the other students to laugh by blurting inappropriate things. He seemed to have no filter and would use inappropriate language and put down classmates when he felt "dissed."

After many months of learning about Kenny's background and finally receiving his cumulative folder, school staff found that Kenny had been in special education at his last school. Kenny had both academic and behavioral goals in his IEP. He was diagnosed with ADHD and has been on and off medication since he was in second grade.

In communications with the family, the staff discovered that Kenny had many ACEs. His parents were divorced, and he had not seen his mother in years due to her substance abuse issues. He had witnessed his father hit his mother when he was younger and was often left home alone while his father worked. Recently, his father's girlfriend had gotten pregnant.

Kenny's behavior escalated beyond the verbal issues. He had meltdowns that his teacher reported "came from out of the blue." This included yelling, throwing things, hitting, and shoving desks and students as he walked out the classroom door when he was sent to the office. Kenny was suspended due to safety concerns.

The principal, counselor, behavioral intervention specialist, special education teacher, fifth-grade teacher, and dean tried the following interventions: wiggle seat, reinforcement for good behavior, behavior chart, special seat at lunch, escort to special events like assemblies, time out tickets, and an adult mentor.

Ms. Abrams reported having a great deal of stress this school year. She has spoken about her lack of sleep and guilt about her lack of attention to the other students in her class. She has taken sick days because of "incessant flu-like symptoms." At the spring break, she told the principal that she would need to remove herself from the classroom for the rest of the year. The team spent many hours on this one student.

occurs in about 5 percent of children (NAMI, 2016), and many schools are contending with anxiety and depression, even among students in elementary school. Mental health issues can affect the student socially, emotionally, and behaviorally. Students who have difficulty developing and maintaining relationships with their peers may be at a greater risk for anxiety, behavioral and mood disorders, substance abuse, and delinquency as teenagers. Ninety percent of those who committed suicide had an underlying mental illness (NAMI, 2017).

Schools work with students who have mental health issues and are undiagnosed and with those who are diagnosed but are not receiving care. Lack of care can be due to many factors including lack of access, being underinsured, or other problems. Students with mental health issues and learning disorders are twice as likely as students without such issues to be suspended, expelled, referred to law enforcement, or be involved in a school-related arrest (National Center for Education Statistics, 2013–14). Students who receive severe discipline consequences in school are more likely to drop out. The overall school dropout rate is 7 percent, but for students who qualify with emotional disturbances under the Individuals with Disabilities Education Act (IDEA), it is 38.7 percent (Snyder & Dillow, 2015).

Adverse Childhood Experiences

Adverse childhood experiences or ACEs is becoming a more commonly understood term within school districts. The Centers for Disease Control and Prevention and Kaiser Permanente worked together in one of the largest studies of childhood abuse and neglect and their effects on lifelong health and well-being. In 1998, the study was published; it was based on the results of a standardized questionnaire that was sent out to almost 18,000 adults during a two-year period. It was found that more than half of respondents reported at least one category of childhood exposure to sexual, physical, or psychological abuse and neglect, and one-fourth reported more than two (Felitti et al., 1998). The ACEs were categorized as 10 types of childhood trauma: physical abuse, sexual abuse, emotional abuse, physical neglect, emotional neglect, mother treated violently, household substance abuse, household mental illness, parental separation or divorce, and incarcerated household member. Researchers found that adults with ACEs had an increased rate of cancer, alcoholism, heart disease, depression, and other negative health outcomes (Felitti et al., 1998). For students who have experienced trauma, there are effects not only to their mental health but also to their academic and educational behavior outcomes (Centers for Disease Control and Prevention, 2018).

Students who have a history of ACEs can exhibit some of the signs of trauma during the school day. Students may exhibit externalizing behaviors, such as being aggressive to people or things, argumentative, or noncompliant on a regular basis. Or they may exhibit internalizing behaviors such as avoidance or withdrawal from social situations, not standing up for themselves, and generally not interacting with their peers. Teachers will see these types of behaviors regularly in classes, and it is difficult for them to understand the cause of the behavior. It can be a temporary situation, like a move or a new sibling. It can be developmental. It is easier to pick out the students who are at risk when they regularly exhibit externalizing behaviors. I often tell teachers that we are lucky because at least we know that something is going on with those students. Flipping the desk over or shouting at the teacher is a cry for help. Whereas, the students who don't overtly communicate their feelings and internalize their adverse experiences can be difficult to help. We don't know if these students are just shy, reserved, or perhaps introverted. Or are they suffering silently?

The Changing Dynamics of Our Classrooms

In many schools I have worked with, there are one or more students, like Kenny, who are labeled "a challenge." There are times when we know that something is not working, but it is difficult to put our finger on what can be done to solve the issue. We may struggle to put together a plan that works, not just for Kenny but for all the students.

In 2018, the National Educators Association wrote an article about the "10 Challenges Facing Public Education Today" (Litvinov, Alvarez, Long, & Walker, 2018). Three of those challenges directly affect the mental health of our students. The first is school safety. Students are worried that a shooting could happen at their school. Teachers who are on the front lines of school shootings and are responsible for the lives of the students can be impacted by this fear. The fear of shootings appears on a regular basis as we prepare our students for active shooter drills, arm personnel, and invest in bulletproof backpacks and shatterproof glass. The second trend is the high levels of anxiety among students of all ages due to many factors, including social pressures, testing pressures, college entrance pressures, and social media pressures. The third challenge is making a change from "zero tolerance" discipline policies, which were damaging to students who were suspended or expelled, to policies focused on teaching them new skills and strategies to manage their emotions (Litvinov et al., 2018).

These dynamics exist and can inhibit the ability of schools to function in a productive manner. Behavioral issues in the school setting can wreak havoc on the classroom learning and well-being of the staff and students. There may be an uptick in challenging behaviors, mental health issues, teachers' inability or unwillingness to work with specific students, complaints of too many students, and recognition that the population and needs of kids and families have changed over the years.

Without understanding the changing dynamics in our classrooms, stakeholders are often left looking at the one or two or twelve students who exhibit challenging behaviors. This misunderstanding causes undue stress for all parties. The task of the change agent is to look beyond one student or one type of student and try to uncover the dynamics that trigger these challenging behaviors.

Burnout and Stress of Teachers

Burnout: What Is It and Do I Have It?

The impact of these challenging behaviors is evidenced in teacher stress, burnout, and sometimes educators leaving the profession. The daily stressors of the life of a teacher can impact performance. In fact, coping with negative emotions toward their students can be a major stressor for teachers that impacts their ability do the complex work of teaching. Experiences of anger (when students are not performing expected behaviors) may lead to teachers engaging in emotional labor to suppress the anger, which can correlate to the teachers' emotional exhaustion (Keller, Chang, Becker, Goetz, & Frenzel, 2014). Anyone who has had to suppress emotions for a long period of time will experience negative impacts. Some of the negative consequences include the physical health of teacher, poor teacher performance, poor student outcomes, teacher turnover, student achievement declines, and inequity in educational access (Greenberg, Brown, & Abenavoli, 2016).

The signs of burnout can include being physically depleted; isolating oneself from friends, family, and colleagues; negative self-talk, being overly critical about work; overreacting; and inability to recognize the resources around them. It should be a priority to be aware and to note when and how teachers openly receive support. Teacher burnout has been recognized as a serious occupational issue. Some of the outcomes of burnout are exhaustion, cynicism toward teaching and education, and poor interactions with students and colleagues (Pietarinen, Pyhalto, Soini, & Salmela-Aro, 2013). Burnout is a factor that affects teacher performance. A recent search of Google Scholar listed over 52,000 citations that referenced teacher burnout.

Burnout can be compounded when there is a lack of social support (Pietarinen et al., 2013). Teachers who feel that they are struggling with the behaviors in their classes on top of the academic and curriculum demands can be isolated, because they may feel that they "should" be able to handle their class. I have seen this particularly in schools where there is competitiveness among teachers or where an evaluation system makes the teachers feel pressured to project the picture of a class with no problems.

Teachers who feel this pressure may withdraw from getting help or support:

When the pattern of social relationships is such that many teachers are disconnected from the flow of resources in their school, that school's ability to achieve its goals may be hindered. Moreover, teachers can only benefit from the resources that are available in their school's network, and a lack of valuable resources or an abundance of less desired or undesired resources may also constrain a school's capacity for improvement. (Moolenaar, 2012, p. 11)

While it may be easy to say to a teacher, "Here are these resources, why aren't you using them," there may be underlying reasons why teachers do not feel able to access other teachers, coaches, or administration for help.

Secondary Trauma in the Schools: How What You Experience Secondhand Affects You

If you have worked with children for any length of time, you have probably heard horror stories: stories of neglect, abuse, and trauma; stories that cause you to bring extra snacks to school because you know a child is not eating enough; and stories that make you cry, wondering if the children you work with during the day are safe at night. School provides continuity and comfort for many students. When school is not in session some students are denied regular meals, warm buildings, or adults who pay attention to them. It is likely that kids in these stories act out prior to any break in the regular school schedule. And as mandated reporters, those of us in education have a personal responsibility to report when abuse is observed or suspected.

This worry, concern, and disruption can be difficult for those in education to manage. And in some cases, it can cause compassion fatigue, burnout, or even secondary trauma. According to the National Child Traumatic Stress Network (www.nctsn.org), "Secondary traumatic stress is the emotional duress that results when an individual hears about the firsthand trauma experiences of another" (National Child Traumatic Stress Network, 2018).

While much of the information about secondary trauma is geared toward helping professionals (counselors, case workers, social workers, therapists), it is my experience that teachers are also impacted by secondary trauma. Teachers see the impact of the student who doesn't come to school properly dressed for the weather on a regular basis. They get to hear the stories that keep them up at night. They get to smell the child who does not bathe. And they get to experience the student's reactions to the trauma in their classrooms.

You may have also experienced reporting abuse and seeing nothing change. You may have had uncomfortable conversations with parents or caregivers about the student. You may have had to use your own resources to help the student pay for food, for supplies, or to go on a class field trip. These experiences can build up and make you feel ineffective and lead to compassion fatigue. Compassion fatigue is feeling tired from caring.

Stress and Teacher Support Through SEL

Burnout is normal, and reducing burnout symptoms requires adopting strategies and fostering the acceptability of teachers reaching out for help. Social interactions play a big part in the school community. Negative interactions contribute to burnout. Social support is thought to mediate stress among teachers (Walker, 1997). "This support will be best accepted when it comes from colleagues that face similar problems and can understand the peculiarities and challenges of the teaching profession" (Tatar, 2009, p. 121).

As a change agent, you can improve the chances that teachers will get help in your school. Tartar (2009) interviewed 281 teachers in 16 schools about the factors related to getting help at school. There are seven factors that facilitate teachers getting assistance. Two of them are especially important in the work of SEL implementation: (1) Educators must know what support is available for them, and (2) educators must be given time to receive the support. In my work, there is not a bigger stated obstacle to SEL implementation than a lack of time. Prioritizing SEL means that administration provides not only the training but also the time for teachers to get help to implement it. Another reason teachers seek help is the creation of a process to solve their problems that is effective and practical (Tatar, 2009). This is something I have often seen in SEL intervention. The curriculum is not explicitly connected to the problem that teachers need to solve.

For teachers to reach out for support, the change agent must create positive relationships. These relationships can lead to benefits not only for the teacher or staff member but for the students. Students will benefit from decreasing burnout among teachers. It has been found that teacher stress can be contagious for some students. In a 2016 study about stress contagion, it was found that teachers' occupational stress is linked to students' physiological stress regulation. The higher levels of classroom teacher burnout significantly predicted the elevation in morning cortisol (a stress hormone) in their students (Oberle & Schonert-Reichl, 2016).

Positive relationship skills can be learned and reinforced when schools practice SEL strategies. When teachers are experiencing stress, they will reach out for help only if schools provide the conditions where they feel supported in getting help. Those conditions can be created in systems that adopt SEL practices. When teachers and students regularly use social and emotional competencies, everyone benefits.

Prevention

The *whys* that are listed here—mental health, ACES, behavioral challenges, burnout, and stress of teachers—are some of the reasons to engage in SEL interventions. You may (and should) have your own reasons to propel you to seek something better. The evidence base for prevention efforts and SEL outcomes has grown exponentially. We can no longer deny the power of this work to affect our staff and students.

Many schools have adopted a continuum-of-care approach. This includes the use of a multitiered system of support or MTSS framework to identify students in need and intervene with them. MTSS includes three levels or tiers of intervention. The first tier is universal (prevention) and provides learning and practice for all students. The second tier (selective) is employed for students who require more direct and individualized attention. Students are often selected for the second tier based on universal screening or adult referral. And the third tier (targeted) includes students who need more intensive support. There are two major areas, in my experience, in which MTSS is lacking in some school systems. The first is that MTSS is often in the academic or instructional realm only, and the second is having a system for tiers 2 and 3 but not a solid prevention program that uses data-based decision making, problem solving, and fidelity of implementation as a core practice of the MTSS process.

Prevention includes adopting practices to affect the well-being of students, staff, and parents/families before a major problem arises. Implementing preventative measures is the first step in cultivating a positive school culture. Preventative measures involve the whole school—adults and students: all hands on deck for cultivating social and emotional health. The research on the importance of prevention has been ongoing for years and is conclusive. Back in 1990, Lewis, Battistich, & Schaps found that narrow, problem-focused prevention efforts were inadequate in addressing the socialization needs of children and adolescents. This research suggested that there were seven characteristics of effective school-based prevention programs.

1. The first was that programs should have a theoretical basis that recognized that problem behaviors were multiply determined. There was not one variable that caused issues within the schools, which meant there was not only one solution to solve them.

2. The second characteristic was that school-based prevention should be directed at influencing a positive, interpersonal climate that facilitates socialization. It was important not only to concentrate on the individual's social skills but also on the school environment characteristics.

3. The third characteristic was promotion of positive influences on social development. The study found that programs of this kind were more effective than programs that counteracted negative influences.

4. The fourth characteristic was that effective prevention programs were comprehensive and carried out over time. These types of programs allowed for progressive skill building and practice with feedback.

5. The fifth characteristic was that school-based prevention programs should be a part of the school curriculum.

6. The sixth characteristic was that prevention programs should begin prior to the emergence of problem behavior. For prevention to be effective, it was important that the necessary skills were promoted before the problem arose, to preempt it or to minimize its effects.

7. The final characteristic was that implementation of prevention programs must be monitored. It was important that the people who worked on the program were properly trained. (Lewis, Battistich, & Schaps, 1990)

For years, a group of dedicated researchers has been working to find the critical components for beneficial social, emotional, and behavioral programs for youth. Durlak and Wells (1997) conducted a meta-analysis of primary-prevention programs designed to prevent behavioral and social problems in children and adolescents. They defined *primary prevention* as "an intervention intentionally designed to reduce the future incidence of adjustment problems in currently normal populations as well as efforts directed at the promotion of mental health functioning" (Durlak & Wells, 1997, p. 117).

The outcomes for an average participant in a primary-prevention program ranged from 59 percent to 82 percent above those in the control group. This means that students who participated in prevention programs demonstrated fewer behavioral and social issues than those who did not participate. This study confirmed the importance of primary prevention as a strategy to achieve change in school populations. It also was implied that these interventions both reduced risks and increased protections for target populations. Durlak and Wells (1997) postulated that successful primary-prevention programs can reduce the rate of maladjustment in children and adolescents.

SEL emphasizes the promotion of programming that benefits the whole system. And it begins with prevention of mental health issues and advancement of well-being for all.

A brief word about prevention for the students in middle and high school. It may be perceived that prevention is only for the young students, but middle and high school students also benefit from developmentally appropriate skill development. After all, the adolescent brain is still creating connections and can use strategies to improve their connections with others.

Outcomes

The benefit of developing social and emotional skills can be found in the student outcomes. One of the ways that social-emotional skills have been measured is by connectedness to school. Connectedness to school has many positive outcomes. The Centers for Disease Control and Prevention (US Department of Health and Human Services, 2009) published the following reasons why school connectedness is an important factor in both health and learning:

- More likely to attend school regularly, stay in school longer, and have higher grades and test scores

- Less likely to smoke cigarettes, drink alcohol, and have sex

- Less likely to carry weapons, become involved in violence, and be injured from activities such as drinking and driving or not wearing seat belts

- Less likely to have emotional problems, suffer from eating disorders, or experience suicidal thoughts or attempts (US Department of Health and Human Services, Centers for Disease Control and Prevention, 2009)

The relationship between teachers and children can impact their long-term connectedness to school. Students who have difficult relationships with their teachers may

"That" Student Becomes "Our" Student

Over the summer, the staff prepared for Kenny to return as a sixth grader. The school staff added a few new things to their approach. First, the school committed to teaching SEL in every classroom. Teachers integrated social, emotional, and behavioral concepts into their academic learning and classroom management. Also, Kenny was immediately recommended for a social skills group where he got to help other kids learn what he was taught. The next step was to strengthen the relationship with Kenny's father's girlfriend, who took more interest in helping Kenny succeed academically, socially, and behaviorally at school. SEL was integrated into Kenny's school, class, small group, and meetings with his special education teacher and counselor. Most of all, Kenny's teachers, classmates, and family members demonstrated consistency in maintaining positive relationships, reinforcing positive social skills, and helping Kenny reflect on his behaviors in and out of school.

At last report, the staff had seen a dramatic change in Kenny. He was becoming a school leader, and none of the previous restrictions (escort, special seating) were necessary. There were many potential causes for this change of behavior. Some of them may have been influenced by the normal changes of maturation and development. But the staff agrees that the relationship and trust from the family to the school and the consistency of relationship, reinforcement, and reflection helped to make Kenny's sixth-grade year successful.

not feel connected or supported and may disengage from participation in school. Ladd and Burgess (2001) found that when teacher-child conflict was greater, students were less engaged in the classroom, were less likely to enjoy school, and were at increased risk for poor academic performance. Classroom context has been found to predict school engagement. This includes things such as instructional quality, social-emotional climate in the classroom, and student-teacher relationship quality (Dotterer & Lowe, 2011).

These outcomes can be demonstrated in large or small groups. Shechtman and Mor (2010) conducted a study with 164 children placed in 18 small groups for 10 weekly sessions. Social support is known to be an important variable in dealing with anxiety and trauma. A reduction in anxiety was predicted by gains in social support and group cohesiveness (Shechtman & Mor, 2010). The group becomes a source of social support that further helps in dealing with a difficult situation. Teaching social and emotional skills can support group cohesiveness.

The Who Is You

As someone who has been in a variety of positions in the educational system for the past 20 years, I feel it is incumbent on me to honor my professional responsibility as a school counselor and educator to advocate for systems change that will serve our students and the faculty and staff that we entrust with our children. Advocacy was a part of my educational journey as it was emerging in the field of counseling. The book *Social Action: A Mandate for Counselors* (Lee & Walz, 1998) was published while I was receiving my master's degree in counseling and educational psychology. And while I gladly took on the role of advocating for my clients (students), I did not consider myself an advocate in any of the other domains. I did not feel like it was within my power to affect a system.

It wasn't until I was in a new role and working in a new district that I learned that indeed it is also my responsibility to be a systems advocate. Systems advocacy focuses on identifying systemic problems through understanding the challenges and strengths of the community. The American Counseling Association's (ACA) advocacy competencies indicate, "Regardless of the specific target of change, the processes for altering the status quo have common qualities. Change is a process that requires vision, persistence, leadership, collaboration, systems analysis, and strong data" (Lewis, Arnold, House, & Toporek, 2003). The advocacy competencies include analyzing political power and recognizing resistance, and these are embedded in my strategies to implement SEL in my work.

What I know now is that we must not wait to become "perfectly empowered" to work toward making change. As Gargi Roysircar (2009, p. 289) says, "Counselors must use their psychological understandings, interventions, and the counselor relationship to help people develop their capacity to join together in social justice advocacy and make the world a better place for themselves, their neighbors, and others." This book is written with the hope of helping others who are involved in systems change, regardless of their role, in the development of SEL strategies in and out of schools and school districts. Although I am a counselor, and the framework I use is embedded in the ACA advocacy competency domains, these strategies can be implemented for all who embark on this journey. The power is within you to make the lives of children, and the people who teach them, better.

Better for You *and* Better for Them

The good news is that this work is beneficial for students, but it can be beneficial for you too. Stakeholders can improve their well-being with the development of their social emotional competencies. Strengthening teachers' emotion regulation through reflection and teaching the skill of perspective taking improves their ability to respond directly to the child (Swartz & McElwain, 2012). The ability to self-regulate by teachers allows them to feel more confident about their interactions with students even when the students are behaving negatively. Also, a more positive environment affects both teachers and students, making school a more productive and welcoming place to be. Students must feel connected to their schools and have a positive relationship with the adults at the school (especially with their teachers). And teachers need a culture that values their contributions and allows for collaboration. But do you know what makes a difference? Educators who can form positive relationships with children and employ social psychological interventions as needed make a difference. Positive relationships provide the ground on which learning grows.

The First Step—Self-Care: Putting Yourself on the To-Do List

Before embarking on this adventure toward implementing whole-school SEL, it is a good idea to understand your own needs. As we know, systems change can be personally challenging and demanding on the system but especially on individuals. People who are responsible for implementation of a program or process like SEL must have additional personal resources to deal with the unpredictability and stress of systems change. Self-care is a *significant consideration and must be a planned event for implementers.*

There Are a Few Things You Can Do:

1. Knowledge is power! Identify whether you are experiencing some of the symptoms of secondary stress: avoidance, anger or cynicism, social withdrawal, exhaustion, illness, sleeplessness, et cetera.

2. Determine the preventative strategies you can use to increase your resiliency when you experience secondary trauma.

3. Employ your safety net. Talk to the people who support you—your friends, family, coworkers, a professional counselor or therapist, your administrator.

The good news is that your care for your students is what makes a difference in their lives. It is now time to develop strategies to also care for yourself. Figure 1.1 lists some questions to ask yourself in this process.

> When one looks at self-care from a prevention perspective, the central focus of an advocacy organization is to prevent burdening its teams with one member's unresolved personal problems. An organization's focus is to make satisfying and energetic contributions amidst the frequent chaos, unpredictability, and stresses involved in advocacy work, thereby adding to the spirit of stability, humor, good cheer, and mutual respect in social justice organizations and collective action. (Roysircar, 2009, p. 293)

Figure 1.1   Reflections on Your Practice: Self-Care

- What are my favorite things about teaching or counseling or administration? Have they changed since my first year?

- Am I being challenged at an optimal level—where new learning feels invigorating versus overwhelming?

- Are the relationships that I have with my colleagues affirming? Do I seek them out to share good or bad news?

- Do my actions reflect my beliefs about students?

- What is the mindset that I go into staff meetings with?

- What things am I currently doing that I could remove or cut down and still meet the demands of my role?

- Do I have a good understanding of my priorities and make time to eliminate what is not a priority from my day?

- In what ways am I focusing on my own mental, emotional, and physical health every day?

- Am I excited to go to work today? What motivates me?

- Are my students excited to see me?

Practitioner's Voice

I want school to be a place where all students are supported to be and grow. Not just academically, but socially, emotionally, and behaviorally. Students come to school with complex backgrounds and circumstances. Many students don't have much time with parents and are navigating the trials of growing up alone much of the time. I want school to be a supportive place that helps students grow into caring, responsible, healthy, and respectful people in the world. Teaching is a more and more challenging profession. It is my calling and I truly love teaching students. I want to support teachers to be successful and enjoy this crucial role.

—Allison Lehr, PBIS/SEL Support Coach

Resources

Printed Material

- *Fostering School Connectedness: Improving Student Health and Academic Achievement* (CDC, 2009)

- *Mental Health Facts: Children and Teens* (NAMI, 2014)

- ACEs pyramid graphic: (https://www.samhsa.gov/capt/practicing-effective-prevention/prevention-behavioral-health/adverse-childhood-experiences)

Videos

- *Theory of Action:* www.youtube.com/watch?v=NbMIhCZVW-U

- *Taking on the Urgent Need for Change:* www.youtube.com/watch?v=EZ3DAl6cEVU

- *Rethinking the Scale-Up Challenge:* www.youtube.com/watch?v=bllazKRgwHM

Strategies

- Communicate your process: Write a leadership newsletter: Example—the Illinois Principals Association put together a newsletter to address, among other items, "What should principals focus on as they plan next steps to address the Illinois SEL standards?": https://casel.org/wp-content/uploads/2016/08/PDF-20-the-illinois-sel-standards-leading-the-way-for-school-and-student-success.pdf

- Keep a leadership log: Leaders should try to keep all details in order so that they can pinpoint their journey and what the ingredients for success might be for their specific culture. Some ideas for leaders to keep in mind:

  o Keep a journal for first school year of SEL work.
  o Ask: What questions do I have? What is not making sense?
  o Capture the major milestones—what happened?
  o Form relationships in different departments. Who are your allies?
  o What happens when you are no longer the new innovation in town? Who are your naysayers?
  o Have personal vision, mission, and goals to keep accountable.
  o In the second year, use the journal to capture larger-scale changes.

REFLECTION QUESTIONS

1. What issues do you see in your school?

2. Do you have experience with students with ACEs?

3. What environmental factors could be causing problems or issues at your school?

4. If you were to walk into your school for the first time, not knowing anyone, what do you think you would notice?

5. Do you recognize yourself or your colleagues in the descriptions of burnout? If so, do you have a support system within your school?

6. What are the challenging behaviors you see in students? What are the adults doing or not doing in response to these behaviors?

7. How do you practice self-care?

Whole-School Social-Emotional Learning
Research on SEL

Social and emotional learning (SEL) is the process through which children and adults acquire and effectively apply the knowledge, attitudes, and skills necessary to understand and manage emotions, set and achieve positive goals, feel and show empathy for others, establish and maintain positive relationships, and make responsible decisions.

— **Collaborative for Academic, Social, and Emotional Learning (https://casel.org/what-is-sel/)**

What Is Social-Emotional Learning?

For many educators, the competencies and practices of social-emotional learning (SEL) are not new. Schools across the country have worked to improve students' social skills, helping them to learn about their feelings, develop empathy, prevent bullying behaviors, and cooperate with others. These practices have been demonstrated in morning meetings, small group counseling, and conflict remediation sessions in the principal's office. The term "social and emotional learning" was created when national leaders met at the Fetzer Institute in 1994 to address concerns about ineffective school programming and lack of coordination (CASEL, 2018). The goal of most SEL interventions in schools is to provide proven programs to improve skills and strategies for youth and those who serve them.

Researchers, school administrators, teachers, counselors, community leaders, and child advocates are all a part of moving this effort forward. Programs focus on student behavior and SEL benefits for students and teachers while supporting classroom learning (Greenberg, Brown, & Abenavoli, 2016). Researchers advocate for the adoption of SEL practices and strategies in the same way that strategies for academic teaching are adopted. It is important to think about social-emotional skills like academic skills, rather than pathologizing them. The whole system gains when we think of students as learners, even when it comes to social and emotional skills. The response to students who exhibit behavioral, emotional, or social issues can be changed from punishment to teaching and positive skill building for these problems.

SEL Core Competencies

Throughout the years, there have been many iterations of what the SEL core competencies look like. They have been considered by many titles, such as *soft skills, character development,* and *twenty-first-century skills.* CASEL (2018) has identified the five competency clusters that are most widely known. They include the following:

- **Self-awareness:** Individuals' ability to identify emotions in themselves and others, understand their own individual strengths and challenges accurately, be self-confident, and believe in their ability to accomplish goals.

- **Self-management:** Individuals' ability to control their emotions, manage their personal stress, motivate themselves, discipline themselves to follow through on tasks, set goals, and be organized.

- **Social awareness:** Individuals' ability to take others' perspectives, be empathetic, appreciate diversity, and respect others.

- **Relationship skills:** Individuals' ability to communicate with others in a clear manner, engage socially with individuals and groups of people, build and maintain relationships, work cooperatively, negotiate and manage conflict, and ask for and receive help when needed.

- **Responsible decision making:** Individuals' ability to identify and analyze problems, solve those problems in a manner that respects others, evaluate the outcomes of a solution, reflect on decisions, and take personal, moral, and ethical responsibility for the health and safety of themselves and others.

These five core competencies are useful in determining what skills and abilities to focus on, because they are based on years of research and the positive outcomes that are associated with attaining these competencies. Along with the five core competencies, a group of Harvard researchers determined the 12 social and emotional skills linked to child outcomes (Jones et al., 2017). Most of these skills are directly related to the five core competencies; however, there are two additional skills that have been found to increase positive outcomes for youth. They are character and mindset. *Character* is defined as "a set of culturally determined skills, values, and habits required to understand, care about, and act upon core ethical values (e.g., respect, justice, citizenship, responsibility for self and others) and to perform [to] one's highest potential in achievement or work contexts." *Mindset* is defined as "attitudes and beliefs about oneself, others, and one's own circumstances that impact one's interpretation of and response to events and interactions throughout their day" (Jones et al., 2017, p. 18). Many schools implement character or mindset programs that can be the beginning of introducing SEL or as additional competencies that increase positive outcomes.

Systems change advocates can use their knowledge of the competencies and skills to develop goals. School districts have used these competencies in many different applications to drive learning of these skills. Some districts use a rubric that is developmentally designed to set goals that students can attain at their age and typical developmental stage. Some districts develop scope and sequence documents that help teachers to understand the expectations of what skills will be taught and in what order. We can use the skills and competencies to enrich our work and provide a goal to move forward.

SEL: A Protective Factor

It is vital to understand the assets that produce positive student outcomes. Students who are mentally and physically healthy and safe will be better able to contribute to our society and economy. Schools can play a pivotal role in teaching students skills and strategies to be successful in an increasingly complex world. As we begin the challenge of helping students to develop these competencies, we must attempt to measure where we are currently to develop goals for where we would like to be.

Multiple studies have found that protective factors increase resilience and buffer students against the negative influence of risk factors. SEL is tied to the concept of a

SEL for All: Same Competency, Different Strategy

The ability to be socially aware (one of the five competencies) is the same for all individuals. What differs is the way these skills are taught. For example, one of the qualities of someone who is socially aware is to understand others' perspectives.

In **prekindergarten** we could teach students how to respond appropriately to other students' expressions of their needs (taking turns/sharing).

In grades **K–2** we could read aloud and discuss potential solutions to social problems.

In grades **3–5** we could model respect for students with different learning styles.

In grades **6–8** we could write about how social media gossip feels for the person on the receiving end.

In grades **9-12** we could have discussions about making responsible dating choices.

Among **adults** we could learn how to have politically engaging discussions by taking other's perspectives.

---

protective factor. Some of the protective factors that overlap with SEL include social skills. Youth who are socially competent and engage in positive interpersonal relationships with their peers are less likely to participate in negative risk behaviors. Youth who interact with prosocial peers or those who are a positive influence are at a lower risk for engaging in problem behaviors.

To focus on actively teaching the competencies and skills that fall under the SEL framework, we will increase the protective factors and decrease the risk factors that lead to poor outcomes for students. However, these outcomes do not get accomplished overnight. They require investment in infrastructure and training to support SEL in schools. The emphasis must be to work with districts and schools that support SEL and developing the system that will support SEL for *all* K–12 school students. Due to the different levels of funding and access, student participation in SEL can be dependent upon a student's zip code. All students gain from learning these skills. The benefits do not end after graduation. All students deserve our investment in these outcomes. With care and attention to the SEL competencies in relationship to the developmental milestones, you can implement programming that increases the protective factors for all students.

Powerful Evidence Supporting the Impact of Enhancing Students' Social-Emotional Skills

Research has demonstrated that SEL can have many positive outcomes. But all types of stakeholder may be interested in how SEL impacts them. Whether you are working with parents, teachers, administrators, or mental health practitioners, you need to provide them with the evidence that speaks to them. New studies on the efficacy of SEL are being done every year, but Figures 2.1 through 2.5 list some of the currently most relevant studies that you can discuss with stakeholders without being too overwhelming. This section is designed to give a few take-aways that will appeal to a group of stakeholders.

Figure 2.1   Evidence for Teachers

1. Students who participated in quality SEL instruction demonstrated improved attitudes and behaviors (Durlak J., Weissberg, Dymnicki, Taylor, & Schellinger, 2011). Students showed greater motivation to learn, deeper commitment to school, increased time devoted to schoolwork, and better classroom behavior.

2. The lead teacher is the best provider of direct instruction of social skills to students (Pelco & Reed-Victor, 2007). The lead teacher is the adult who is most often available throughout the school day to provide the students with the ongoing practice they need before they can independently demonstrate the learning-related social skills that they have learned during explicit lessons. This practice can include modeling, role-playing, and acknowledging examples of positive student behavior.

3. Students will learn best from interventions if they are done in the classroom environment (Lynch, Geller, & Schmidt, 2004). Classrooms are particularly appropriate for the implementation of prevention programs for young children, because the structured, supportive environment creates a protective factor.

4. Teacher implementation of SEL curriculum can lead to the experience of less stress, greater teaching efficacy, and greater job satisfaction (Collie, Shapka, & Perry, 2012). This study investigated whether and how teachers' perceptions of SEL and climate in their schools influenced three things—teachers' sense of stress (workload and student behavior stress), teaching efficacy, and job satisfaction. It was found that SEL has an important impact not only on students but on teachers. "In the short-term, learning new skills for SEL appears to be stressful; however, in the long term—once teachers' confidence for implementing SEL increases—they are likely to experience less stress, greater teaching efficacy, and greater job satisfaction" (p. 1198).

5. Social skills can be generalized by embedding them in lessons (McIntosh & Mackay, 2008). To create an efficiency of efforts, attention should be paid to lesson design and delivery so that multimodal prevention (behavior management, social skills, and learning strategies) is intentionally embedded within the lesson delivery of classroom teachers, paraprofessionals, and tutors.

6. Students need opportunities to practice and apply SEL skills in actual situations (Lane, Menzies, Barton-Atwood, Doukas, & Munton, 2005). To increase their mastery of social skills, students need to be provided skill instruction, and they need sufficient opportunities to master the skills that they learn, become fluent in their use, and adapt the use of these skills to a wide variety of social settings. Students are more likely to generalize the social skills they are taught if the social skills instruction focuses on targeted social behaviors that are valued and likely to be reinforced in students' natural settings. Generalization is enhanced when the social skill instruction is provided across persons and settings that the student is likely to encounter daily.

What does this evidence mean to me? And my students in class?

Figure 2.2   Evidence for Administrators

1. Students who participate in quality SEL instruction demonstrated fewer negative behaviors (Durlak J., Weissberg, Dymnicki, Taylor, & Schellinger, 2011). This included decreases in disruptive class behavior, noncompliance, aggression, delinquent acts, and disciplinary referrals.

2. Learning and behavior are interconnected, and schools that systemically address both academic learning and SEL have shown increased student achievement (Elliott & Kushner, 2007). Schools that use a proactive, systematic process for identifying and addressing student needs through universal and early screening across both academic and social/behavioral areas are better able to provide supports and promote skill development in the key areas before many students develop a more serious or prolonged problem that requires intensive, formalized, and expensive supports.

3. SEL enhances students' knowledge about empathy, anger management, impulse control, and bullying prevention (Edwards, Hunt, Meyers, Grogg, & Jarrett, 2005).

4. SEL programs return eleven dollars on every dollar spent (Belfield et al., 2015). This cost-benefit analysis included the reductions in aggression, substance abuse, delinquency, depression, and anxiety and their resulting costs to the education system.

5. School environments high in connectedness promote a sense of security (Blum, 2005). A report supported by a grant from the US Department of Defense demonstrated the importance of a school environment that promotes a feeling of security through connectedness (Blum, 2005). A sense of belonging and relationships with other students and teachers were important in feeling connected to school, and nonacademic aspects of school were a significant contributor to those feelings. This report revealed seven qualities that influence students' positive attachment to school: had a sense of belonging, liked school, perceived that teachers were supportive and caring, had good friends within the school, were engaged in their current and future academic progress, believed discipline was fair and effective, and participated in extracurricular activities.

What does this mean for my school?

Figure 2.3 Evidence for Parents/Families

1. Students who participate in quality SEL instruction perform better academically (Durlak Weissberg, Dymnicki, Taylor, & Schellinger, 2011). Their achievement scores are an average of 11 percentile points higher than those of students who have not received SEL instruction.

2. Classrooms high in emotional support may be particularly helpful for children whose temperamental characteristics are not well matched with the demands of the classroom (Rudasill, Gallagher, & White, 2010). Highly supportive classroom climates (teacher is in tune with the needs of the students and readily responsive to them) may buffer children from lower academic achievement associated with poor attention, and children's temperamental attention and classroom emotional support work together to predict academic achievement.

3. SEL is a good return on investment (Belfield et al., 2015). The overall goal is for children to identify and understand their emotional state and to manage and communicate their emotions appropriately and so increase social competence and reduce aggressive and delinquent behaviors. The overall result suggests a good return on an SEL investment under a variety of assumptions.

4. Programs that promote academics, social skills, and school connectedness have long-term positive outcomes (Lonszak, Abbott, Hawkins, Kosterman, & Catalano, 2002). Longitudinal gains from theory-based programs that promote academic success, social competence, and bonding during elementary school can prevent risky sexual behavior and adverse health consequences in early adulthood.

5. Social competence in kindergarten predicts future wellness (Jones, Greenberg, & Crowley, 2015). A longitudinal study that followed students for 20 years determined that those rated high in social competence in kindergarten were more likely to graduate from high school, attain a college degree, and have a full-time job at the age of 25.

6. SEL competencies of middle school students predict current and future grades and test scores (Fleming et al., 2005). Results of this study indicated that higher levels of school connectedness and better social, emotional, and decision-making skills were related to higher test scores and higher grades.

What does this mean for my child?

1. Kindergarteners' social-emotional skills are a significant predictor of their future education, employment, and criminal activity (Jones, Greenberg, & Crowley, 2015). Kindergarten teachers were surveyed on their students' social competence. Researchers used that data and compared it to follow-up data collected 19 years later, when these same students were approximately 25 years old. It was found that students rated as having higher social competence in kindergarten were more likely to have graduated college, to be gainfully employed, and to not have been arrested than students rated as having lower social skills.

2. SEL can improve the factors known to help students through college (Taylor, Oberle, Durlack, & Weissberg, 2017). This study analyzed results from 82 different programs involving more than 97,000 students from kindergarten through middle school in the US, Europe, and the UK. The effects were assessed at least six months after the programs completed. The researchers found that SEL continued to have positive effects in the classroom but was also connected to longer-term positive outcomes. Students who participated in programs graduated from college at a rate 11 percent higher than peers who did not. Their high school graduation rate was 6 percent higher. Drug use and behavior problems were 6 percent lower for program participants, arrest rates 19 percent lower, and diagnoses of mental health disorders 13.5 percent lower.

3. The top five attributes that employers seek in their applicants include leadership, ability to work in a team, communication skills (written), problem-solving skills, and communication skills (verbal) (National Association of Colleges and Employers, 2016). Four of these attributes are intentionally taught through SEL.

4. The US Department of Education has an "Employability Skills Framework" that includes effective relationships though interpersonal skills and personal qualities, critical thinking skills, and communication skills (Office of Career, Technical, and Adult Education, 2018). These skills are improved using SEL practices.

5. Students with high self-efficacy or self-awareness appear to adapt more successfully to college than students without these attributes (Ramos-Sanchez & Nichols, 2011). This study found that learning to be self-aware and self-sufficient before entering college helped students to adjust to the first year of college.

What does this mean for your student's future?

1. Students who participate in quality SEL instruction have fewer emotional distress and conduct problems than students who have not participated (Durlak, Weissberg, Dymnicki, Taylor, & Schellinger, 2011). This meta-analysis found fewer reports of student depression, anxiety, stress, and social withdrawal. Students who participated in SEL programs implemented by their teachers showed these gains in diverse communities across K–12 grade levels and locations.

2. Integrated approaches of PBIS (positive behavior interventions and supports) and SEL produced greater improvements in overall mental health than either approach alone (Cook, Frye, Slemrod, Lyon, & Renshaw, 2015). Findings from this study speak to the power of implementing a more comprehensive structure of universal supports by integrating PBIS and SEL interventions together using a blended approach both theoretically and practically speaking. This combined approach produced additive effects on mental health outcomes, including internalizing and externalizing behavior problems, beyond changes that occurred when implementing only one intervention.

3. SEL is an effective component in bullying prevention (Smith & Low, 2013). Skills taught in SEL programs contribute to the prevention of bullying at school.

4. The school environment offers an ideal setting in which to work with child survivors of trauma, as all students have accessibility to school mental health resources (Thompson & Trice-Black, 2012). Children exposed to the trauma of domestic violence tend to experience difficulties with internalized and externalized behavior problems, which

can include deficits in social skills and academic functioning. Domestic violence can be a hidden issue that the school may not be aware of, so school staff cannot provide individual support to students who are living through this trauma. Whole-school SEL approaches can support those students who are experiencing trauma at home that the school and mental health practitioners are not privy to.

5. Students with disabilities can benefit from small group social instruction (Ledford & Wolery, 2013). Small group instruction provides multiple opportunities to observe social and other behaviors performed by peers, which may increase the ability to understand and perform the social skills that are reinforced at the school.

6. Nurturing environments promote well-being and reduce the impact of mental and emotional disorders (Biglan, Flay, Embry, & Sandler, 2012). Environments that are nurturing have impacts in the following ways: They minimize biologically and psychologically toxic events; teach, promote, and richly reinforce prosocial behavior, including self-regulatory behaviors; monitor and limit opportunities for problem behavior; and foster psychological flexibility— the ability to be mindful of one's thoughts and feelings and to act in the service of one's values even when one's thoughts and feelings discourage taking valued action.

What does this mean for students' mental health?

Figure 2.6   Student Inclusion

What do your students need to know about SEL?	
How do you get students to buy in to learning social skills?	
What expectations need to be set for students when discussing SEL?	
How can you make these concepts relatable to students?	

Multitiered Systems of Support and SEL: Universal Support for *All* Students

What Is MTSS?

As mentioned in Chapter 1, multitiered systems of support (MTSS) is a model that integrates the resources in the school to meet both academic and behavioral needs of students. Instructions and interventions are developed to meet the needs of students. This model reflects practices aligned with the Every Student Succeeds Act (ESSA, 2015) and the Individuals with Disabilities Education Act (IDEA, 2004). While each school and district may implement MTSS at their own pace, I have generally seen adoptions begin with academic instruction and intervention. Behavioral instruction and intervention in a tiered fashion have lagged in implementation. And often the tiered intervention occurs at the Tier 3 or intensive level with just a few students needing extra support for social-emotional or behavioral issues.

Whole-School Tier 1 SEL: Universal Support for All Students

At the Tier 1 level, core instruction is provided to all students and is differentiated to support all students in a continuum of care. It is reported that 75–80 percent of students gain from Tier 1 supports alone (Shapiro, 2014). This is true when MTSS is implemented with high-quality evidence-based strategies and programs. One of the key components of successful Tier 1 implementation is fidelity. This means implementing the lessons and activities as intended by the program's developer. Like many difficult concepts, we stress the importance of it and how we must strive to obtain fidelity. But it isn't easy; it doesn't always come naturally for how we work. Generally, those who go into education are creative. This is what makes teachers unique, and this is why students—even when in the same grade, learning the same curriculum, using the same learning standards—will not be taught the same. The challenge is to stay true to the intent of the intervention (fidelity) while making decisions that feel natural for you, and to feel you are a part of the process.

One of the biggest hurdles to face when working to integrate whole-school Tier 1 SEL is starting at Tier 1. School staff look at their current issues and feel that the school should be concentrating on the students who have the highest impact on the school day—the students who are having behavioral issues that are keeping them from participating in class and causing a disruption for other students. Working with schools, I emphasize the need for a strong Tier 1 for all students.

Rathvon (2008) discussed the best practices for maximizing success of interventions. One of her strategies is to enhance the function of the entire classroom rather than just the target student. There are a few reasons that Tier 1 strategies are supportive of a positive school culture. The first is that Tier 1 strategies are more efficient in time and labor. For example, when we teach social practices such as cooperation, the goal is to impact the entire classroom. We hope to see proximal outcomes where students can demonstrate their cooperation skills. We can also look for distal or long-term outcomes such as improved classroom and/or school climate. Proximal outcomes demonstrate changes in the skills of students based on the intervention. These can be measured more immediately and should impact the distal outcomes. Distal outcomes are reflected in long-range school-level data. Distal outcomes measure the collective impacts of interventions on the whole school.

The second reason to use Tier 1 strategies is to avoid singling students out. Some of the interventions that we use on a regular basis have the unintended consequence of causing students to be labeled. Students notice when other students are treated differently or have different rules of engagement. This does not mean that we get rid of interventions that are working for students who need those strategies. But have we had a discussion with students about equity versus fairness? Do the students understand that we all need extra help in some way, and that they may not understand why one student gets to leave the classroom when he wants or has a wiggle chair? Explicit discussions around these topics are helpful if the perception from the other students is that one child is selected to get special allowances. Classwide strategies are more acceptable to teachers, because they avoid the fairness issue.

One Counselor, 500 Students

Mr. Castellanos was a new counselor at Greenleaf Elementary School. He was learning about his new job, the new students and staff, and his administrator's views about the role of the school counselor; and he was trying to develop a comprehensive counseling program for 500 students. Because the school was also adopting an SEL curriculum, he was asked to introduce the lessons in the classrooms. Mr. Castellanos had used this curriculum at his previous internship, so he felt that this was something that he could do. At the beginning of the year, he met with each grade-level team and learned about which lessons they wanted and how they wanted them scheduled. He also delivered lessons outside the curriculum as teachers requested on things like growth mindset and bully prevention. In addition, Mr. Castellanos asked for teacher recommendations for small group work for five different Tier 2 groups. By the end of the year, Mr. Castellanos had taught 245 social-emotional lessons and held nine Tier 2 social, emotional, and behavioral small group meetings with a total of 46 kids throughout the year. Mr. Castellanos reported that he was struggling to keep up with this schedule on top of the other demands of the school counselor role. The principal, seeing this overwhelming schedule, helped to truly make Tier 1 SEL a schoolwide priority and had the school counselor perform a supportive role in the universal implementation of their SEL curriculum for the next year.

One of the positive outcomes of whole-school or whole-class Tier 1 strategies is that peer influence can affect outcomes. The students can reinforce and model the strategies that they are working on in class when they are out of class, on the playground, or in other areas of the school. If an entire school is working on a specific strategy—for example, respecting others—all students can reinforce respectful actions when they see them. When Rob helps clean up his lunch tray, or Sadie speaks to her teachers kindly, they are demonstrating active participation in the goals of the school.

And finally, Tier 1 strategies can have a positive impact on the functioning of all students in the class (Rathvon, 2008). We can do our best to screen students for academic, social, and behavioral issues, but we may not catch them all. Using Tier 1 strategies for all students gives those who we may not have identified the skills that they may need, and provides others with learning that can benefit them far outside the classroom.

SEL and School Culture

The culture of a school is represented by its shared beliefs, its ceremonies, its nuances, the traditions and the things that make the school unique. School culture takes a great deal of time to create. It doesn't happen overnight. It happens over years.

—David Jakes (Jakes, 2013)

SEL is beneficial to the individuals who adopt the skills and strategies to deal with a complex world. These skills affect the overall school climate, which as previously mentioned then go on to impact school culture. It is imperative to first look at "the way things feel around here" to change "the way we do things around here." The positive school culture begins when adults begin to challenge their previous understandings and approach this new learning with a growth mindset. We learn how positive changes can emerge from what schools do best—educate! Adults and students learn self-awareness, empathy, cooperation, self-regulation, and problem-solving skills, among many other social-emotional practices. Stakeholders who are positive role models develop healthy relationships with students and build resiliency in those students. This changes the way things feel in the school environment, and after a few years of being engaged in this positive climate, a new normal emerges, through positive school culture.

There is a direct overlap between school climate and the social and emotional competencies and attributes (Berg, Osher, Moroney, & Yoder, 2017). The American Institutes for Research offered the following conditions for learning and social-emotional development (Berg, Osher, Same, Nolan, Benson, & Jacobs, 2017). These school climate conditions allow adults and students to practice and build on their competencies:

- Supportive, respectful, trusting relationships

- Emotionally and physically safe environments

- Cultural competence and valuation of diversity

- Culturally responsive, participatory, and diverse instructional approaches to meet diverse needs

- Shared and consistent expectations and norms across contexts

- Shared narrative and support for different viewpoints

- Strengths-based approaches

- Necessary additional supports for those who need them

- Leadership and staff modeling of social and emotional competencies directly through behavior and indirectly through fair and equitable policies

- Open communication and partnerships with families and community partners

- Measurement of these components for continuous improvement

Altogether, this list may seem overwhelming. But remember, every journey begins with the first step. Here is one exercise to help you understand your school climate: Imagining you are new to the school, observe the physical environment and interactions between staff members, student and staff, students with each other, parents and staff, certified and classified staff. What do you notice about "the way things feel around here"?

Figure 2.7   Perspectives on Your School

Looking at My School as a Newcomer	What Is the School Climate?	How Does That Impact the School Culture?
From the outside the school seems. . . .		
On the Great Schools website and other websites, people are saying. . . .		
When I enter the front office, I experience. . . .		
Communication between parents who come to the school is. . . .		
When there is an emergency on the campus, the staff is. . . .		

Families who are new to the area experience. . . .			
Teachers collaborate with. . . .			
Students resolve their difficulties by. . . .			
During holidays or special occasions, we. . . .			
Staff receive appreciation when. . . .			
The pressure to succeed academically at this school feels. . . .			
The staff room is. . . .			
Certificated staff feel. . . .			
One special tradition at our school is. . . .			
Our school is known for. . . .			
Our afterschool programming promotes. . . .			
Teachers say _____ about the professional development offered.			
Administration helps teachers to. . . .			
The feeling in the lunchroom is. . . .			
The best thing about our school is. . . .			
The most challenging thing about our school is. . . .			
Community members think _____ about our school.			

Positive School Culture at the Front Desk

Mrs. Bashir was a school secretary. But her role was much more central to the school than her daily secretarial duties would suggest. She was the first person that the community encountered when entering the school. Mrs. Bashir would welcome anyone who came in, even if she was in the middle of a task. She knew all the families, the district staff, and the UPS delivery person. She made them feel welcomed. Many of the parents were non-English speakers and Mrs. Bashir would do her best to communicate. And despite the language barrier, they would get their questions answered. Mrs. Bashir was often in charge of the students who had been removed from class as they waited for the principal or dean to meet with them. She had a special place in her heart for these students, and they often came back years after and would tell her how much her kindness meant to them. Mrs. Bashir was very big on celebrations for the teachers and staff. She remembered everyone's birthday and special occasions. She would often have special treats made for holidays. When she retired, there was a big retirement party, and many people came to celebrate her and what she meant to that school. The way that she infused social and emotional learning into her everyday actions was something to be admired. She was an expert at social awareness and relationship skills. She provided an experience for those students, families, and staff that made the school a place they wanted to be.

Practitioner's Voice

I truly believe that social and emotional learning instruction is needed in all schools. In the four years I have been implementing SEL and incorporating all aspects within my schools, I have seen tremendous growth in respectful and kind behaviors between students. We have seen fewer problem behaviors between students and truly identify those SEL competencies when reteaching behavioral expectations or creating counseling groups and guidance lessons for students. In addition, I've seen a significant difference in test scores across all grade levels in both formative and summative assessments. When students feel happy, [and] are confident and respected in the classroom and across all areas of campus, they are much better able to perform both academically and socially.

—Erin Lane, Elementary School Principal

Resources

Printed Material

- "School Culture, School Climate: They Are Not the Same Thing" (Gruenert, 2008).
- Employability Skills Framework: A Crucial Component of College and Career Readiness (Office of Career, Technical, and Adult Education, 2018).
- *The Practice Base for How We Learn: Supporting Students' Social, Emotional, and Academic Development* (Berman, Chaffee, & Sarmiento, 2018).

Videos

- *Nice Kids Finish First:* www.npr.org/2015/07/16/42305191
- *The Big Picture: Integrating SEL Across a District:* https://youtu.be/xxTeO8T4Kag
- *Morning Meetings: Building Community in the Classroom:* https://youtu.be/U6_pLkwaCeY

Strategies

- Learn some conversation starters that support social and emotional development for students of all ages: www.parenttoolkit.com.
- Make sure your expectations are consistent with your students' typical developmental levels by checking the developmental benchmarks for the five core competencies (self-awareness, social awareness, self-management, relationship skills, responsible-decision making): http://www.parenttoolkit.com/explore-your-toolkit.
- Understand more about ACEs by checking your own ACE score and resilience score: https://acestoohigh.com/got-your-ace-score/.

REFLECTION QUESTIONS

1. What problems would SEL solve in your environment?

2. How do you address SEL in your instructional strategies?

3. Which core competency do you think your staff would benefit from learning more about?

4. Which stakeholders will need to hear more about SEL research? How can you present the research in the most palatable way?

5. What is your current understanding and use of MTSS? What are your colleagues' opinions?

6. What roadblocks may you experience when rolling out a Tier 1 whole-school intervention?

7. What improvements do you think need to be made in your school climate?

Strategy #1:
Identify Your Why

Everything around you, including what you see, hear, feel, and smell, are all artifacts of the culture. Reaction to each of these senses is influenced by the culture because culture taps into belief systems and helps to decide preferences, dislikes, who to trust, when to go home, what to wear, how fast to drive, and how to teach. The culture will provide you with the information about customs and how you should react to certain situations.

—Steve Gruenert (2008, p. 58)

Inspiration Leads to Action

To lead is to inspire. Once people are inspired, great things can happen. Change agents begin by tilling the soil or uncovering their "why." What is the reason you are involved in this work? The why can be a feeling, a goal, or an inspiration. But many times, the why involves a person or people. Why is improving school culture by integrating SEL for everyone? Individuals who are transparent in their efforts to improve school culture by integrating whole-school SEL will work toward increasing school connectedness and improving relationships.

Clarity of purpose for SEL can be achieved in several ways, the first being to invest in the relationships between staff members and students. When individuals are connected to their schools, they may feel safe to try new ideas and work toward a mission of SEL for all. The second way is to understand what staff believes about SEL. Understanding this will guide the direction and pacing of your work. The third is to learn what motivates your staff. What makes them want to invest time and energy in SEL? In the remainder of this chapter, we discover more about the keys to identifying the answer for, Why SEL?

Increasing School Connectedness as a Prerequisite to SEL

Relationships cannot be underestimated during the process of systems change. When involved in trusting relationships with colleagues, teachers and staff members can allow themselves to be vulnerable and adapt to change more easily. That level of inclusion is created when the adults have respect and trust for each other. (It does not mean that everyone agrees all the time—this is the real world after all!) But respect (I am willing to hear you out because I believe you to be worthy), and trust (I may not agree with what you have to say but I believe you have good intentions) are essential.

This is difficult! As I reflect on some of my coworkers over the years, I can think of people who I didn't take the time to get to understand. But as I have learned, until *you* try to build that bridge, you will not have a relationship that can guide change. Some individuals are unwilling to grow, to learn from others and the children and adolescents who depend on them to provide a healthy, positive role model; help them to see that this is not an avocation for everyone. There is no shame in learning that and moving on to something else. Educating children is not for the faint of heart!

But for those who choose to dedicate their life to educating children, support each other. *Make your workplace one where everyone belongs! The students will know the difference.*

Three Relationship "Musts"

Let students know

1. They matter to you.

2. They belong in the classroom and school.

3. You accept them even if their behavior in the moment is unacceptable.

This may seem like common sense, almost insulting, advice for those of you who actively practice these things. But human beings are complicated, and we can at times think that what we are doing is working without checking. Right now, think of the students in your life: For high school/middle school teachers, administrators, counselors, and other school personnel, there could be hundreds. So, my suggestion is to pick out one group or one class.

Ask yourself these questions:

1. What do I know about these students outside their immediate grade status? Do I know about their home lives? Their hobbies? Their friends? Their interests? Would I know if they were in trouble? *When I see them in the morning, does my face light up?*

2. In what ways do I make all the students feel like they belong? Is there any outreach to the kids who just seem to be barely hanging in there? Are there clubs, events, or school activities that appeal to all types of interests at our school?

3. Am I able to separate the behavior from the student? Can I treat the student fairly and allow the consequences of the action (natural or regulated) to be enough? If students are asked to leave, do I have a reentry strategy for them once they come back into my classroom?

As educators, we have a big responsibility: We are not only teaching our students to be academically proficient—good readers, thoughtful thinkers, problem solvers, and responsible people. We are also helping them to become productive members of society, teaching them life skills that will last a lifetime.

Identifying Students Without a Significant Adult Relationship at School

One of the schools I worked with modified the "relationship matching" activity that many schools use to identify students who do not have strong relationships with an adult at school and to match the teachers up with these students. Faculty were asked to put a star next to the names of the students that they could report they knew things about outside of their academic progress. For example, if a teacher knew that Mike had a younger brother, liked soccer, and was a huge Fortnite fan, he would put a star next to that student's name. In this middle school of over a thousand students, they found students the faculty could not identify as being known. The faculty then chose those students to try to make a connection with. The students were also asked if they connected with any faculty members, and in this way the staff found additional students who had no adult connections. Staff used the data to identify the students they could learn more about. This activity helped the faculty see that they could work toward developing better relationships with the students at their school.

Beliefs as Barriers to Action

Change agents should try to understand their staff's beliefs about SEL. Staff beliefs can help or hinder implementation. Beliefs lead to thoughts, which produce actions, which affect the school climate, which creates the school culture. Below is an example

---

Graphic 3.1   Beliefs graphic

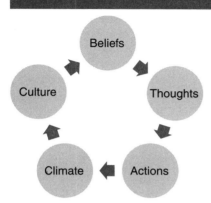

Belief: Teachers have a powerful role in students' lives and in how students see themselves.

Thought: I can affect students' lives in a positive way.

Action: I make a point to *tell* students when I recognize their talent and abilities.

Climate: Teachers feel positive about their relationships with students.

Culture: Teachers regularly practice social-emotional skills with their students.

Understanding Staff Beliefs

Beliefs are models of how the world works for us—a road map or representation of our experiences. Beliefs are formed by our why, and they are based on our perceptions. If our perceptions are skewed, our beliefs will be affected. Beliefs affect our everyday actions and reactions. Therefore, without an understanding of our own individual beliefs and the beliefs of those we work with in the school environment, real change will prove almost impossible. For example, we might believe that a student's negative behavior is based solely on the student's home training. We may want to blame the parents' parenting style as the reason the negative behavior is occurring in the school environment. And if we choose to look at parenting as the reason for negative behavior, we might be less likely to look at whether our own behaviors could be causing the student's negative behavior. This makes it unlikely that we will look at strategies to change our own behavior to impact the behavior of our students.

When educators use an open-minded perspective on their own beliefs, they can see errors in belief and gain new insights. It is important to understand the growth potential of the change process. The self-improvement perspective of being lifelong learners can help lower the barrier to change. Change is a part of life, and it is vital that we learn from our mistakes and our accomplishments. That learning happens when individuals challenge their beliefs, especially when the beliefs are a barrier to action.

Graphic 3.2   How Can We Understand Our Staff Beliefs?

Questionnaire

Interviews

Round table

School climate survey

Correlational data

The Mascot, the Carrot, and the Competition

As you begin to dive into understanding your staff's beliefs, you may learn that individual staff members have different motivators to do what they do. The motivator may be a personal why or a collective why. I have seen three main types of motivators for systems change specifically as it relates to SEL: the mascot, the carrot, and the competition.

The mascot represents the moral purpose. Sometimes it is a charismatic leader, a tragedy that occurred, or a child that everyone rallies around. One of the main missions for the systems change agent is to find a positive motivator for change. Michael Fullan (2003) suggested that if people are asked to do something that they perceive as worthwhile, they will be more likely to put in the extra effort to help achieve successful outcomes. Achieving a moral purpose is possible when people are interacting, new knowledge is being produced, new solutions are being discovered, individuals feel invested and committed to finding a solution, and there is a process whereby solutions are looked at critically to continually seek the best ideas (Fullan, 2003).

The carrot is the tangible motivator—a reward or recognition. Being recognized for doing good work is a motivator for many individuals and schools. Schools that are known in their communities for having award-winning teachers or innovative practices can attract teachers to want to work there. Because financial rewards are not usually the motivation of people who enter the educational field, recognition is an important motivator. It is a way of acknowledging the dedication of the individuals engaged in the work.

The competition reflects a desire to keep up with other teachers, schools, and districts in the state or nation. Another way to build motivation is to demonstrate to stakeholders how this process or program has affected other schools and communities across the country or world. Enhancing the feeling of missing out on what is happening on a national level can be an important motivator. Individuals who fall in this category do not want to be left out of the national conversation. They want to be a part of the movement.

What Motivates Your Staff?

Your staff may be motivated by something else as well. The important thing is that you know what your staff motivation is and that it may change as leaders change, as policy changes, and as your community changes. When you are developing an understanding of the people who work alongside you, it may benefit you to keep in mind their motivations. Motives will push us to act toward a goal. Psychologists theorize that motivation

The Kindness Garden

A Mascot Motivator

Jasmine was a little girl with third-degree burns over most of her body. Her body was scarred, and her face became leathery in appearance. Students would often make comments about Jasmine's appearance or avoid her altogether. The school administration and her parents decided to face this challenge head on. Because she had difficulty using the playground equipment but loved to be outside, they decided they would build a garden with flowers, a little path, and a bench that all students were welcome to use. The administration rallied the classes to volunteer to work on the garden. Meanwhile, they discussed how they treated all their classmates with kindness and respect. It became known as the kindness garden. Students had a place to sit in the shade and talk with Jasmine, when she was there. Jasmine became their unofficial kindness mascot.

comes from different sources, such as instinct, return to homeostasis, optimal level of arousal, intrinsic and extrinsic causes, and sources related to Maslow's hierarchy of needs. But why should we care? For change agents, the beliefs and attitudes of the people around them can *directly affect the success of their change efforts.* Those individuals may have established patterns of working with others that can create obstacles for change. Well-established preferences for forms of helping behaviors are often impediments to the adoption and scale-up of evidence-based approaches (Aber, Brown, Jones, Berg, & Torrente, 2011).

If you can learn more about what motivates your specific group, you have a better shot at making your change efforts work. Motivation can be a very important determinant for action. There is an activity based on McClelland's need theory (McClelland, Atkinson, Clark, & Lowell, 1953) to help individuals determine their own needs or motivations. Motivation can be broken down into these four areas:

- Need for achievement—desire to excel and improve on past performance
- Need for affiliation—desire to interact socially and be accepted by others
- Need for autonomy—desire to work for self, rather than others
- Need for dominance—desire to influence and direct others

You and your team can take the quiz shown in Figure 3.1 to help you identify what motivates you.

Figure 3.1   Motivation Quiz

#	Using the 0–2 scale shown to the right, please rate the extent to which each of these statements applies to you:	Scale: Not a motivator for me = 0 Somewhat motivating for me = 1 Very motivating for me = 2
1	I like to work with others.	
2	I like to improve on my past performance.	
3	I like to oversee others.	
4	I prefer individual projects.	
5	It is important for me to be accepted for my work.	
6	I like to influence people around me.	
7	I am self-directed.	
8	I want to be the best in my work setting.	

These statements reflect the four kinds of motivation:

1. Statements 1 and 5 = affiliation motivation
2. Statements 2 and 8 = achievement motivation
3. Statements 3 and 6 = dominance motivation
4. Statements 4 and 7 = autonomy motivation

Do you recognize any of these motivations in your coworkers? How can you tap into those motivations to increase adoption of your ideas to improve school culture?

Some Strategies to Meet Staff Needs

1. If your staff has a need for *achievement,* work with them to develop goals to move further beyond their past performance.

2. If your staff has a need for *affiliation,* provide social time and create more opportunities for them to support each other.

3. If your staff has a need for *autonomy,* recognize their accomplishments as individuals and encourage them to share their process with others.

4. If your staff has a need for *dominance,* make your mission about being the best place for kids, and quantify your results (e.g., fewer referrals, better ratings in specific areas).

The first step in discovering the motivations of your staff is to observe and ask thoughtful questions. Educators often find internal motivation in interesting work, professional and personal growth, and learning. Tap into those motivators. Getting to know what will motivate your staff to implement SEL is yet another opportunity to develop those intentional relationships.

Why Is the Driver for *Who, What, When,* and *Where*

Social connectedness can also enhance motivation. This is why relationships are so important. Sometimes individuals acquire goals and motivations from others in their work environment. Motivation from others can be a consequence of small cues of social connectedness. Those social relationships, especially when groups of people are working together on a challenging task, increase intrinsic motivation for individuals (Carr & Walton, 2014). You must also understand the social traditions of your school culture. Traditions can promote connection to the school, including events such as the school carnival, fall festivals, harvest festivals, cultural celebrations, graduation ceremonies, talent shows, arts and music performances, and sports competitions. The more your staff is connected to the school through the events they plan and the colleagues they work with, the more opportunities there will be

The "You Should Know Better" Cognitive Dissonance Example

Teachers at Bell High School took a survey, and an overwhelming majority felt that "students should know better" how to behave at school. However, these same teachers agreed that SEL should be taught at school. While the teachers saw the value of SEL at school, they also believed that students should behave well and be ready to learn the material. Some of the teachers had discussions about implementation of SEL that included caveats such as "with funding" and "in health class." We looked at this as an opportunity to talk about how "students should know better" takes you out of the learning stance that they will need to acquire the social and emotional skills that are needed in the very specific context of school. Yes, we want all students to come to school prepared to learn and behave in ways that are consistent with our expectations. But this is not always the case. Instead, we must look at our imperfect situations and think of our students as being immersed in learning not just academic but behavioral, social, and emotional skills; and adopt the mantra, "We teach what our students do not know."

for connection. These opportunities are even more beneficial because students are involved, and their involvement can create an even greater sense of connectedness to schools. Students will have the opportunity to practice their social-emotional skills.

When all else fails, cognitive dissonance is a powerful motivator for change. When people recognize a difference between what they currently think or do and what they would like to be or have, this can create an uncomfortable state with which they will need to reconcile. Discussions that are gradual and nonjudgmental may help them see that their current beliefs are leading them away from rather than toward their goals.

Questions to Inspire Thinking About Motivation

1. Do we share the same goals?

2. Do all stakeholders share the same level of understanding for the need for change? (certified, classified, administration, parents, community)

3. What are the potential barriers for implementation?

The *why* needs to fit the values, culture, and needs of the local context. It is the driver of your next steps. When thinking about your school environment, you must be clear about how SEL relates to other initiatives and how it will solve problems for the people who are asked to adopt SEL practices. Figure 3.2 is a template with questions to help your thinking about motivation.

My Why (an Example)

In school, I experienced many of the things that students today experience—stress, loneliness, anxiety, isolation, and uncertainty about the future. And I had my share of teachers who did not appear to recognize or respond to my struggle. But I also had adults who

---

Figure 3.2 Why Do I Do It?

What is your story that connects you to this work? _____
_____
_____
_____
_____

Why do you think it is important? _____
_____
_____
_____
_____

Would you feel comfortable sharing that? _____
_____
_____
_____
_____

provided me the support and caring to build my resilience. My first-grade teacher, Ms. Day, became my first "friend" as I tearfully followed her around the playground. I was a scared and shy kid at a new school, in a new living situation, in a new state. In fourth grade, I was involved in a counseling group for kids of divorced parents that allowed me to express my sadness. My sixth-grade teacher, Ms. Getto, saw my potential and recommended me for honors classes when I had no thought of them for myself. And in high school, when a student teacher used my biology class to conduct a social experiment, my principal, Mr. Howton, interceded on my behalf. Those examples of care helped me to understand the power that one teacher, one counselor, one administrator had to make a difference not just in my academic life but my personal life as well.

Many of these individuals are no longer in education. I wish that I could tell them how much they meant to me for that small moment in time. This is what drives my why. My why then became the students that I served, and then later, the other stakeholders that I work with. As a change agent, I may never know the people I impact, as I was never able to tell the individuals who impacted me. But I have come to learn that the why lives in the doing, not in the accolades. I aim to pay forward the good. If you don't have any of those individuals from your past, think about the way you wish it had been, and make that your why.

Practitioner's Voice

A positive and effective school culture comes from a shared understanding and agreement of the mission of the school. By facilitating a collective engagement within our staff regarding SEL instruction, our team was able to identify potential concerns within our student population and begin formulating a plan of action. This identification of the "why" resulted in shared vision and decision making at all levels of our school community.

— Kyle Moore, K–8 School Principal

Resources

Printed Material

- *Florida Teacher Starts Each Day Complimenting Students One by One:* (https://abcnews.go.com/Lifestyle/florida-teacher-starts-day-complimenting-students/story?id=35259600)

- "8 Ways Principals Can Build Positive School Culture Now" (https://schoolleadersnow.weareteachers.com/8-ways-build-positive-school-culture-now/)

- *High-Risk Children in Schools: Constructing and Sustaining Relationships* (Pianta & Walsh, 2013).

Videos

- *Every Kid Needs a Champion:* https://youtu.be/SFnMTHhKdkw

- *How Great Leaders Inspire Action:* https://youtu.be/qp0HIF3SfI4

- *If I Knew Then/A Letter to Me on My First Day of Teaching:* https://youtu.be/miPYLJI247g

- *What Happened When Teachers Learned How Students Feel About Them: A Plus:* https://youtu.be/gANeGBBoSBs

REFLECTION QUESTIONS

1. What is *your* why?

2. What are the similarities between your why and the whys among your colleagues?

3. What changes do you think would be most impactful for the students at your school?

4. What motivates you to come to work every day? What motivates your staff?

5. Are the relationships with your colleagues conducive to creating a collaborative culture?

6. Can you think of an example of a student who inspired you?

7. What are the differences between you and your colleagues in the way you approach this work?

Strategy #2: Adopt a Framework

If you don't have time to do it right, when will you have time to do it over?

—John Wooden (1997)

Framework, Model, and Intervention, Oh My!

Systems change is built on a theoretical basis formed over many years, scientific studies, and thought leaders' recommendations. We can benefit from this knowledge and apply it to the things that we want to change in our schools specifically as it relates to the adoption of SEL. However, if we dig into the details, we may find ourselves stuck in Oz, where we become confused and overwhelmed by all the terminology, opinions, and research.

Vare and Scott (2007) write about education for sustainable development. They suggest that to make real change, it is crucial to build capacity to think critically about what experts think, and to become involved in testing sustainable ideas. The purpose is learning as a collaborative and reflective process; to make changes sustainable, those most closely related to the change effort must be involved in the decisions and meaning making (Vare & Scott, 2007). The best collaboration that I have seen often involves learning from theories and processes developed by others, but using critical thinking and group work to build solutions that work for the individual school or context.

A *framework* is an organized structure used to view concepts and practices. It is often seen as the "how-to" support for conducting the implementation efforts. A *model* is a theoretical construct often used to represent the goal or ideal that a school is trying to achieve. And an *intervention* is an actual process or procedure meant to bring about change in an individual, group, or system.

Adopting a framework is an important next step after identifying your why for SEL. A framework provides a structure to guide our efforts. Systems change agents will benefit from having a logical order to follow. Just as if we were building a house, we need to start with the foundation—the why. Then we begin to frame the house—the framework. Before we discuss specific frameworks to guide the organizational structure of our SEL implementation, we must begin with a discussion of implementation science and evidence-based practice.

Implementation Science

Effective implementation includes changing the beliefs and behaviors of educators and administrators, creating the setting conditions to facilitate these changes, and creating the processes to maintain and improve these changes in both setting conditions and behavior of well-intentioned adults (Fixsen, Naoom, Blase, Friedman, & Wallace, 2005).

We can look to medicine to see how poor implementation robs us of good outcomes. Woolf and Johnson (2005) wrote,

Society invests billions of dollars in the development of new drugs and technologies but comparatively little in the fidelity of health care, that is, improving systems to ensure the delivery of care to all patients in need. Health, economic, and moral arguments make the case for spending less on technological advances and more on improving systems for delivering care. (p. 545)

Three Methods of Evidence-Based Practice

Most educators understand the need for evidence-based practice (EBP). EPB helps to guide educators to make the best decisions for their students based on understanding of research. There are three types of evidence to inform our use of EBP (Technical Assistance Center on Positive Behavioral Interventions and Supports, 2010):

1. **Scientific evidence:** Studies based on empirical evidence, where information is determined through observation or experimentation. These research studies are designed to answer a specific question or test a specific hypothesis. Such studies follow a strict scientific protocol to discover how to understand, improve, prevent, or treat a specific issue with specific variables.

2. **Program evaluation:** A systematic method for understanding specific programs, specifically the outcomes of a program and the program's effect on its participants.

3. **Participant voice or social validation:** An exploration of outcomes and life experiences to determine a collective meaning. This practice considers the preferences and understandings of those who the intervention is meant to help.

School Versus District Framework

Frameworks should be used at both the school and district levels. The difference, of course, is the amount of time and organizational capacity you would need to get all necessary stakeholders on the same page when choosing a framework for an entire district. Most frameworks involve an environmental scan of the current evidence-based practices. In a large district, this can require time to discover all the resources you currently have. This chart gives an example of resources a district might need to evaluate:

Goal	Curriculums to Evaluate for SEL Competencies
Staff will evaluate curriculums currently in use to determine whether they are evidence based.	1. Health curriculum 2. Second-step curriculum 3. Character counts 4. Kelso's choice (counseling)

Having completed this evaluation, you would then add information about who is receiving the lessons or curriculum; who is providing them, how often, and when; whether assessments are being made to determine current skill level, et cetera.

This information forms the basis of the choice you make as to how to achieve your goal of giving students the social and emotional skills they need. Gathering this information can also help you as you consider adopting a specific intervention that addresses the gaps in the action planning stage.

Evidence-Based Practice in the Real World

Interventions should be evidence based. However, the process of determining how to implement is context dependent. This can be a difficult task. How do schools maintain the integrity of the intervention while working through their real-world issues that may be unlike those in the settings in which the evidence for the interventions was collected? For example, School 1 and School 2 decided to work on parent education for SEL. School 1 gathered ideas from the parents/families about what they wanted to learn about SEL through the school's website. School 2 used the implementation guide for parent/family meetings provided by the curriculum company. Both schools held parent/family education workshops about SEL, but *how* they conducted these was based on what they knew about their people.

In evidence-based science, there is the concept of active ingredients, which are the actual ideas or concepts that need to be learned to improve the outcome of an intervention. Because schools are so different in population, size, priorities, et cetera, it is nearly impossible to replicate the conditions where the original scientific study took place. In his study of the practice and policy of SEL, Durlak (2015) discovered that adaptations are common and may improve program outcomes. This does not give schools license to take a program or curriculum and completely make it their own. Instead this is a thoughtful process that looks at the school culture, and any adaptation that is made should ensure the active ingredients of the program are retained (Durlak, 2015). Active ingredients come from a strong theoretical and empirical background.

> In summary, to ensure the appropriate blend of fidelity and adaptation in new programs, it is important that those bringing the program into schools (funders, researchers or original program developers) collaborate with staff in the host setting to determine an acceptable way to decide on the proper blend of fidelity and adaptation. (Durlak, 2015, p. 398)

A Caution: Data's Siren Song

Starting with data before investing in a framework can result in false reasoning. We may first start with the problem, because this is the thing that we want to immediately solve. In systems change work, we must assume that the problem is just a symptom of something else, and we must dig deeper. It may be easy to get wooed into the false sense that if we just got rid of _____ (fill in the blank), all would be better. And to make it more complicated, the data may tell us that too. For example, if we think the problem is bullying, we take a survey that looks at bullying behavior, and we find that there is bullying going on, we may choose interventions that address the bullying. But lo and behold, we still have problems. The identified "problem" may only be one of the issues, or the issue that is most present and identifiable.

Because of this focus on the problem, based on one piece of data, we have chosen an intervention that we hope will address that problem. Almost every school can relate to various interventions that they have tried over the years. School storage facilities are the intervention bone yard. In them, you will find books, kits, VHS tapes, and guides for interventions that have been tried and failed for many reasons, not necessarily that they weren't great work based on great science. Perhaps it wasn't the right time or right place for these discarded interventions. Perhaps a principal attended a conference and found an intervention that was thought to be a great idea, but the staff didn't buy into it. It may be that the intervention was too complicated, and teachers had too many other things to do. It may have been the next new thing that the staff heard a lot about and wanted to try. Whatever the reason, implementation of the intervention is no longer occurring, so the boxes collect dust in storage.

The cumulative effect of these half-baked intervention attempts may have changed the beliefs of some of the educators about the efficacy of interventions. And we have an example of how beliefs impact thoughts, which impact behaviors, which impact school climate, which impacts school culture. For example, if the staff does not believe that social skills interventions work because these interventions have failed in the past, they may not believe in future social skills interventions. This can lead to staff not fully believing or participating in an intervention, which affects its success. These staff may not feel like part of the team (a school climate issue), and that impacts the norms of nonparticipation (a school culture issue).

Therefore, choosing a framework before investing too much time on the data is so important. A good framework will provide support in an organized fashion to your change efforts. The framework should provide a structure and overview of the practices that will allow you to see the whole picture and solve problems with a systematic approach, rather than merely a problem-solving approach.

Read the Directions Before Application: Choosing a Framework

Back to the visual of the house we are building where the foundation is the why, the framework is the wood frame, and the competencies are the rooms. The competencies are skills that we want in a fully functional house. We can easily identify the room or skill such as self-awareness. When building self-awareness in students, we will be using strategies to enhance, improve, or install their capabilities to understand themselves and the place they have in the world. When building a kitchen, we will have specific tools and appliances that work best in the design of the room. At the end of the process, we can evaluate whether the individual can demonstrate self-awareness. We can also evaluate whether our kitchen has running water and a working stove.

Listed below are some frameworks, as we define them here, that will help organize your understanding of whole-school SEL as systems change. As you begin to read more about systems change, you will learn about building capacity, scaling up, and outcomes. Many of these models have flowcharts and discuss frameworks; there are a few them to look at and one that frames our discussion here. Some of these frameworks may work for your school:

1. **UCLA's Center for Mental Health in Schools (Adelman & Taylor, n.d.):** This framework includes the vision/aims/rationale for applying the intervention in the school setting. The resources (tangible, human, and social capital) will be deployed, created, or brought together to bring about improvements to the organization. The general functions, major tasks, activities, and phases are decided with the vision in mind. Then infrastructures and strategies allow for connection between functions and outcomes of the system change. The positive and negative outcomes are evaluated for the short, intermediate, and long term. This also allows for accountability to the system.

2. **CASEL District Framework (https://drc.casel.org/).** CASEL's District Resource Center's framework includes communication, vision, alignment of resources, building of expertise, needs assessment, professional learning, integration, programming, standards, and continuous improvement.

3. **Frontiers of Innovation, IDEAS Impact Framework (Harvard University Center on the Developing Child, 2018):** This framework includes the following steps: Innovate to solve unmet challenges, develop a usable program with a clear and precise theory of change, evaluate the theory of change to determine what works for whom and why, adapt in rapid-cycle iterations, and scale promising programs.

4. **Getting to Outcomes (GTO) Framework (Elias, Zins, Graczyk, & Weissberg, 2003):** This framework includes these steps: conduct needs/resources assessment, establish goals/desired outcomes, consider best/promising practices, assess fit, address capacity issues, develop a plan, implement plan, conduct outcome evaluation, engage in continuous quality (evidence that program worked), and address sustainability issues.

5. **National Institutes for Urban School Improvement Systems Change Framework (National Institutes for Urban School Improvement, 2018):** Different types of activities and different roles of people are highlighted in each of the levels of this framework. The levels are differentiated by the professional effort rubric, the school effort rubric, and the district effort rubric.

Choosing a framework that looks at the big picture of systems change with an organizational path that seems reasonable for your school culture is ideal. It is important to begin with the frame and then move on to the intervention. Figure 4.1 provides an outline for adopting a framework.

Recommendation: Frameworks That Use Program Evaluation for SEL

As mentioned, there are three methods of evidence-based practice: scientific evidence, program evaluation, and social validation. Program evaluation may be the most user friendly. The practice of performing a program evaluation based on what is currently happening in the system will be helpful in determining the usefulness of your framework. The first step is to identify problems with the data collection procedures to minimize the risk of losing valuable data. Then collect data to evaluate program effectiveness. Look at other programs already in use in your school, and integrate them into your SEL program; this means not doubling efforts by wasting time and energy. Leaders should examine and evaluate the whole idea or system and not throw out parts that will still work. There are many great resources for implementing and scaling up evidence-based practice strategies. Most strategies include a process that tests hypotheses and documents the program's implementation, including changes and outcomes.

Change agents may want to use qualitative methods as well as quantitative methods to evaluate their SEL interventions. Due to the complex nature of improving school culture, it is vital to use tools to uncover the complexity of what makes interventions work

Figure 4.1 Adopting a Framework			
How User Friendly Is It?	How Much New Learning Will We Have to Do?	How Much Effort Will It Require?	What Is the Estimated Timeline to Integrate the Framework?

and how we interpret and honor student voice. Qualitative methodology illuminates the process and outcomes of the intervention. The intent of qualitative findings is to deepen understanding through the eyes of the participants or to "put faces on the statistics to deepen understanding" (Patton, 2003, p. 2).

Evaluation is a form of social science research that studies the effectiveness of existing knowledge to inform practical action (Clarke & Dawson, 1999). Evaluation research is a valuable tool in assessing interventions. Good evaluation research should inform practice and not just be a summary of the past. It should be collaborative, should work from participants' perceptions of good practice, and should enhance learning (Savin-Baden & Howell Major, 2013).

This type of research looks to quantify and qualify information about implementation, operation, and effectiveness of programs created and designed to bring about change (Clarke & Dawson, 1999). This method is valuable because it is sensitive to the different voices of program participants, it allows feedback using the natural language of the participants, and it shifts the locus of formal judgment from the evaluator to the participants. There is an emphasis on positive as well as poor practice, and it provides an environment that facilitates change (Savin-Baden & Howell Major, 2013). Elliott and Kushner (2007) wrote an evaluation manifesto based on their reflections over three decades of evaluation research. They discovered that evaluation should be designed to provide insights into educational purposes and practice, including matters of curriculum, philosophy, and social implication (Elliott & Kushner, 2007). Program evaluation can take make different forms. But the method may vary depending on your school resources.

The Importance of Process When Choosing a Framework

As change agents, we can tend toward a solution-focused way of thinking. Frameworks that are solution focused and time based have decision rules, well-defined job roles, specific outcomes, and a timeline for implementation. And while those things are significant and necessary, they don't tell the whole story of how a large-scale implementation of a program works.

This solution-focused model is valuable for eliminating "problem admiration," which can occur when working in problem-solving groups. I have been in more than one meeting where we focused solely on the problem at hand, and these meetings can turn into complaint sessions. We may leave the meeting feeling good that we had an opportunity to vent, but we come away with no real plan for moving forward.

I advocate for a model that integrates both a process focus and a solution focus. In my experience, practitioners at the school level haven't put much of a focus on the process of systems change. *Process* describes the collective discussions that happen as an intervention is taking place. It is not time dependent. There is a priority for conversations about the data and experiences that the practitioners are having with the intervention. There is an openness to a mindset change, and individuals may experience discomfort.

The success of your change lives in the process. Process can be messy and not follow a linear formula. Change agents can prepare themselves by assessing the areas where they do have some measure of control and the areas where they should allow time and space. Start by asking the question: What is working and not working about this intervention? Collect this information to evaluate what the stakeholders are telling you. Change is maximized when you can capitalize on successes and offer solutions for any issues. The change agent can accelerate change by maximizing opportunities for discussion of successes and problems during the process.

No Quick Fixes

This process of taking social-psychological interventions to scale is difficult. It may require grassroots movement, where early adopters implement the change that they want to see to influence others to join them. Change takes time; it is a slow process for it to be embedded into the culture. As I have seen in many districts, there is not one program or intervention that works the same way and in the exact same timeline in all districts. It is important to take the perspective that we are in this for the long haul. We celebrate the small victories but realize that the work will never truly be done, as we are revising it as we learn more about our students, teachers, parents and the community. There must be collaboration between researchers and school districts to look at both the raw data and the lived experiences of students to inform the process of systems change.

Reflection on SEL Implementation: An Integral Part of the Framework

Whether it is specifically a part of your chosen framework or not, curiosity and inquiry should be a part of your systems change effort. When all stakeholders are actively participating, providing support and counterpoints, and thinking about ways that the whole school social-emotional learning can be improved, that is when you get real change. Reflection is weaved into all parts of the framework. Maintaining a stance that promotes inquiry in a way that is not blaming or judgmental can cause a shift in the school climate that becomes a norm within the school culture.

Permission to Find What Fits

You may feel pressure to make this work, make it work in the correct way, and to choose the "right" intervention. You will need to allow yourself permission to fail. It may happen. This is the reason for choosing a framework. Hypothetically, if you stumble at Step 3 of your chosen framework, you can go back to review Steps 1 and 2 to make sure you had all the necessary information. And if you had all the information and made the choice that seemed right at the time, that's OK. We are here to learn, correct the direction, and press on. Adopt a mission that gives you room to grow. What if this were your mission?

> **We work together to come up with the best solutions based on evidence. We practice with meaning and integrity and we reflect on the process and outcomes. If we don't hit the mark, we are resilient, and we try again.**

Framework

Lessons From a Middle School SEL Curriculum Adoption

Schools with curriculum adoption processes can also include SEL curriculums. In one district, we used this process to determine what the needs of the schools were and how SEL curriculum could meet those needs. The process of vetting the curriculums was based on our specific needs. We understood what our needs were by relying on the framework. The schools understood through their needs assessment and program evaluation that they had a good process for establishing rules and keeping order. They had good teaching strategies for some of the SEL competencies. We learned that teachers felt that they wanted strategies to integrate brief SEL practices daily. When looking for a curriculum, the team kept the needs, the desired goals, and their specific context in mind. This helped with buy-in and acceptance of another curriculum, because we kept the needs and goals of these middle schools a priority.

Practitioner's Voice

The development and careful planning of a districtwide framework is the lynchpin of a successful and sustainable evidenced-based practice. The responsibility lies within the leaders at both the district and school level to develop a clear vision, mission, and common language. This is necessary in order to rally and motivate others in an organization around that common vision, with the goal of empowering and building staff expertise through ongoing professional development and feedback cycles. Establishing systems and structures, such as adding staff positions to provide teacher coaching and support and scheduling regular trainings and feedback groups, can help support the long-term sustainability of that initiative.

—Stephanie Wright, PBIS/SEL Support Coach

Resources

Printed Material

- *Guidelines for Selecting Evidence-Based SEL Programs* (https://casel.org/guidelines/)

- *In Pursuit of Equality: A Framework for Equity Strategies in Competency-Based Education* (https://www.competencyworks.org/wp-content/uploads/2017/06/CompetencyWorks-InPursuitOfEquality-AFrameworkForEquityStrategiesInCompetencyBasedEducation.pdf)

Videos

- *Building Adult Capabilities to Improve Child Outcomes: A Theory of Change:* https://youtu.be/urU-a_FsS5Y

- *Re-Thinking the Scale-Up Challenge: West Wind:* https://youtu.be/SFnMTHhKdkw

- *Theory of Action: West Wind:* www.youtube.com/watch?v=NbMIhCZVW-U

- *Taking on the Urgent Need for Change:* www.youtube.com/watch?v=EZ3DAl6cEVU

Strategies

- Learn about the differences between research principles and program evaluation principles in a helpful chart put together by the Centers for Disease Control and Prevention: https://www.cdc.gov/eval/guide/introduction/index.htm

- Develop a protocol for discussing frameworks. A protocol will help guide the conversation in a productive manner. School Reform Initiative has a template called "Why Protocols?" that can guide your work: www.schoolreforminitiative.org

REFLECTION QUESTIONS

1. Have you used frameworks to guide your work in other areas? If so, what did you find useful about them?

2. What are the pros and cons of the frameworks discussed here?

3. How would you introduce the concept of this framework to your stakeholders?

4. Which framework seems most adaptable to your school culture?

5. What efforts need to be made to braid together the framework and intervention?

6. What learning opportunities can you provide stakeholders about the timeline for your framework?

7. How do you plan to use the collective discussions of your stakeholders to inform your path?

Strategy #3: Do Your Detective Work

Data Collection and Data Analysis

The capacity to see the big picture is perhaps most important as an antidote to the variety of psychic woes brought forth by the remarkable prosperity and plentitude of our times. Many of us are crunched for time, deluged by information, and paralyzed by the weight of too many choices. The best prescription for these modern maladies may be to approach one's own life in a contextual, big-picture fashion—to distinguish between what really matters and what merely annoys.

—Daniel Pink (2006, p. 143)

Ask Questions

The education system is burdened with the number of things that need to be taught, assessed, intervened in, mediated, and achieved in the 12 years students work their way through to graduation. These expectations can feel like a burden for teachers who are also trying to cope with new curriculums, ever-changing evaluation measures, testing requirements, parent demands, et cetera. When any type of change is put in front of them, their immediate reaction may be a swift NO. Therefore, it is imperative to take stock of the environmental factors that exist.

You can find out more about your system by identifying the factors that work against your mission. This can be done many ways. I recommend trying to gain information in three ways—through surveys, interviews, and observations. Start with the question that Daniel Pink imposes: *In your environment, can you distinguish what really matters and what merely annoys?*

Who Are We? Considerations of Local Context

It is vital to understand what the implementation of an SEL program looks like in the local context of the school/district. The program can look different depending on the culture of the system. These differences could include an evolution of the program/process (e.g., the program was delivered somewhat differently from how it was designed). For example, the intervention may call for a specific type of data to be collected; however, your school would have to redesign its data collection procedures and processes to collect meaningful data.

The focus on the SEL implementation process should include considerations of local context, group behaviors and motivations, relationships and interactions, and an acceptance of the complex and multifaceted nature of systems change. Context can also be affected by outside influences or events in the world. For example, a traumatic event in the community can impact the local implementation. Also, as we learn more and do more empirical research in the developmental and prevention sciences, we must be willing to adapt to the new information.

While it may take additional time, learning as much as you can about the local context where your change will take place will bring better gains in the end. Developing a roadmap of most accessible roads, knowing where the potholes are and dangerous territory is, will allow for a safer journey for your SEL adventure.

One of the most difficult challenges for the change agent is managing the two sometimes conflicting goals: implementing best practice versus respecting the local contexts. *A systems change agent must be aware of the dos and don'ts of best practice while maintaining an understanding of how the specific environment will receive these practices.*

My best suggestion when managing through this work is to maintain your *openness*. Openness will allow you to see how your skills and attributes fit into your specific context. And for the areas that you need more help in understanding or skill development, it is a perfect opportunity to collaborate with others.

Questions About Your Local Context (School, District, Community)

1. What are the norms of your building?

2. What is okay or not okay to talk about?

3. How do individuals treat each other?

4. What would an outsider say the priorities of the school are? What would an insider say?

5. How are the everyday practices determining the overall personality of your school/work environment?

6. Are your colleagues engaged? Is there chronic absenteeism? Or do they miss important meetings?

7. Do the staff gather socially outside of school?

8. Does your supervisor create a trusting environment?

As you think about these things, also try to observe your environment. If it were your first day in this environment, what would stand out? What are the expectations? What are the rules? And do those rules and expectations make things better for those individuals who work and attend school in those environments? Be clear about the unspoken rules of your context.

What Do We Know? Making the Best Use of the Data That We Already Collect

There are many ways to collect social-emotional-behavioral data. The acceptability of data collection—and who will be responsible for design, collection, and analysis of data—can

Who "Gets" Air Time?

When entering any school or environment for the first time, particularly for a meeting or structured event, I reflect upon the people who are "allowed" to talk. In some settings I have been in, there was an unspoken rule that only specific individuals get asked to speak, are asked for their opinion, and are not cut off when speaking. This information is useful when thinking about local context. Generally, the individual who gets air time is the one who has power in the system. Learning about who gets important information, how much, and when can also be useful. Gathering data about the local context often requires us to imagine that we are new and learning the system for the first time. This will help us build a more thoughtful SEL implementation plan.

Figure 5.1 Data Currently Collected

Data Source	What Does It Measure?	What Trends Do We See Over Time?	Potential Impact on School Climate
Student/teacher ratio	Total students per teacher for the last 10 years	In the last 10 years, the student/teacher ratio has increased from 25/1 to 32/1.	Teachers are frustrated, and building is burdened by need for extra supplies.
Unexcused absence rate (attendance)	The total absences of students without a valid excuse such as illness	Unexcused absence rate has decreased by 15 percent over the past 20 years.	Efforts made to contact families and provide transportation vouchers may have proved a valuable resource.
Graduation rates			
Suspensions or expulsions			
Minor/Major discipline (ODR)			

be very context dependent. Positive behavior interventions and supports (PBIS) offer many types of data collection resources for schools that are free or cost little. However, PBIS may not appeal to all schools. Data collection can be quantitative (numerical data) or qualitative (not numerical). Examples of quantitative data collections include universal screeners, surveys (health information, soft skills, beliefs, school climate), and assessments of attendance data, discipline data, school records, et cetera. Qualitative data includes words that can be developed into themes or descriptions. Examples of qualitative data collections include interviews, focus groups, exit tickets, et cetera.

When determining the need for data, the purpose must be understood by all stakeholders. While we often hear about how necessary data is, unfortunately, collecting it is also seen as a burden to the system. A clear comprehension of the purpose and need for data collection to drive the work is the first step. The purpose can also include a way to track the level of improvement and determine what is not working to change course if necessary. There should be a general understanding of why there is a need to collect data, and a direct relationship between the data that is collected and the next steps based on that data.

For you as a systems change agent, the next step is to gather all the data that has already been collected. This is the historical data that every system collects. Then, determine what the gaps are, and consider whether you have access to instruments and tools to gain access to data to fill the gaps. How much time and effort are required for this data collection? To get schools used to data collection, I often suggested conducting a data blast (more about this later in the chapter). This would be a two- to four-week period where everyone is on board to collect data on a specific thing for a short length of time. Once you have identified the gap, the instrument to collect the data to fill it, and the time necessary to collect the data, the actual data collection will go much more smoothly.

Schools across the country are already collecting numerous data points, as required by state and federal law. What are the demographics of your school? Is there cultural diversity? What are the extracurricular activities that take place? What is the free/

reduced-price lunch rate? How many students qualify for special education services? What is the student/teacher ratio? How many students are considered English language learners? Examples of data already being collected include attendance information, academic grades, discipline data, and various surveys such as healthy youth surveys, exit surveys, community surveys, climate surveys, et cetera.

The question is how you are using this data to answer questions regarding SEL competencies or school climate or teaching practices that support SEL. You can also learn about previous interventions. What happened before and after other interventions? Did you see the improvements that you were hoping for? If not, why not? Figure 5.1 lists examples of data often collected by schools, as well as trends for some of the data and potential impacts of these trends.

Once your team goes through this process a few times, they will begin to understand how valuable it can be to look at your current data, create further areas to investigate, and discover the gaps in your data. Adding whole-school SEL programming will not affect all the areas that need to be improved in your environment. However, you will have a better idea of the ways SEL can potentially impact your outcomes.

Using Data Thoughtfully

The Tim Gunn Way

One of my favorite TV shows to watch with my daughter is *Project Runway*. We love Tim Gunn, a warm yet direct presence. He has a few things that he often says to the designers. Before he leaves the work room, Tim turns to the accessory wall and says, "Use it thoughtfully." This is appropriate for our work in SEL as well.

Determining what works should be driven by data. Data drives next steps for implementation, direction, pacing, content, getting buy-in, and the problem-solving process. Documents should be made that illustrate this process. But with all of that, it should be noted that all documents are a work in progress, never set in stone. Data can change over time, and if data is truly driving your process, the system should change too. It is the process of the intervention that gets us closer to our vision.

As you are thinking about what data to use, keep in your mind what data is useful for your specific target group. For example, it might be interesting to think about how budgetary trends changed over the years, but if teachers can't do anything about it in their direct job duties, it is not useful to present the data to them. The data that you work with should be in direct relationship to change in practice. Once we know what the data says, we can ask what can we do about it. Using data to tell a story about systems change may be the most effective way for individuals to hear difficult information without being overwhelmed. *Ask yourself, what is the most thoughtful way that data can be used to tell your story of systems change?*

Team Training on Data

Many schools use teams to look at data. These smaller groups allow for self-selection to increase the involvement of individuals who understand or even enjoy looking at data. Those involved in the data collection teams have a powerful role in understanding, interpreting, and disseminating the data to the larger staff.

When Disseminating Data to Staff, Teams Should Consider the Following:

1. There is a balance between the staff's understanding of the importance of using empirical research (to support their evidence-based work) and their ability

to translate the research using their own data. Research that has been done by other schools or districts may not apply to your school or district. Try to understand where the staff is before presenting new data to them

2. Always begin with acknowledgment of work done—previous practice. Staff need to know that their hard work up to this point has been noticed and is appreciated.

3. It may be helpful to connect current learning with societal issues that impact your students: ACEs, anxiety and depression, technology, future college, and career goals.

4. Just like students, staff members are building schema for new concepts. They may be familiar with the concepts that you are discussing, but they may not have the deep knowledge that you do because of your discussions with the team and interest in the subject. Be patient and offer numerous opportunities for learning.

5. Offer additional training around data collection.

The takeaway message that teams should deliver is how the information will be a benefit to students. Rather than delivering the information in a way that generates fear (e.g., this data reveals something that we are not doing or even doing wrong), frame the data with curiosity (e.g., what does this data tell us about what we are doing). Systems change leadership requires recognition that change can mean loss, a feeling of incompetence, or disloyalty to the practices we adopted in the past. But as Maya Angelou says, "Do the best you can until you know better. Then when you know better, do better." A spirit of curiosity when confronted with data can bring home the importance of investing in new strategies. Team members can demonstrate that process of learning from the data with an open mind. Other staff members may model this openness, and that is when real change can happen.

Data-Driven Decision Making: A Method to Use SEL Data

Part of our work as change agents is to gather and present the data to show urgency for change. This includes both national and local data. Change agents use data to make sense of what is happening and why it is happening, and to begin to get an idea of how to make something better.

Data-driven decision making is key to systems change. Data collection and analysis drive the next steps in our SEL work. We use data to drive our decisions systemically and with individual students and scenarios. Looking at systemic data may involve a multistep process that looks at different parts of the problem and tries to solve for all the parts.

There are many variations of the problem-solving process. The MTSS/RTI approach uses the four-step model of problem identification, problem analysis, intervention design, and response to intervention (Florida Department of Education, 2017). The problem-solving process is a great way to gather data about interventions that are used in your building (see an example in Figure 5.2). And it can also be used to offer suggestions for social and emotional interventions as well as behavioral interventions.

There are many benefits to using this type of problem-solving process during your SEL implementation. This information can be collected to see if there are specific problems that you are seeing schoolwide, to design trainings for specific SEL strategies that are regularly used, and/or to determine which curriculum to purchase based on student SEL competency needs. When gathering data about the outcomes, you may want to talk with the students. What do they feel about the process? Do they feel like they can apply this skill to other contexts? All this information will inform your SEL implementation.

Figure 5.2 Example of the Problem-Solving Process

Step in the Process	Steps	Data Collection	Example
Problem definition	Teacher requesting help	Name/date/grade or class	Smith/3.15.19/4th
	Details of problem	Who, what, when, where, potential reasons why	Students reported to be disruptive in class/during math lessons. Teacher finds that students don't ask questions despite being given the opportunity.
	Things already tried	Details and results	Offered tutoring, sent info for how to get help to families, students sent out of class for disruption.
Problem analysis	Factors contributing to the issue at hand	Student factors? Peers? Classroom? Curriculum? Changes in school or home environment?	Unknown
	Brainstorm	Specific SEL strategies	Relationship skill "asking for help"
Intervention design	Purpose	Reason we selected this strategy	Because many students seemed to require this skill, teaching the skill to the whole class was selected.
	Goals of intervention	Outcomes of proposed strategy	Teach students the steps to asking for help.
	Materials and/or training needed	Types and time	Time to review strategy before class, and talking with teacher after class
	Steps or checklist	Steps to or outline of procedure	1. Focus on what you know and don't know about the lesson. 2. Put a star next to the areas that are confusing on your workbook. 3. Use SMART question format. 4. Find three people who might be able to answer this question. 5. Ask them if they have time to help you. 6. Bring list and SMART questions to them.
Response to intervention	Measure outcomes	Teacher perception and/or assessment	Students had a decrease in disruptions, with only four interruptions in Week 1 and zero interruptions in Week 2. Students are more regularly asking for help.
	Next steps?	Maintain, modify, lessen, intensify, or remove	Maintain and continue to reassure and reinforce good practice of asking for help.

Large Data Sets: Needs Assessment, Universal Screeners, Skill Assessments, and Surveys

The benefit of developing a grassroots movement for SEL is that people often understand the reason why they need it, and their heart is in it. Naturally, we are interested in finding out more about the social and emotional wellness of our students and staff. Whole-school data collection can be useful. Over the past few years, there have been many more assessments developed for use in schools.

There are instruments aimed to measure specific skills, needs, risk factors, competencies, strengths, attitudes, and awareness of our students' social and emotional abilities. The method and rationale for data collection will depend on the direction that the school or district is planning. This section will give a brief overview of different types of large data sets. Leadership and change agents should be thoughtful about the type of data they collect and what they plan to do with the data. Before you begin, learn how your school or district makes decision rules. How are schools receiving services, and how do students qualify for additional supports? Are the decision rules documented? What is the cut score for students who get the additional interventions? Change agents who understand how students have historically received services at each tiered intervention level will help you use the data you collect more efficiently.

Needs Assessment: Mind the Gap

A needs assessment is used to understand your school's strengths and weaknesses. This assessment identifies the needs and goals of your school. It can be comprehensive and involve things like school safety, mental health, school climate, family engagement, connectedness, or student learning.

CASEL (2018) identifies the needs assessment for SEL as including the following:

1. Existing programs and practices that your district can build upon

2. Gaps where new programs, practices, and policies may be needed

3. Resources that may enable your district to maximize the impact of SEL

Conducting a needs assessment is a great way to understand the system and use the strengths of your system to your advantage. It can also help you shore up and prepare for weaknesses. In my work I like to assess four areas: staff SEL competencies, school infrastructure, school culture/climate (including equity and cultural competence considerations), and student SEL competencies. Overall, this gives me a good idea of the school's infrastructure needs, school culture assets, and student and adult competencies. I then can develop a more informed plan of action to work with the school and its unique culture.

Some of the introductory questions to investigate include these:

1. Are the teachers in your school using a specific SEL curriculum or other schoolwide programming?

2. What are the perceptions of the students of the program? The teachers? The administration? All other stakeholders?

3. Systematically review to identify strengths and gaps in current programming.

4. Have any teachers integrated SEL programming into their academic instruction?

5. What are the qualities of the instruction that are impactful to the students?

Universal Screeners: To Screen or Not to Screen? That Is the Question

Universal screening is used to identify individual students who are at risk. Universal screeners for academics identify students at risk for learning difficulties. Universal screeners for behavioral and emotional risk are used to identify students at risk of emotional or behavioral problems. Learning more about the specific risk factors related to emotional or behavioral problems can be useful information for school leadership.

The Unneeded Needs Assessment

Mrs. Garofolo was asked to conduct a needs assessment at her school to determine the social, emotional, and behavioral needs of her staff. The needs assessment was four questions long, with two check-the-box questions and two fill-in-the-blank. The open-ended questions asked about what types of support the staff needed.

This way of conducting a needs assessment is a recipe for disaster. Asking staff open-ended questions about how they can be supported results in blank responses, general responses, or super-specific responses. This assessment was not helpful in designing the next steps for implementation. Because all teachers may not be versed in the specifics of SEL competencies, ask them questions that they can answer, and find out if the teachers' needs can be met with SEL. Here is an example of such an assessment:

Common Practices	Majority of My Students Exhibit This Skill	Majority of My Students Need to Learn This Skill	How I Would Like to be Supported In Helping Students Learn This Skill?
Group work			
Following expectations			
Goal setting			
Working individually			
Taking others' perspectives			
Listening to the speaker			
Taking turns			

Multiple choice answers for the last column could include these:

A) I have some ideas. Let me get back to you if I need support.

B) Let's brainstorm!

C) I would love to see an SEL practice modeled.

D) I would love to observe a classroom where the teacher is doing this well.

E) Please refer me to a curricular lesson that I could teach.

Note: All these common practices can be taught.

Universal screeners provide a structure to identify students in need of additional supports, which can be helpful when using a tiered system of support. At the universal level or Tier 1, all students receive services. Universal screeners are designed to identify students who are "at risk" and are often used in MTSS models. The application of this data to help students who are at risk is appealing for school staff.

On the other hand, universal screeners provide challenges that schools would be remiss if they didn't address before using them. Some of the challenges include their oversized use of resources (time and money), the need to maintain the security of the information collected, the question of whether student consent (versus assent) is necessary to use them, alignment of needs assessed with programs to meet those needs, lack of outside referral resources, misunderstanding or misinterpretation of results, the possible inappropriateness of clinical instruments in school settings, an

Figure 5.3 Universal Screener Comparison Sheet

Universal Screener Name	Screener 1	Screener 2	Screener 3
Timing and frequency of administration			
Constructs relevant for determining an individual's risk status			
Format and content validated by previous research			
Contextually and developmentally appropriate			
Reliability is confirmed (internal consistency, test-retest, interscorer)			
Validity is confirmed (predictive, concurrent, construct, content)			
Cost			
Number of personnel necessary to administer			
Ease of interpreting assessment data			
Accommodations for learners with special needs			
Treatment validity—outcomes useful for guiding intervention			
Informants (rating type)			
Constructs measured			
Grade level(s) appropriate for			

increased need for Tier 2 or Tier 3 interventions as a result, et cetera. There is a saying: "If we screen, we must intervene." This does not mean that we should wait until the perfect system comes along to begin this process. What it does mean is that schools need to weigh the pros and cons and come into the process as informed and prepared as possible.

When choosing a universal screener, it is important to consider the following (Cook, Volpe, & Livanis, 2010):

1. Appropriateness for the intended use
   - Compatibility with the service delivery needs
   - Alignment with constructs of interest
   - Theoretical and empirical support
   - Population fit

2. Technical adequacy
   - Refers to evidence in support of the reliability and validity of the screening instrument

3. Usability
   - Actual costs, time, and energy needed to conduct, carry out, and administer the assessment

4. Determination of the optimal informant
   - Teacher, parent, student
   - Depends on many factors, developmental level

5. Treatment validity
   - the extent to which any assessment procedure contributes to beneficial outcomes for individuals

It may be helpful to use a template like the one in Figure 5.3 to compare different universal screeners.

SEL Skill Assessment

CASEL (2018) recommends strengths-based assessments. These assessments measure competencies specifically such as relationship skills and empathy. Currently there are new skill assessments that are being developed to address the social-emotional competencies. *The Handbook of Social and Emotional Learning: Research and Practice* (Durlak, Domitrovich, Weissberg, & Gullotta, 2015) offers suggestions for the six recommended SEL assessment tools. Strength-based assessments provide schools with information that they can use to focus on skill building with students. SEL Solutions at American Institutes for Research has published its *Are You Ready to Assess Social and Emotional Development?* toolkit (Moroney & McGarrah, 2015). The toolkit includes a decision tree for thinking through the use of assessment for SEL in your school or district. The considerations include purpose, rigor, practicalities, burden, and ethics. It also has all of the current assessments, constructs measured, and other considerations. The beneficial quality of SEL assessments is that they can be used for formative assessment to monitor student learning and provide ongoing feedback in the moment. This is helpful for targeting specific skill deficits. They can also be used for summative assessments to evaluate the students' learning at the end of the year or semester. This helps us understand both the needs of individual students and the overall skill attainment for all the students. Systematically we can improve our instruction based on the gaps in knowledge that the students demonstrate through the assessment.

Formative Assessment Examples

1. Observation tickets—Adults can take a day or a few hours to observe students in various areas of the school. Do they observe SEL in action? They can tally those results and the details of the observation.

2. Have students draw a concept map to represent an SEL competency or skill. What does cooperation look like?

3. Assign students to write an essay about an SEL competency.

4. After an SEL lesson, have students write one or two sentences identifying the main point of the activity or lecture.

5. Invite students to design a project that integrates SEL competencies. Challenge them to think about how they might appreciate the diversity in their own community.

6. Have students teach others some of the SEL competencies. If you were to teach someone how to communicate something when you are mad, what would you say?

Surveys: If You Have a Moment....

Most of us have taken surveys. The school survey is given to students, faculty, staff, administrators, parents, community, et cetera. It can provide a lot of good information at a relatively small cost. Surveys are convenient, as they are often directly sent to your e-mail address and can usually be completed in five to ten minutes. This may be a good way to understand some of the systemic challenges you face as you begin to implement SEL in your school. Because surveys are anonymous, you will get more honest opinions.

The disadvantages of using surveys are the anonymity. To solve problems, it is important to be as detailed as possible about the problem at hand. If we don't know who is responding to our survey, we can't ask follow-up questions or disaggregate the information to make the solution more nuanced.

When asking staff to complete a survey, make sure they understand the purpose of gathering the information and the potential future uses of the data. Keep your staff apprised of where this survey fits in your overall goal of SEL implementation. When I have given surveys in the past, I have sometimes heard the feedback, "I don't remember taking this." That was when I had to reevaluate the messaging around the data. Yes, educators are very busy, but it is up to the change agents to make sure that the intent and use of any survey is clear. Connect the dots between the information that you get from the survey and the next step of your implementation.

In the Moment: Data Collection

In some of the schools I have worked in, I recommend "guerilla" data collection practices: tactics with which a small group uses irregular methods to understand the larger group. These brief hit-and-run methods do not give you the large amounts of data that a screener, needs assessment, or survey may give, but they will help you understand the system a little better with only minor costs in time and energy:

1. **Team-only data collection**: If you have a well-dispersed team, have them collect data on their own practices to get an idea of how intrusive the data collection process is.

2. **Data blast**: For two weeks, the whole staff collects data on one thing. For example, relationship issues. How many times have you had to mediate a relationship issue between two or more students? What was the issue? How did you resolve it? Did it reoccur?

3. **Drive-by observations**: A few people walk through the building to count how many times they observe a specific behavior. They do not need to intercede unless there is a dangerous situation; they just make a visual confirmation and count. For example, how many students are actively participating during class?

4. **Staff or student vote**: This is useful for getting an idea about things that they find important and worthy of discussion. It can be used to determine the direction of interventions.

5. **Exit tickets**: These should pose questions that will help you get to a better understanding of the efficacy of professional development or other learning opportunities. The exit tickets should have at least three questions and ask about what participants learned, what more they want to learn, and what feedback they have for the teacher or presenter relating to the educational session.

Knowing What They Do and Building upon It

One of my favorite questions to use to gather data from educators is this: What strategies do you use to increase social and emotional competencies in your classroom or school? The answers to this question can help you to determine your next steps. What trends do you see? What resources are they using? What grade level seems to be most and least involved in teaching SEL? Are they using a curriculum, and if so, which one? What modalities do they prefer using to incorporate SEL? This data can be used during all your next steps—growing interest and leadership in SEL, forming a team from those who are already doing it and seeing success, action planning, identifying training needs, combatting resistance, and determining the outcomes of the SEL effort.

How Do We Gather Data About Our School and Community?

This type of data can also be easy to obtain, or it may require some work to put together a data set. When looking for school or district information, look at district data collection sites as well as state and local data collections. Some schools collect information on student health, rates of referrals to outside services, and soft skills. Direct information from students may be hard to come by depending on what access you have to that information, or on whether the district or school has invested in school climate measures. Most districts do have records about attendance, discipline rates, students with disabilities, graduation rates, et cetera.

After you have reviewed all of the accessible local data, you may find that there are gaps in information needed to understand your school and community. Demonstrating this gap to stakeholders may help build your case for more data collection. It is also suggested you connect with other school districts in your area. They may have already developed or gained access to the data to provide urgency for change in your region.

Data can be obtained through surveying other stakeholders outside of the students themselves. This includes teachers, parents, classified staff, educational assistants, support staff such as counselors, special education staff, psychologists, behavioral specialists, or union representatives. At times, information can be "siloed," so it is not being shared between parties of the same organization, school, or district.

Change agents must be comfortable learning more about the different stakeholders and the information and data that they have access to. Then they can build bridges between the different data sets to create a more comprehensive picture of the school and community.

Developing Your Own Accountability Tool

Use a Tiered Fidelity Inventory (Modified for Your Culture)

The primary reason to develop a tiered fidelity instrument is to help track progress year over year. This is often called progress monitoring; it is the process of systematically and repeatedly assessing performance with easy and quick tools to make decisions while the intervention is occurring. School teams can use this to demonstrate school improvement to the faculty, administrators, district personnel, parents and families, and community. There are great examples of tiered fidelity inventories out there. Generally, they are used for formative assessment, progress monitoring, annual self-assessment, and state recognition purposes. However, I believe the most powerful use occurs when schools build

Figure 5.4 Accountability Tool

Category	Expectations/ Agenda Items	Action Steps	Data Sources Documentation	Scoring Criteria	Score
Vision	Goal 1				
	Goal 2				
	Goal 3				
	Goal 4				
Teaming	Tier 1 team				
	Tier 2 team				
	District team				
Professional Staff Development	Administration				
	Teams				

(Continued)

(Continued)

Certificated staff				
Classified staff				
Out-of-school-time (OST) staff				
Whole-School SEL Competencies				
Self-awareness				
Self-management				
Social awareness				
Relationship skills				
Responsible decision making				
Staff SEL Practices				
Social teaching practices				
Instructional interactions				
Adult SEL competencies				

Data			Communication			Outreach		
Needs assessment	Universal screener	Surveys	Internal	In district	External	Students	Family engagement	Community

the tool to the specifications of their culture. Designing one yourself will help to guide your data collection specifically to meet your needs. Change agents at the school level can use this to gauge progress year over year. Inventories that I have designed include things like a self-score sheet with the categories shown in Figure 5.4.

The inventory is divided by the action steps, expectations/agenda items, data sources, scoring criteria, and scores. Developing your own accounting tool can be a powerful way to invest in a system-specific and detailed accounting. It also provides a way to communicate your process of systems change and the steps that you took along the way. Another benefit is that it helps the team be accountable for follow-through.

Data Threshold—Death by Data Collection

While all the data is required to understand systems and can be used to influence systems change, we must also be sensitive to data overload. There is a limit to individuals' capacity to hear, and interest in hearing, statistics about the state of education. To learn where this limit is, one strategy is to ask specific stakeholders who can give you a realistic sense of your audience's willingness to hear statistics. I somewhat jokingly talk about death by data collection. But if you have ever introduced the idea of data collection to a room of educators, you may understand what I mean. Data is critical for our understanding of where we are and where we need to be in the integration of whole-school SEL. However, we must also be sensitive to data overload. There is a data threshold—a limit to the amount of discussion, planning, and thinking about data that educators will do. Many hours of looking at charts, graphs, and dot matrix plots can drive most people out of the room.

One solution is to unpack one or two things at a time to work with as an entire staff. Large surveys may be full of data. And eager change agents may want to look at it all. But for most of the staff, they will need to begin these discussions with baby steps. Teachers may be used to looking at academic data, but data about social, emotional, and

A Case of Data Overload

Once I went to a training about Tier 1 implementation. The topic was "Success, Gaps, and Equity." This was of interest because I am always hoping to learn from other schools and districts about ways that they were successful, what they learned through the process of implementation, what they recommended, and how I could apply some of the things that they learned to my work.

For a three-hour meeting, the agenda read as follows:

- Introduction and purpose of meeting (15 min)
- Updates on implementation status, establishing baseline and sharing the story, school climate survey, staff self-assessment survey, data analytics (45 minutes)
- Coaching tools, resources and articles to promote fidelity and equitable outcomes, coaching as an action, fidelity inventory, building and district audit tools, implementation, professional development, evaluation blueprint, district capacity assessment (45 minutes)
- Professional development needs—poster activity (45 minutes)
- Shared calendar of events and training (15 minutes)
- Next steps, homework, and next meeting (15 minutes)

Notice there wasn't a bathroom break? I came out of that meeting very frustrated, because it did not meet my needs in any way. It was very datacentric and provided very little information about how I could take their success story and adapt it to my setting. While many educators, including me, have been overenthusiastic about the power of data, it can be overwhelming and frustrating for those who were hoping to walk away with usable ideas but instead heard a lot about assessments.

behavioral competencies and outcomes may be new. For qualitative data sets, discuss the themes in the data and potential ramifications of these themes.

When you are presenting the data, ask trusted stakeholders to give you a realistic assessment of the amount and type of data that will be most readily accepted. Think of data as the seasoning for a meal. Too much can make us turn away. Without seasoning, there is no depth. As with all things, we must find the happy medium. Use data to tell a story about systems change. Use the power of personalization: These are your kids, Joey and Josephina. They are not merely points on a plot. The story can be a very effective way for individuals to hear difficult information without being overwhelmed.

Data is a very important part of the work we do. Use data to inform your next steps in the problem-solving process. Use data to understand your population, their strengths and challenges. Use data to find out whether what you are doing is working. But most important, be clear about the *what and why* of data collection. And use your data intentionally to tell the story of your SEL implementation.

Practitioner's Voice

For content areas, I had been using data from assessments, along with standards, to determine what I needed to teach students. However, I was not using this same approach to teach students social-emotional skills; I often grabbed lessons or books because I liked them or they were recommended. The SEL content was disconnected from the student needs. Thus, I started to collect data on SEL skills through surveys, observations and screeners. I quickly learned what my students needed me to teach them in relation to topics such as how they solved problems, self-talk, friendship skills, assertiveness, etc. Using data to drive the social-emotional learning of my students was a game changer, as SEL instruction was targeted to the students' needs.

—Shelly Ward, PhD, PBIS/SEL Teacher on Special Assignment (TOSA)

Resources

Printed Material

- *Social-Emotional Learning Assessment Measures for Middle School Youth.* This report, by the Raikes Foundation, identifies valid, reliable, and useable schoolwide assessments. It can assist schools and districts in finding tools to assess SEL programs. (http://www.casel .org/wp-content/uploads/2016/01/DAP-Raikes-Foundation-Review-1.pdf)

- *Compendium of Preschool Through Elementary School SEL and Associate Assessment Measures.* This resource gives educators a list of the social and emotional learning assessments available for preschool and elementary school students, as well as assessments for other related learning behaviors. (http://www.casel.org/wp-content/uploads/2016/06/ compendium-of-preschool-through-elementary-school-social-emotional-learning-and- associated-assessment-measures.pdf)

- *Empowering Teachers With Tech-Friendly Formative Assessment Tools.* This article gives specific tips and applications for using observations, checklists, and quick quizzes to gather formative data about students. (https://www.edutopia.org/blog/tech-friendly- formative-assessment-tools-monica-burns)

(Continued)

(Continued)

Videos

- *Making Sure Each Child Is Known:* https://youtu.be/xjZx0VdmgkE

- *Learning Walks: Structured Observation for Teachers:* https://www.youtube.com/watch?v=AUTIIOfma90

Strategies

- Have staff take a survey about their beliefs or perceptions about your social, emotional, and behavioral intervention. One example is the *Staff Perceptions of Behavior and Discipline (SPBD) Survey:* www.spbdsupport.com

- Assess your student's feelings about physical and psychological safety through mapping. This strategy can be used to get student voice in understanding the safe and unsafe spaces in your school. Give students a map of the school and have them label areas on it as follows:

  1. Green—spaces where they feel comfortable

  2. Yellow—spaces where they feel unease

  3. Red—spaces they want to avoid as much as possible

- As a staff you can use this information to determine where you need to concentrate your efforts at promoting safety (which will help with connectedness) in the physical environment of your school.

REFLECTION QUESTIONS

1. What data collection procedures have taken place at your school?

2. What did you do with the data collected?

3. What training or professional development needs to take place to make staff feel comfortable with data discussions?

4. What are the perceptions among stakeholders for the various forms of data collection—screeners, needs assessments, surveys, accountability tool, et cetera?

5. What type of data will provide you the best next steps?

6. How do you plan to disseminate the results of your data collection?

7. What would you include in an accountability tool for your systems change work? How will it be perceived?

Strategy #4: Work With Others to Develop a Vision to Guide Change

People cannot learn by having information pressed into their brains. Knowledge has to be sucked into the brain, not pushed in. First, one must create a state of mind that craves knowledge, interest and wonder. You can teach only by creating an urge to know.

—Victor Weisskopf (1998, p. 194)

Vision Statement

A vision statement is a one-sentence statement that describes the change you hope will result after implementation of the program/process. A mission statement describes the why or reason for the change, and it is used to create goals and priorities. A feedback loop should be considered that addresses how information is routed through the system from the state, superintendent, principal, and leadership team to staff via professional development, and back to the leadership team with feedback from staff. Begin with the vision statement, and have as many stakeholders as possible offer feedback in the creation of the vision. Stakeholder buy-in is key to sustainable change. Program goals should also be consistent with district goals.

When collaborating, the why should drive the need and must be included in the rationale/vision. This is the best way to influence teachers. Many teachers can agree to the concepts of student-centered learning environments, focus on relationship, social and emotional growth, and real-world learning. Another important component when fleshing out the vision and goals of system change is to connect to school realities. Will this help them with their day-to-day responsibilities and their evaluation system? How does it connect to the realities of teaching?

Braiding District Vision With SEL Vision

Change agents need to think about how to braid the vision of SEL for all students and adults within the school system to the overall vision of the school. Many district and school vision statements include improvement for the whole child or the future of youth. SEL can usually fit within this type of vision.

It is important to align or braid together these visions to demonstrate that our goal for teaching and promoting SEL is just another piece to developing and preparing students for life outside of formal education. Academic knowledge and SEL go hand in hand. With these two pieces working together, students are given the skills to succeed in college and career, in relationships and in their communities, and be resilient in the face of adversity.

In 2016, American Institutes for Research came out with a report, *When Districts Support and Integrate Social and Emotional Learning (SEL): Findings From an Ongoing Evaluation of Districtwide Implementation of SEL* (Kendziora & Yoder, 2016). One of the recommendations from this report is to coordinate efforts to support all systems. Change agents can use the vision to braid together the various initiatives, projects, and/or committees in schools. This process helps schools to consider the items that need to be braided together to provide continuity between the goals, strategies, measures, and outcomes of all initiatives that improve social and emotional competencies. An example template to use for this process is shown in Figure 6.1.

Figure 6.1 Braiding Example

Vision: (District/School or Initiative) Vision Statement Here
Goal 1:
Goal 2:
Goal 3:

Initiative, Project, or Committee	Purpose	Aligns With Which Goal	Target Group	Staff Involved	Outcomes
SEL curriculum	Teachers will deliver the selected SEL curriculum to increase their students' social and emotional competencies.	Goal 1	All students	All staff	This school year all students received 20 SEL lessons. Competencies were measured through teacher reports.
Growth mindset book study					
Bullying education					
School improvement plans					
PBIS (positive behavior interventions and supports)					
Academic curriculum					
School-based mental health services					
Afterschool programming					
MTSS/RTI					
College and career readiness					
Discipline practices					

Results of the Braiding Activity

In Fairview Junior High, the staff had been using a discipline referral form that listed nine of the most common issues that teachers observed. The form listed the demerits that students would receive because of the referral. When it came time to integrate the practices of SEL, the team discovered that the discipline referral process was antithetical to the changes they were trying to make in the building. The staff had many good discussions about the role of discipline and intentional teaching of expected behaviors. The discipline discussions weren't always easy. The staff did not always agree. But they worked through the process, gave their feedback, listened to and learned from each other, and eventually agreed upon a progressive discipline process that aligned with the school vision.

Each of these separate programs and processes should braid into a central vision for your school or district. These are the practices that produce the outcomes that fulfill the vision that you see for the students at your school.

A Sales Problem

Getting everyone on board with the vision can be challenging. Once, when I was working with a school district, we were having a very difficult time gaining traction with our change efforts. We seemed to encounter resistance at every turn, and people had a difficult time understanding what we were trying to do. My staff was frustrated, and I was struggling with how I could move us forward. As I often do when I am looking for the answer, I return to my resources—my books, papers, and notes that I have taken over the years. There on the shelf was a book I had bought but hadn't had the time to read, Daniel Pink's *To Sell Is Human: The Surprising Truth About Moving Others* (2012). This happy accident helped my staff and me to conceptualize our issue. We had a *sales problem*. Our change effort seemed so large, the components so multifaceted, and the role so new that we didn't have the language to explain what we were doing in a way that our constituents could understand, let alone get behind and support.

In the book, Pink discusses the Pixar pitch (Pink, 2012). Pixar stories follow a narrative structure that involves six sequential sentences:

1. Once upon a time _____
2. Every day _____
3. One day _____
4. Because of that, _____
5. Because of that, _____
6. Until finally, _____

For example: Once upon a time, the principals, teachers, deans, administrators, and special services staff worked with kids who had challenges that impacted them at school. Everyday these employees would work tirelessly to help these students. One day, X school decided to integrate SEL to help all students.

Figure 6.2 Sound Bite Examples

Question	Sound Bite
What is my role in this systems change effort?	I am advocating for whole-school SEL at our school. Would you like to learn more?
Where do I practice my role?	I use SEL in my classroom and I am working with school leadership to form a team. Would you like to join the team?
When do we practice?	Team meetings will be monthly, but I practice weekly in my classroom. Would you like to drop by and watch?
How do I support this change effort?	You can support the change effort by participating in the training and advocating for SEL with me. Would you be interested in participating in a training?

Because of that, students and adults learned how to become more self-aware and more socially aware, developed relationship skills, and became more able to self-manage and more responsible decision makers. Because of that, schools became even more positive, which led to better school culture and student outcomes. Until finally, all students and staff felt supported, and they learned social and emotional skills that enriched their lives.

Going through this process helps to refine your vision and ability to verbalize what you are doing in a way that is meaningful to people not immersed in your work. It is effective for creating "sound bites" for individuals who are working on systems change but need to explain what they are doing to stakeholders who do not have the experience or time to understand all the detailed work that the individuals are undergoing.

Have these answers ready for stakeholders by completing the exercise in Figure 6.2.

Vision for Leadership

In *Ready to Lead: A National Principal Survey on How Social and Emotional Learning Can Prepare Children and Transform Schools* (DePaoli, Atwell, & Bridgeland, 2017), the results of a survey of 884 preK–12 public school principals were published, along with interviews with 16 superintendents and 10 district-level research and evaluation specialists representing diverse school districts with varying levels of experience in implementing SEL programming. The good news is that principals and district leaders across the nation found potential in SEL. Although they see the value of SEL, they need support, resources, and tools to help them fully implement systemic SEL initiatives that can improve students' SEL competencies (DePaoli et al., 2017). One recommendation was that the schools perceived as most successful in integrating SEL usually involved more people in systemic implementation. Change agents get many different stakeholders invested in the vision.

Insider Versus Outsider

Change agents must consider those participants and the leverage they have in the system. Someone who is an insider may know more about the internal workings of the

Graphic 6.1 Vision for Leadership

Administrative	• Principal • Vice or assistant principals • Deans
Certified	• Teachers (grade levels represented) • Counselors • Psychologists
Classified	• Paraprofessionals or educational assistant • Secretary • Nurse
Students	
Parents/Families	

Figure 6.3 Identify Change Agents

Who are your proponents for change in your school?	
Are your change agents able to collaborate across grade levels and job roles?	
Do your change agents have the trust of the staff?	
What skills do your change agents possess to advocate for change?	

system and may have more success building strategic alliances that support the vision. Change agents who are considered outsiders must use their perceived expertise to their advantage. Figure 6.3 lists ways to identify change agents.

Staff Consensus

Consensus is crucial when forming a vision for the work. Staff consensus does not necessarily mean that everyone agrees. Formal consensus procedures work well in systems where the expectation is that we work together but we may not always agree. These procedures help stakeholders work together to find a mutually acceptable solution. If your school does not practice consensus-based decision making, it may be worth considering. It can help with the process of determining a vision for your work. And it can be used at many other decision points during implementation of SEL.

There are five levels of consensus:

1. I can say an unqualified "yes."

2. I can accept the decision.

3. I can live with the decision.

4. I do not fully agree with the decision; however, I will not block it and will support it.

5. I refuse to enter consensus.

Do we want the fourth level of consensus as our typical response? It isn't ideal, but we have to expect that, in a school with a variety of personalities, this will happen. If you have more than one member who strongly believes that this is the wrong thing to do and refuses to enter consensus, it is time to take a pause. At that point, it will be a good idea to try to understand the point of view of the dissenting members. They may be your canary in the coal mine. It may require more negotiation to get to a point where true consensus can be achieved.

Your School Leaders—Are They on Board?

In my experience, it is requisite to invest principals in understanding the data that is gathered. In many districts, principals are "keepers of the vision." They can make or break an innovation based on their interest, comfort level, and perceived need of the intervention.

Principals have a lot to balance when running their schools, and if they are not convinced of the need for change, it may not take a priority in their building. When discussing the urgency for change with principals, emphasize the positive outcomes that can occur after implementation. One must address any concerns or questions to get to the heart of any misconceptions. I have found it important to get feedback in many different forms from principals—through informal conversations, exit tickets, meetings, and visiting their schools. Exit tickets can be used as a source of data where themes can be developed to get a sense of what needs clarity and what direction would be best to inform the next steps.

Change agents can learn more about feedback in an educational context from John Hattie and Helen Timperley. They suggest that effective feedback answers three questions (Hattie & Timperley, 2007): Where am I going? How am I going? And where to next? When you ask for feedback, make sure students or staff have time to process your request. Most of the items that you will be asking for feedback on will require deep thinking. This kind of processing requires time (Hattie & Timperley, 2007). Think about this when you are asking for feedback from any educational stakeholders, and allow them the time to process their thoughts.

A word of advice: Make sure that you *use the data* that you collect, and be explicit about how it guided your next steps. Principals, stakeholders . . . really everyone will not want to take the time to give opinions if you aren't using them in some way to inform your next steps.

Follow the Leader

Principals and district administrators need to forward the vision to their constituents. When the change agent is not the principal, an important first step is to understand how the leaders plan to forward the vision. Be open to their input even if you don't see things the same way. Colvin and Sprick (1999) suggest these action steps:

1. Make public statements of support.
2. Continue to work toward obtaining faculty/staff consensus.
3. Develop leadership teams to support the vision.
4. Maintain standards for the vision.
5. Embed the vision in the decision-making/problem-solving process.
6. Reinforce actions that fall in line with the vision.

Increase Principal Buy-In

The best way to promote SEL is in collaboration with your school principal. Principals have many responsibilities, and they may need to know the best way to support you and the effort within a brief amount of time. Preparing information in advance is one way to increase principal buy-in. Here are some suggestions to achieve this goal:

- Give principals actionable steps that fall in line with their current needs and goals.
- Provide opportunities for collaboration and sharing.
- Seek ongoing feedback throughout the year from stakeholders to see how things are going. What are their highest priorities?
- Tailor support based on self-selected goals.
- Consistently acknowledge gains—one-on-one and in small groups.
- Give them control (if not over what, then over when)—If a curriculum or intervention has been identified for implementation, can they choose when they start or who they will start with? Do they think their staff is ready? If not, what do they need to help get them ready?
- Give opportunities for principals doing good work to shine among peers by asking
  - What are they proud of?
  - What steps did they take to accomplish it?
  - What strategies did they use?
  - What feedback did they collect?
  - What recommendations do they have?

Principal Concerns

Whether the principal is the lead of the change advocacy effort or not, it is critical to be able to address questions the principal will naturally have as the leader of the school. Having a sense of how you might answer these questions will accelerate the change process. Figure 6.4 will help you prepare these answers.

Changing Paradigms

Everyone involved in systems change will come at the work with a different academic background. They will have varying levels of experience in and out of schools. They may have been administrators or supervisors before, or they may have not. With each unique individual comes a unique point of view. Even within my field, a psychologist,

Figure 6.4 Principal Checklist

Need Procedures for _____		Steps:
A checklist		
Timeline		
Professional development		
Resources		
How can they support?		
How do they evaluate?		
How do they communicate?		

a counselor, a psychiatrist, and a social worker may all approach an issue from different vantage points. The differences will hopefully add to the depth of understanding of your school culture. But as you develop your vision, you will want to adjust the paradigm, thinking about things and the way you approach them in a new way. As a teacher or counselor, you may be used to people coming to you. But as a change agent, you will have to reach out to people. Seek them out to discover their thoughts and opinions. A change agent must be selfless in pursuit of understanding and coming to a compromise that promotes the well-being of students and staff.

Live the Vision

The reason there is such an investment in developing your own leadership skills is that you will need to demonstrate them regularly as a change agent. Your ability to practice and model these advocacy skills will be challenged. You model the behavior that you want to see daily when you work with kids. You demonstrate to the students the way that you want them to act based on the way that you act. This is also how we need to work with adults: living in a way that brings the competencies of SEL to life. This is true especially with relationships. Relationships are sacrosanct. Good relationships with your colleagues are built on keeping an open mind, positive presupposition, and listening. These practices that you demonstrate on a regular basis help others to see what is possible and how they can potentially use it in their own lives. You will represent service to the school as you live the vision.

Vision Standards

Best-case Scenario

At this point, you have a foundation for the work, a framework to organize it, competencies that you want to enhance, and data that drives the work. Determining your vision and the standards to support your vision can also be driven by data—data about what it takes to be successful in the future. It is the process of the integration of SEL that gets us closer to our vision.

Standards to Support the Vision

The vision may include a sentence or two, but there need to be standards that support the vision. The words used in the vision must be defined in a way that all stakeholders understand them. For example, if your vision includes the term *whole child,* do your stakeholders understand your definition of that term? Change agents should also understand the standards of the vision. The standards relate to the vision but are not necessarily goals. Some of the talking points to support the vision are listed below. Understanding your stance on these talking points will make it much easier to advocate for SEL.

1. **Key concepts**
   - Importance of understanding and believing in school climate, SEL, and that positive relationships affect outcomes for students
   - Importance of using evidence-based interventions and data collection to ensure fidelity of implementation and gauge efficacy
   - Importance of supporting the advocacy work with the staff

2. **Knowledge of outcomes and expectations for SEL implementation**
   - Brief description of SEL and the research behind it
   - Brief description of whole-school SEL and how it impacts school culture
   - How this information can be integrated into the evaluation system and Common Core

3. **How to communicate the vision, and to whom**
   - Webpage
   - Parent/families monthly workshop
   - Family engagement
   - Resource management
   - Community outreach/resource

4. **Roadmap for SEL implementation**
   - Estimate how long implementation takes
   - Assurances of investment in SEL to stakeholders
   - Professional development/training
   - Meeting schedule
   - What do the first few weeks look like?

Embed Vision in Practice

It is essential to always connect to larger goals. My central role in working with change agents is to provide them with strategies to move toward their vision while immersed in the complicated work of systems change. Change agents must look at the impacts of the implementation on the entire system. The reason you are implementing an innovation can lead to an explanation of how it fits into a district vision or mandate that can impact outcomes.

As you move forward, it is important to embed the vision in the decision-making process. Sometimes interventions can get off track because of a specific curriculum used, or an enthusiastic change agent, or an unforeseen incident. Keeping the vision in sight helps you to avoid the natural detours that come up when you are doing this long-term work. The vision is your North Star, guiding you to the place you want to be. Review your practices with this lens so that the vision is the thing that guides you.

Voicing the Vision

The most successful examples of voicing the vision have similar elements. Voice the vision by using different voices: The more and varied individuals who can voice their enthusiasm and appreciation for SEL, the better. Team members can speak to their colleagues about their successes and challenges. They are good at animating the practices and how they are guided in the vision for the work. Also, individuals can speak to different methods of using SEL. Allow staff to be involved, to hear how they can see the connection between the vision and the practice in their own words. The vision is, at its best, made alive by the practitioners.

Practitioner's Voice

A school needs a healthy school culture in order for students and teachers to thrive. School culture (like soil) should be cultivated by the principal, but leadership must be shared among staff to ensure long-term health for the school as a system. When teachers support and teach the SEL strategies like they do academics, students are more successful inside and outside the classroom and are better equipped for the future.

—Ali West Shepard, elementary school principal

Resources

Printed Material

- *The Power of Feedback* (Hattie & Timperley, 2007)
- *Communicating an Action Plan to Stakeholders* (https://drc.casel.org/communication)
- *Ready to Lead: A National Principal Survey on How Social and Emotional Learning Can Prepare Children and Transform Schools* (DePaoli et al., 2017)

Videos

- *Why "To Sell Is Human"*: https://www.youtube.com/watch?v=J6EjBwrdHgE
- *SEL Expert Roger Weissberg on Academics and Character Education:* https://www.youtube.com/watch?v=oGZKfKjDgVc
- *How Does the WHY Relate to Vision?:* https://youtu.be/C1yPpShOH-s

Strategies

- Learn more about "Unjumbling the Schoolhouse and Assessing School Culture and Climate" from the Academy for Social-Emotional Learning in Schools Certificate Program through College of Saint Elizabeth/Rutgers: http://sel.cse.edu/
- Invest time in learning about this consensus-based decision-making process from the School Reform Initiative: http://schoolreforminitiative.org/doc/consensus_decision.pdf

REFLECTION QUESTIONS

1. What is your elevator pitch for SEL in your school?

2. Who will you involve in the creation of your vision?

3. What is your strategy to communicate your vision to stakeholders?

4. If the principal is not leading this change, what do you need to do to help the principal understand the need for this type of change?

5. What standards will be needed to maintain the vision?

6. How will you set up a system to gather feedback about the vision and the standards that support the vision?

7. How do you plan to empower others to act in service of the vision?

Strategy #5: Understand the Politics of Your Workplace

It must not be left to genes and parents to foster greatness; spurring individual achievement is also the duty of society. Every culture must strive to foster values that bring out the best in its people.

—David Shenk (2010, p. 116)

Understand the Politics of Your Workplace (Yes, Even in Kindergarten)

It is my hope that you haven't had to endure the type of sabotage that can happen in places of work. But this is a real part of education. Part of the role of the change agent is to analyze sources of political power and social influence. Political power can be both obvious—based on employment status and rank—or not obvious and having to do with the social influence that an individual can have in the building.

Bolman and Deal (2003) discuss using four frames to view organizations: structural, political, human resources, and symbolic. The most challenging but necessary frame when working with school or district administration is the political frame. Bolman and Deal (2003) describe how to reframe the political to cope with power and conflict in systems. An effective leader in the political frame is an advocate or negotiator. Therefore, the advocacy competencies align very well in the systems change process when dealing with the political frame. The leadership process includes both advocacy and coalition building.

Coalition building includes finding the common ground or goal that stakeholders can get behind. The essential strategies of the political frame include creating arenas where issues can be negotiated, and forming new coalitions. Change agents should become invested in learning what arenas are feasible in their environment. They will want to meet stakeholders where they are, and that includes a specific location. I found

When Teachers Disagree

At Magnolia High School, Ms. Wu was a team teacher with Mr. Nash. Ms. Wu and Mr. Nash disagreed about a specific student. Mr. Nash wanted the student removed from his class due to her disrespect and sporadic attendance. Ms. Wu felt compassion for the student because of her difficult home situation and was trying to work with her. Mr. Nash went to the administration and complained about the student, explaining that because she was 18, had gone over the unexcused absence limit, and was currently failing the class, he felt she should be removed. Ms. Wu prevailed and was able to keep her in the class even though she still failed the class in the end. Mr. Nash was furious, especially when Ms. Wu entered on the report card that she was "a pleasure to have in class." The next year Ms. Wu was interested in adopting a new program and was trying to talk to her administration and team about looking into it. Mr. Nash campaigned against the initiative and convinced some of the staff members to also boycott it. Ms. Wu knew this was related to the confrontation about the student last year, not about the program, but there was nothing she could do.

that visiting different schools and being willing to see things from those specific locations allowed for more openness to change within those environments.

When working with the political frame, Bolman and Deal (2003) describe the barriers to change to include such issues as disempowerment and conflict between winners and losers. As a change agent, my most vital role is to make sure stakeholders are made aware that their positive actions to improve the lives of children are recognized and reinforced. Within a district there can be political favorites, which may cause other schools and individuals to feel that they are "have-nots." Determine whether this is the case with your schools, and work toward providing equity of services so everyone can experience being in the "winner" category. Change agents need to do their best to be immune to political favoritism and be equitable when offering their time and resources.

Social Network Theory

Social network theory helps us understand how teacher collaboration can support or constrain teaching, learning, and educational change (Moolenaar, 2012). Teacher collaboration includes school culture that emphasizes the norms of collegiality, trust, and support.

When thinking about the use of SEL programs and curriculums for your school, consider that the networks at school may be centralized around informal leaders in the building, and subgroups may have formed that reflect similar ages or other commonalities (Moolenaar, 2012). Another type of social network may develop around school goals or activities, for example, groups who work on a fundraiser, a book study, or as a sports coaching team. And school relationships often look like friendships—they form among people who enjoy spending time together and sharing private details of their lives outside of teaching (Moolenaar, 2012).

Although we can find commonalities among social network structures, it does not mean that all schools will be structured similarly. This makes the importance of understanding and the processing of interventions that much more interesting and unique. These networks can impact student performance indirectly. Political power among stakeholders and relationships between the teachers in the school matter. And as we can see in the above narrative, the relationships affect collaboration. It is central to consider the change agent within the school and district context.

Leveraging Relationships

One of the best examples of leveraging relationships happened at Frost Elementary School. Ms. Harrison was hired as a coach to help the school integrate and learn SEL practices. In her second year on the job, she was relocated to a new school. The principal had not bought in to SEL, and the progress of the initiative was very slow in the first year. When Ms. Harrison was brought on, she knew that it would be an uphill climb to energize the staff. She had worked with some of the staff previously and began her work with them, gaining their trust, supporting them in and out of class. The members of her SEL team were the first to realize how important she was to the school. They were not shy about verbalizing this to me and others. This became the school mantra, that Ms. Harrison was so important to the success of SEL at their school. Because of that, Ms. Harrison was able to move the school in a direction to try new things and develop new processes, and staff felt that this process was worth the time and effort they were dedicating to it. The principal pulled me aside and let me know that her staff would be very upset if she got moved again. Her ability to leverage her relationships undoubtedly led to the progress of SEL in that elementary school.

Power

We do not often talk about power in the school system. But power, who has it, and how it is used affect many individuals in schools. It is important to consider the change agents. Are they insiders in the school? Do they have relationships already established? Are they known within the system to have a specific work style or people they generally work with? Or are they outsiders who have no alliances within the system? This will change the power dynamic among the people involved in systems change.

What Is a Sociogram?

One strategy to discover who has the power and influence in your building is to create a sociogram. Educators may be familiar with the practice of using a sociogram for students in their classrooms. But you can find out valuable information about perceived leaders in your SEL work from doing this exercise. (A brief warning—as with any strategy, make sure you take cautious consideration of your staff before engaging in this exercise.)

A sociogram is a charting of the interrelationships within a group. Its purpose is to discover group structure: that is, the basic network of friendship patterns and subgroups. The relations of any one individual to the group as a whole are another type of information that can be derived from a sociogram. A sociogram's value to a teacher is in its potential for developing greater understanding of group behavior, so that the teacher may operate more wisely in group management and curriculum development (http://www.6seconds.org).

Sociograms may be constructed in a variety of ways. The methods described here are ones that teachers have used and found not too difficult or time consuming. During data collection, the change agent will collect the basic material from which a sociogram is constructed, as group members answer questions such as these:

1. Which three staff members would you ask for help if you needed it?

2. Which three staff members would you go to if you needed an intervention or strategy for your classroom?

3. What three people in this group do you most admire?

4. Which three people in this group would you most enjoy hanging out with outside of school?

The results of this should be kept private. This is merely to determine who the teachers perceive to be most helpful and who they are most connected to. If you can find this information, you could ask those individuals who are ranked highly to work with you too in the SEL effort. If teachers who are the go-to for helping other staff members out can speak positively about your intervention, you will make more headway. To learn more about your current social network, draw a diagram. Who is at the center? Who works with whom? How are these social networks connected to each other? The graphics that follow illustrate the process of constructing a sociogram.

Norms of Collaboration

When analyzing political power and social influence, be aware of the norms of collaboration that have been previously established. Teaching can be a lonely endeavor at times. While it may be a norm to collaborate in an elementary school, middle and high schools can be much more segmented by subjects they teach, buildings across a large campus, and schedules. When I worked in a high school, during whole-staff meetings, staff from similar departments would sit together: the physical education teachers at one table, the

Teacher	Help	Strategies	Admire	Friends
Smith	Washington	Wilson	Wilson	Ortega
Washington	Taniq	Adams	Salazar	Hamilton
Ortega	Salazar	Adams	Jefferson	Hamilton
Lincoln	Jefferson	Wilson	Jefferson	Jefferson
Adams	Washington	Taniq	Salazar	Salazar
Wilson	Ortega	Ortega	Washington	Adams
Salazar	Ortega	Hamilton	Jefferson	Adams
Taniq	Salazar	Adams	Jefferson	Adams
Jefferson	Franklin	Lincoln	Hamilton	Lincoln
Franklin	Washington	Adams	Wilson	Wilson
Williams	Taniq	Taniq	Taniq	Taniq
Hamilton	Adams	Adams	Washington	Washington
Total	Washington = 3	Adams = 5	Jefferson = 4	Adams = 3

Graphic 7.2 Sociogram Results Example

Strategies

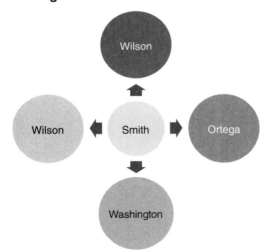

For each category:

1. Who is represented the most? Is it the same person in every category?

2. Is there anyone who was not chosen by anyone?

3. Are most of the choices mutual or one-way, where the choice is not reciprocated?

4. Do you see groupings of individuals who only choose each other?

5. Determine if you can find patterns to discover which teacher might have the most social capital to be on your team?

math teachers at another, and so on. And there may be a power differential even between subjects. That is why change agents should have a good understanding of the norms of collaboration within the school.

History of Interventions

Part of understanding the politics of your workplace is to learn about the history of interventions at your school or district. This includes the history of how the interventions

Figure 7.1 An Introductory Conversation About Previous Interventions

Intervention	Pros	Cons	Suggestions
Introduction to intervention			
Education of staff about intervention			
Training for intervention			
Continuing discussion of intervention			
Discussion of outcomes of intervention			
Revision of intervention as new information is learned			

were introduced, who is paying for them, and who made those decisions. Any SEL intervention will be perceived in the light of former interventions. Much of the pushback from teachers and administrators comes from a poorly designed or received intervention from the past. This is yet another reason to understand the history of interventions with your school. In my experience, two mistakes are most common in previous interventions. The first is an intervention that was mandated without any level of understanding or agreement: Staff were forced to integrate something that they had no voice in. The second big mistake is an intervention for which the staff perceives there has been little return on investment, paying a lot of money with little to show for it, or spending a lot of time with little to show for it. Or even more troublesome is an intervention for which a lot of time, money, and resources have been spent for something that no one fully understands, and it goes away after a few years.

One strategy to find out if there may be roadblocks is to discover the history of interventions at your school. Ask staff the following questions: What have the stakeholders experienced with past interventions? What will be required to accentuate the positives of previous interventions? What will be required to correct the flaws in past interventions? Figure 7.1 is a template you can use to record their answers.

Importance of Who Is on the Team

Raise your hand if you'd like to volunteer to be on a team. Anyone? Working in teams is a major part of education. You may volunteer or "be volunteered" to join teams many times as an educator. Systems change agents must invest in their teams to get the best from them. If the teams are a "sit and get" opportunity or a complaint session, you will not get the best use of everyone's time

The purpose of the school team is to use data and assessments to determine the school's needs, set priorities and monitor practices within the school, identify schoolwide strategies, provide for staff training, identify resources, oversee program implementation, and share team goals and outcomes within the school.

Make sure that your team can discuss and elaborate on your purpose. Can they speak to others about your proposed change? Do they have an elevator speech? Everyone on the team should be able to talk about the benefits of your program or process. *Make sure that they have an answer to the question, What's in it for me?*

Developing an SEL Team

The first step when developing a school-level team is to engage diverse stakeholders, including building administrators, teachers, counselors, school psychologists, social workers, and classified staff. Depending on your district, you may also have a district-level team. A district-level team is designed to address multischool leadership and collaboration. Ideally, the team will consist of representatives of administrators from each school level as well as the specialists that support the tiered system. Over time, teachers, parents, and community representatives will be asked to join the team. The primary function of the team is to engage in leadership and coordination to support and sustain the implementation of evidence-based practice. Members of the team will provide overall leadership related to assessing, developing, implementing, managing, and evaluating the program. The team will work together to craft solutions to emerging issues as they arise. They will also help to revise a long-term action plan to guide the capacity-building and coordination efforts.

Basic Elements of Teaming—How to Approach the Work

Most schools are familiar with the purpose of teaming. Teams are formed to solve problems, organize resources, plan events, or resolve conflicts. Teams can be short-term for a specific issue or event, or long-term, such as a leadership team. Your SEL team should be considered a long-term team, because the implementation will be purposeful and will take dedication from the team members.

The team structure should follow best practice guidelines that are clear for all who are considering adoption of interventions. This team structure should integrate processes and programs currently working well in the system. This will signal to any concerned parties that you honor and respect the good work that took place before, and it does have a place in your new system. *Developing a team that is dedicated to the work of systems change is vital for success!*

The Players on Your Team: Cheerleaders, Power Players, Positive and Productive People

It is not only important to engage diverse stakeholders. The implementation team needs to have a few members to energize and applaud the efforts at systems change. These teams should be chosen specifically with faculty who will cheerlead this change. They are well respected in the building and not afraid to be the first one to try new things. These are your early adopters and they will help guide the work within the building. These individuals should be able to use data/assessments to determine building needs, set priorities and monitor practices within the school, identify schoolwide strategies, provide staff training and resources, oversee program implementation, and share team goals and outcomes within the building.

These team members should be available to meet monthly. They can be responsible for items on the agenda such as collection, management, and analysis of data; taking notes; keeping time; and communication with each member of the team. These jobs can rotate regularly so that everyone has a turn doing the more tedious jobs. Team members should follow an agenda and record their meetings. The agenda should include

- the date
- who is to be in attendance
- previously defined problems (who, what, where, when, why)

The Meeting Dominator

Once I was working with a school team on which one of the members was unable to read the body language of her coworkers. She belabored her points and talked through the valuable time they had together. Her coworkers rolled their eyes and doodled on their agendas while she talked. My feeling was that this person, although intelligent and well meaning, was pushing the other members away. This level of disinterest could become toxic. I spoke with the change agent on the team and asked her what she thought she could do about this. She was initially resistant to discussing it with the team member, but in the end, she did find that the team's work was being stifled. Therefore, it is so important to have the skills of an advocate. You need to advocate for the most productive people that you can find to be on your team, or people will quit just to avoid hearing one member pontificate.

- o solution actions, by whom? by when? (goal and timeline, fidelity of implementation, effectiveness of solution)
- general information and issues
- new problems (who, what, where, when, why)
  - o solution actions, by whom? by when? (goal and timeline, fidelity of implementation, effectiveness of solution)

Teams may use different agenda items, but overall the agenda should be consistent and contain the data that you will need as you appraise the work the team has done over the years.

Sticking to an agenda consistently may be a challenge at first. Typically, agendas have too little information or too much. It may take a few attempts to find the sweet spot in your agenda creation. The important point is at the end it will tell the story of what you did, when you did it, what the results were, and who was a part of this work.

The "What" of School SEL Teams

Choosing who is involved on the SEL team is crucial, but it is also important to think about what the teams need for success. The planning for what teams need in advance will help to alleviate political issues down the line. Team members can use specialized skills such as data analysis, facilitating and leading teams, developing plans, presentation, report writing, and data collection to build a solid team.

What Teams Need

1. **Create comprehensive job descriptions for the team member role.**
   - What will your team members do? What are they responsible for?
   - What are the similarities and differences between this team and other teams in the school?
   - Expectations for team members: These can include extra training, paid meeting times outside their contract, creating and/or leading professional development for stakeholders—teachers, certificated staff, families, community, participation in reflection exercises, data collection and analysis, and active participation and responsibility for action planning.

2. **Identify materials for data collection.**
   - Use the team meeting agenda described previously for organization of data collection efforts at every meeting Data collection to inform your process can include
     - Votes
     - Exit tickets: KWLB (What do we KNOW? What do we WANT to know? What have we LEARNED? How will this BENEFIT us?)
     - Interviews
     - Surveys
     - Observations
     - Needs assessments
     - Team input

3. **Determine the range of strategies for SEL implementation that team members will promote when problem solving.**
   - Teachers will have different needs, and teams should be able to provide them different strategies to try.
   - There needs to be an understanding that there is not one perfect strategy for everyone.

4. **Identify methods to check in—formally or informally—to get a sense of how the intervention is going.**
   - Check in with principals.
   - Check in with change agents and implementers.
   - Check in with stakeholders.

Making Working Together Work

For those of us working in school districts, we know that we may not always have a choice in the "who." My strategy is to choose team members when I can and make plans for those times when I cannot. All the people on my teams have come with different skill sets, and it has been my job to find out what they excelled at, give them room to run with it, and help develop the skills they needed work on. I infuse a growth mindset and the "power of yet" in my work with the individuals I supervise in systems change. The power of yet is a strategy used by many educators to represent that learning is a process, and we may not be where we want to be, but we continue to strive to reach our goals. For example, "We haven't gotten full commitment by the staff to try this SEL strategy…yet."

One quality that I promoted was for us to "take our own medicine." This means that above all we had to practice what we preached. We did not ask our teachers to do what we could not, and we modeled good relationships and collaboration very intentionally. We developed norms and worked together to make them live in our meetings, our conversations, and our day-to-day interactions. The norms included things like keeping an open mind, positive presupposition, and listening to all voices. It was impressed upon my teams that relationship is revered above all other things. This can be a humbling experience.

It is profoundly meaningful to take part in change that affects systems and individuals positively. Your team members will likely grow and develop new skills as a part of this process.

Good Relationships

If we want to have real lasting success in leadership or advocacy efforts, we must prove ourselves invaluable in the process of improving our schools. We must recognize the need for our specific skill sets and how to use our expertise in helping teachers (and other members of the school staff). As relationships are established, the trust and respect will allow us to lead implementation of SEL.

When building good relationships, don't talk at the stakeholders without learning who they are and what they care about or what they are afraid of with implementation of these new strategies. Some ways to build relationships include these:

- Listen deeply.

- Pay attention to others' reactions and one's understanding of problem.

- Build rapport.

- Respect how people define their own goals and self-interests.

- Offer action options, and encourage others—do not force them—to take next step.

Incorporate individual strengths by inviting teachers to contribute strategies about how to build relationships in schools, and encourage other beneficial ideas from staff. Some individuals intuitively create relationships. But how would you instruct someone to do what naturally comes to you? What were the steps before you went in the classrooms? How can you lay the groundwork for teachers to not only accept but want to collaborate? How can you use your experience to provide insight into the perspectives of those with different roles? The best way to get buy-in from teachers might be to share how you bought into SEL. How do you build relationships and navigate the political environment of your schools? Who can help develop strategies? What do you understand from the perspective of your role?

Another piece of building a good relationship is to understand what they bring to the table. In some cases, you have hundreds of years of experience collectively in your building; tap into that. For example, school psychologists may have great ideas about how to be inclusive of students with disabilities. Physical education teachers may have great ideas about classroom management for large groups. Math teachers may excel in data analysis. Use your local talent as a resource for your change efforts.

The Good Practices Ambassadors

In Lincoln Middle School, the team decided that their passion for SEL could be demonstrated in the small everyday moments at school. The team talked about their successes and challenges with SEL implementation whenever they could. It became part of the regular conversation. When they heard classes that were going well, the team members asked the teachers to speak about what they are doing to the rest of the staff. When things were challenging for a teacher, they helped connect the teacher with someone who overcame a similar challenge. The relationships were strengthened through the informal problem solving that happens in the hallway or in the break room.

Conflict Resolution Skills

To maximize the efficacy of their implementation efforts, change agents should be informed how to best alter beliefs. Discussion about beliefs should be nonconfrontational, so the change agents are not singling any person out. All conversations about beliefs should be reflective. If the topic is especially sensitive, it may be better to talk about discussion norms and expectations at the beginning of the discussion. Change agents should understand their own process when it comes to managing difficult conversations.

You can begin by asking yourself the following:

1. What do I typically do when I must have a difficult conversation?

2. What am I most afraid of when I face a difficult conversation?

3. Process: How did the conversation go, and what can I do to improve it for next time?

This may be the most unexpected thing that change agents experience when thinking about implementing SEL, the conflict. To a change agent, it may be inconceivable that individuals who take part in educating youth would not see the value in teaching social and emotional skills to students. They cannot image that their fellow colleagues don't see the value in improving their school climate and culture. They cannot fathom being confronted with a staff member who refuses to implement social and emotional strategies. Dealing with that conflict is part and parcel of the work of a change agent.

Growth Mindset

I find that for the most part, teachers believe that students benefit from having a growth mindset. Change agents can use this concept to promote new learning and discovery, goal-oriented behavior, and hard work. This growth mindset will need to be applied when looking at our teaching practices, our classroom expectations, our discipline procedures, our systems, the way that we see students, and especially, the way we interpret student behavior.

Having a growth mindset allows individuals to understand that it is okay to make mistakes. This way of thinking can help us adapt to change and challenges we face. We must understand what we believe about being wrong. As educators, we are supposed to have the answers. Being wrong can cause shame or other negative emotions. These feelings are difficult to manage and affect an individuals' perceptions about themselves and their judgment. It can also affect their well-being. Therefore, growth mindset is so powerful. It gives us permission to think differently about being wrong, failure, and change. Adopting this new frame of understanding enhances our ability to learn from our mistakes as we engage with students in a different way.

More Issues

Unfortunately, not everyone will support your change effort. Change agents need to learn as much about the system and its hierarchy as they do about the planned intervention. There are many considerations when determining what your position is in the power structure. Here are four of the most crucial questions to ask:

1. **What is the budget for this change effort?** We know that budgets can make or break your SEL efforts. If you do not have direct access to the budget or spending resources, you will need to know who does, and learn the following:

- Who determines the budget
- A clear understanding of how the intervention will be funded, at present and for the long term
- How much is budgeted for
- Training (in and out of district)
- Resources/supplies
- Memberships
- Data collection programs and data analysis

2. **Who has the decision-making power for this change effort?** Budget is not the only determining factor. Decision-making power is important to understand. Most school staffs are hierarchical. At the school level, the decision maker is usually the principal. At the district level, the decision maker is the superintendent. But in very large districts, you may have coordinators, board members, assistant superintendents, or directors who may have the ultimate decision-making power for your effort.

- Who has decision-making power for staffing decisions?
- Who determines the job roles?
- Who determines the agenda at all-school and district meetings?
- Who determines the expectations for the intervention?
- Who has the power to hire or fire staff?
- What precedent has been set for how individuals access resources for the change effort?

3. **How will the implementation plan be rolled out?** When using a cohort or a pilot model of rollout, there can be a perception of inequity. Others in the system may want to know why specific schools or teachers were chosen and whether they will also be trained in the same manner. Individuals may need to be reassured of the fairness of the rollout and what the plan looks like. Ask the following:

- What precedent has been set that guides selection for participation in the intervention?
- What is the timeline for access to materials, resources, and training?
  - o Before school year begins
  - o Two weeks before students arrive
  - o First month
  - o Midyear
  - o End of year
  - o Ongoing throughout the year
- How will later adopters be supported to catch up with teachers or schools who are already implementing?
- Was clear and consistent information provided to all stakeholders when the program was in development?
- What is the procedure if there is a change in the scheduled rollout?

4. **Who determines what the school staff will do and what they won't do?** Things that are not dictated specifically in the contract may fall under the grey area of "other duties as assigned." If your SEL intervention falls into that area, you must understand how much latitude you may have to ask teachers and other stakeholders to add this to their plate. Some districts use memorandums of understanding (MOUs) as agreements for extra duties if necessary. This is important to understand, because not knowing what the teachers can be contractually asked to do can trip your efforts up.

- Is this a mission that staff see the value in and will take on willingly, or is it a mandate they won't fulfill (unless mandated)?
- Will you need a special agreement to teach SEL?
- Are the staff leaders in your school willing to have these discussions with other stakeholders, like the teacher's union?
- Do you have active resistance to change, and do the resisters have power within the school or system?

Exploration of the power and influence can inform your next steps for the intervention. You must know whether your SEL implementation is a "will do" or a "won't do." If those in power will do, it means they believe in it; they see the value. They do not have to be totally convinced that it will work and is worth the time and effort. But those who won't do fall into the mandate category. They will do it because someone above them in the hierarchy has mandated it. This is not the best position to be in for most interventions, because they won't be done intentionally or with fidelity. Lack of knowledge about whether it is a will do or won't do will create more work for you. You should try to understand if there is a norm to allow staff to opt in or opt out of interventions. This will guide you to determine where you should concentrate your efforts.

Things to Consider When Hiring an Expert

It is common practice for schools to bring in outside experts and trainers to help during implementation of any innovation. Bringing in a consultant can increase your chances at success. A consultant can provide expertise, an unbiased opinion, knowledge from working with other schools/districts, and ideas about how to build an infrastructure to implement your change.

However, be aware that hiring a consultant will change the power dynamic among the people involved in systems change. Perceptions about expertise should be explored. Will stakeholders trust information about strategies provided by the consultant or the change agent? What is the impact of the change agent being a consultant versus a school employee? The benefits of consultants are that they have seen implementations in different contexts, so they should provide different experiences; they have no hidden agenda; they have a high level of expertise; and they can be motivational for staff.

However, a consultant cannot provide the meaningful day-to-day work that someone who works for the school district can. Both can be helpful in the systems change journey. Try to get a clear picture of the positional hierarchy in your school. Positional hierarchy refers to how people are treated based on their position in the school. Principals may hold positional power, but they don't always have social influence in the building. This should be explored. And finally, what precedent has been set that guides access and resources? When determining what the power structure looks like in your school or district, think of these questions to guide your decision making.

The power and influence to make lasting change depend upon multiple factors. A consultant may assist in determining the best use of your time and resources. Make sure to think about the role that consultants will play in your implementation efforts to make the most of their time and expertise.

Practitioner's Voice

The first thing I worked on this year is the same thing that I put into practice my whole career as a teacher, counselor, and coach . . . establish relationships with those I would be working with. Establishing relationships can be a difficult and humbling experience, especially when you are working with those that battle with issues that keep "outsiders" far away. My quest was to make connection with as many members of my team as I could, with a particular focus on those that kept their distance. Once that rapport was established and I began to gain trust more and more, that's when the real work began and I was able to have conversations with staff members that would have been impossible without the connection. With the relationship built, then it was time to get to work on the "issues" that prevent progress and success. This is a monumental mountain to climb, but with a focus on each step, we're that much closer to the top. This year has been about building a solid foundation upon which to build the rest of the system and that process has been slower at times than others, but looking back on how far we've come, I am AMAZED at our work this year!

—Jeff Clark, Teacher/School Counselor

Resources

Printed Material

- *Good to Great* (Collins, 2001).
- *Two Mindsets* (https://www.mindsetworks.com/science/impact).
- *Building Teams That Stay,* (Aguilar, 2018).
- *Research Every Teacher Should Know: Growth Mindset* (Busch, 2018).

Videos

- *Teacher Collaboration: Spreading Best Practices School-Wide:* https://youtu.be/85HUMHBXJf4
- *Empathy: The Heart of Difficult Conversations:* https://youtu.be/2UvDMQyBVLs

Strategies

- Enhance your conflict resolution skills. Learn about conflict resolution on a web resource for how to manage and resolve conflict. Includes "About Conflict" and "8 Steps for Conflict Resolution:" https://www.talent.wisc.edu/onlinetraining/resolution/stepsoverview.htm
- Complete a stakeholder analysis to identify individuals who support the work of SEL or other change initiatives: https://www.mindtools.com/pages/article/newPPM_07.htm

REFLECTION QUESTIONS

1. How do you build relationships and navigate the political environment of your school?

2. Who can you work with to develop SEL strategies that benefit your students and staff?

3. What is your understanding from the perspective of your role in this change process?

4. What power do you possess in the system?

5. Who has power in your system? How is the power used?

6. What typically happens when there is conflict at your school?

7. Do I have the skills and/or resources to improve my communication abilities? If not, how do I improve?

CHAPTER 8

Strategy #6: Develop an Action Plan for Implementation

Experience is what you get when you didn't get what you wanted. And experience is often the most valuable thing you have to offer.

—**Randy Pausch (2008, p. 149)**

Making Stuff Happen—It's All About a Plan

As previously discussed, change agents should use the information about power and influence to inform the next steps for the intervention. You must know if this is a will do versus a won't do. If those in power will do, it means they believe in it; they see the value. They do not have to be totally convinced that it will work and is worth the time and effort.

Developing a plan of action is intentionally chosen as the sixth strategy. SEL interventions require all the "prework" of the first five strategies before getting to the planning. This allows the change agent to have enough information and feel prepared enough to structure a reasonable action plan for implementation. During your process, you must know if the system you are proposing to change is fairly flexible or inflexible, for long-term planning. Keep open to change, and base any changes that are made on data, not opinion. It is essential to always connect to larger goals. My central role in working with change agents is to provide that balance between the immediate needs and the larger goals, while investigating the impacts on the entire system. *The reason or "why," as determined in Strategy #1, you are implementing an innovation must be considered when developing all parts of the action plan.*

You Say You Want an Intervention

In many SEL implementations, your school will choose an intervention to meet your specific needs. Tier 1 whole-school interventions are designed as preventative and proactive measures that support all students. Interventions are everywhere these days. Some work so well, we can't imagine life before the intervention arrived. It feels great when a strategy works and the adult and student feel a sense of accomplishment. But there are other instances where an intervention can feel like another job, and it is not helping the child, the adult, or the situation.

Educators are often saddled with the issue of knowing they need a solution to their problem (an intervention) and not having enough time and resources to determine which intervention is the right one for their classroom, their school, or their district. One way to think about an intervention is as a tool. And like all tools, it can be used successfully or unsuccessfully, and it is dependent on many variables. Does the child respond to this kind of learning? Is it difficult to implement? Does the teacher feel resentful about the demands of the curricululm? There are many other considerations. The point here is that educators may be convinced that an intervention alone will solve their issues.

Although I know that this is an issue, I cannot stress enough the importance of choosing an intervention after you have determined your why, chosen a framework, looked at the data, established your vision and goals, and assessed the political environment that the intervention will be implemented in. Once you have completed those steps, the first and most important question is this: *Is the intervention or strategy evidence based?* Evidence-based practices have been validated using scientific methods to evaluate and measure outcomes. Many of these practices are rated according to strength of evidence of effectiveness, effect size, number of studies that have been done on the practice, and quality of studies of the practice (Slavin, 2008). When deciding to implement an intervention or program, it is essential to choose things that have been proven successful in the areas that you would like improvement.

Take some time to find out if the intervention you want to use for the youth in your school works for other youth with the same challenges. It will save you a lot of time and effort.

Interventions—Less Magic, More Mindset

Interventions are not magic. Magic is illusory and quick, and we don't often know how it happened. Interventions are tools that are grounded in research and that have been found to have beneficial outcomes on targeted areas.

> These interventions grew out of basic laboratory research and theory investigating these processes. They have produced long-lasting gains in achievement in multiple studies, but they are dependent on the capacities, meanings, and recursive processes present in local contexts. If scaled up in appropriate ways, social-psychological interventions have the potential to contribute, in conjunction with other reforms to the solution of endemic problems in education. (Yeager & Walton, 2011, p. 293)

Change happens when you choose the best intervention for your specific conditions.

As mentioned previously, we must change the mindset from brands to essential ingredients. Our intervention theories need to solve the problem of identifying and reliably measuring the essential ingredients, the causal agents that lead to positive change, rather than the brands that package the causal agents (Aber, Brown, Jones, Berg, & Torrente, 2011). Many times, we buy the brand without truly understanding why it works. If we don't understand the conditions under which it works, we will not get the greatest benefit from the intervention.

To illustrate this point, imagine I was car shopping, and I had heard great things about a Ferrari. People I respect rave about the Ferrari, so I think that that is the car I should get to meet my transportation needs. And they were right, the Ferrari is great for driving around during the summer in the Midwest. But winter is coming! As you can imagine, the Ferrari did not fare well in four feet of snow.

You need to evaluate—*What will lead to positive change in YOUR school, rather than what is the intervention du jour?*

SEL Intervention

Unfortunately, SEL curriculums can be among the interventions that we purchase without consideration of how they will fit in our culture. SEL is beginning to be the intervention du jour. Curriculums and assessments are selected, paid for, and implemented, and that is where it begins and ends.

Supporting the Intervention

A Common Teaching Practice

When teaching about the Civil War, teachers may have students read *The Red Badge of Courage*. When learning about science, the teacher may have students build a wind gauge. When learning about literature, the teacher may have the students recite Shakespeare. SEL is no different. In one elementary school, the team came up with read-aloud books that supported the SEL curriculum. In one high school, there was a mandatory community service component, where students volunteered time at local nonprofits in the area. This requires connecting the practices to the competencies. Supporting the evidence-based curriculum with activities, projects, books, et cetera provides for a richer experience that is not context dependent. We want to support these evidence-based interventions by expanding their use. Students could say, I learned about empathy in advisory, we talked about empathy in my language arts class, we did an activity in PE called "walking in another person's shoes." I demonstrated empathy when I worked at the local homeless shelter and I told my little brother about empathy when he was being mean to our sister.

Systems should have a specific rationale for which curriculums they choose, what they are targeting, how these curriculums meet their needs, and how they are being implemented with fidelity. The rationale for using any intervention is to align our organizational process so that we can make the best use of implementation science, the specific intervention, and evidence-based practice with whole-school SEL. Before the SEL intervention and/or curriculum is integrated into the school day, we must consider the diffusion of intervention. How will your SEL intervention be weaved into the fabric of your school life, including staff training, differentiation, and integration into all three tiers of your MTSS system? Will any additional supports be required? Your use of SEL may be considered an innovation, an application of better solutions to meet the needs of your students and staff.

Diffusion of Innovation

Systems change includes the knowledge of the what—planning for the general functions, tasks, activities, and phases requires understanding of the diffusion of innovation. Diffusion of innovation is the pace and path of acceptance of new ideas and innovations. It is essential to mobilize recipients of the innovation to learn and use the new behaviors (Adelman & Taylor, n.d.). There are four strategies to connect with an audience. The first is to elaborate on the benefits of the innovation. Explain what can be gained from the intervention use and action. The second is compatibility or fit. How is the intervention consistent with the values, experiences, and needs of your school? The third strategy is usability. How can the innovation be used, understood, integrated, and experimented with? And finally, the evidence of impact. The data can speak to some of the outcomes that can occur with implementation (Wilson, 2015).

"In the end, our effectiveness as leaders is not determined by our own abilities, but rather, our ability to develop capabilities for making all things better and new in much larger groups of people" (DeGraff, 2009, p. 199). Innovation can be made in your school or district. DeGraff suggests a few ideas that apply to our work with SEL and developing an action plan. Take a portfolio view. He suggests that if you value one approach too heavily, you may lose focus on the big picture of creating a positive, productive school culture that helps students learn social and emotional skills that will benefit them for life. Your approach should be balanced in your team and with your practices while keeping an eye on effects to the system. Learn about what practices are the most appropriate and effective when constructing your action plan. Another suggestion is to bet on people, not just processes. People will drive this movement. Be on the lookout for individuals who get results from their innovation. Celebrate those individuals and get them involved in a leadership role. Another suggestion DeGraff proposes is to "leave room for the stuff you don't know now." Implementing SEL requires flexibility in thinking, asking questions, and finding new answers and new possibilities. Think about your plan as something that evolves based on experience. You will learn from your first iterations of your plan, and you will develop a stronger plan based on that information. This process is not a checklist, although there are checklists involved. If you are the change agent working on implementation, it is important that you and your team come to understand this. The deeper work of implementation will require you to think outside of the curriculum box.

Action Planning

Districtwide Goals and Schoolwide Goals

In Chapter 6, vision standards were established. The formation of goals is important as a part of the vision. The goals will be the guide for action planning. Action planning uses data to drive decisions, included in the beginning of the plan. It guides what the teams do. Therefore, it is important to include this type of action planning for each step of the intervention. It creates a sense of responsibility and accountability for the team members. But remember to set concrete, short-term goals or SMART (specific, measurable, attainable, relevant, timely) goals to keep the intervention going in a meaningful way. Figure 8.1 is a template for you to use in creating an action plan.

Include in the action plan

- ❑ Goal
- ❑ Action steps
- ❑ Phases or timeline
- ❑ Who is responsible?
- ❑ How do we know when we have accomplished our goal? How will we measure success?

Figure 8.1 Action Plan Template					
Action Steps	**Who Is Responsible**	**Resources Needed**	**Leadership Check**	**Due Date**	**Notes**
Step 1					
Step 2					
Step 3					
Step 4					

Practicing SEL

How We Practice

The issue becomes this: What does each component look like in action, and what do we do to make it happen? How do we infuse personal ownership and action? Can we drill down the competencies into actions that can be demonstrated, taught, modeled, and reflected upon? Durlak, Weissberg, and Pachan (2010) recommended four practices for social-skill training within an intervention program. The first practice was sequential components, using a connected set of activities to achieve skill development. Secondly, the programs needed to use active forms of learning. The third practice was to develop personal or social skills as part of the program. And finally, the programs needed to have explicit personal or social goals (Durlak et al., 2010).

Durlak, Weissberg, Dymnicki, Taylor, and Schellinger (2011) conducted the seminal meta-analysis of 213 school-based, universal SEL programs that involved 270,034 students in kindergarten through high school. One hypothesis the researchers proposed was that programs in which staff used the practice of SAFE (sequenced, active, focused, and explicit) in SEL interventions would be more successful than those that did not. The researchers completed an extensive literature search with inclusion and exclusion criteria. The multiple cohorts were coded and analyzed separately. The independent variables were the intervention format, use of SAFE practices, and reported implementation problems. The dependent variables were six student outcomes: social and emotional skills, attitudes toward self and others, positive social behaviors, conduct problems, emotional distress, and academic performance (Durlak et al., 2011).

As mentioned, the SAFE training approach is sequenced (step by step), active (it requires students to practice new skills), focused (specific time and attention is focused on skill development), and explicit (social/emotional skills are defined) (Zins, Weissberg, Wang, & Walberg, 2004). It was found that programs following all four recommended training procedures (SAFE) produced significant effects for all six outcomes, whereas programs not coded as SAFE achieved significant effects in only three areas (attitudes, conduct problems, and academic performance) (Durlak et al., 2011).

This study added to the importance of understanding social-emotional programs conducted in schools. The implications for schools were that SEL programs do have significant positive effects, as evidenced by increased prosocial behaviors and by reduced conduct and internalizing problems. They also found that for programs to be successful, they should be well designed and well conducted. This meta-analysis focused exclusively on universal, school-based, social-emotional development programs (Durlak et al., 2011).

Strategies That Promote SEL

The Collaborative for Academic, Social, and Emotional Learning (CASEL) put together a report in 2017, *Sample Teaching Activities to Support Core Competencies of Social and Emotional Learning,* that promoted four strategies that promote SEL. They included free-standing lessons, general teaching practices, integration of skill instruction and practices, and systems considerations to make SEL a schoolwide initiative.

Each of these strategies requires a different approach for schools, especially as they are implemented schoolwide. Before you begin, identify the time and resources available, the training required for the strategies, and your school's willingness to use them. The number one priority is willingness. The rest is just negotiation of details. Schools can find the money, the time, and the training. But without the willingness of the teachers to promote or practice SEL, you will fight an uphill battle.

Figure 8.2 SAFE Implementation

How Can We Implement SEL in Our School or District?	Ideas	Are They Sequenced, Active, Focused, and Explicit? (SAFE)
Freestanding lessons		
Teaching practices		
Integration of SEL into academic practices		
Systems change to support SEL		

Assuming you have a staff that is willing, let's move on to deciding the approach that will work in your specific environment. Freestanding lessons work best in a school environment that has the financial resources to pay for the curriculum and time in the day that they can allot to provide instruction. General teaching practices can be easiest to integrate, such as refining the behavior expectations for the class, changing the flow of classroom traffic to accommodate group work, or instituting a morning meeting. But this strategy may require the staff to change their current practices, which can cause many other issues. Supporting SEL through the academic curriculum is a great option. It requires staff to look at their current scope and sequence for their academic subjects and find ways to naturally support SEL. Using general teaching practices and skill instruction in the academic curriculum should be intentional and systemic, and data should be collected to demonstrate effectiveness. Finally, schoolwide initiatives require strong leadership, advocates for SEL in the school, and a plan for dissemination. Figure 8.2 provides a template for considering how these four strategies can be used in your school.

Instructional Practices Questionnaire

When looking at the many types of SEL curriculums, one of the most important questions is, How will this fit with our school culture and practices that we already feel competent doing? Teachers will better integrate SEL practices if they feel comfortable doing them. For example, not all teachers feel comfortable doing role-plays or using puppets. This can be a barrier to successful implementation. One exercise is to look at the types of instructional practice and determine what your staff feels comfortable using. There will be more discussion of selecting curriculums and interventions later, but for now, Figures 8.3, 8.4, and 8.5 provide charts for rating comfort with several instructional practices.

Putting It All Together

As you create your action plan, your main objective is to align the overall goals with practices. What strategy connects to your goals? If you have more than one goal, how do you prioritize the goals? This can be done by sequentially ordering the goals based on skill development and child developmental norms. You have learned what strategies your staff feels most comfortable using. How are you applying this information in the design of your action plan? Have you thought about other elements that may have to be pretaught before implementation? For example, do you need to work with students

Figure 8.3 Instructional Practices Questionnaire—Elementary

Elementary Instructional Practice as Defined in Jones et al., 2017	Definition	I Would Feel Comfortable Using this Practice to Promote SEL Skills (Yes or No).	Order of Preference for Each Skill You Marked Yes in Column to the Left
Discussion	Discussions can occur in pairs, small groups, or class.		
Didactic instruction	Teacher provides specific instructions outside of an open discussion. This might include providing definitions, teacher modeling, or imparting specific information.		
Book/story	Teacher reads aloud a book or short story that may or may not include pictures.		
Vocabulary	Activities used to teach language, words, or terms related to specific concepts.		
Handout	Use of a tool or material to promote specific strategies, often used to help students visualize concepts in a concrete way.		
Writing	Students are asked to write about personal experiences related to a specific theme or to record the experiences of others.		
Drawing	Drawing activity with a goal other than depicting an event or experience. The focus is on the artistic expression.		
Art/creative project	Art or creative project other than drawing that can be individual projects or a collaborative project.		
Visual display	Charts, posters, or other visual displays.		
Video	Videos that demonstrate challenging situations used to prompt group discussions.		
Song	Songs and music videos or chants used to reinforce skills; these often involve dances, hand movements, and/or strategy practice.		
Skill practice	Students actively practice skills or strategies outside of a game or role-play scenario.		
Role-play	Teacher role-plays, entire class role-plays in pairs, or two students perform in front of the class.		
Game	Can be used to reinforce themes, build community, practice specific skills, or transition students in/out of a lesson, et cetera.		
Kinesthetic	...ing student movement and		
Teacher choice	...ted to choose their own ...e of options, such as ...ion of different games ...s preferences.		

Figure 8.4 Instructional Practices Questionnaire—Middle School

Middle School Instructional Practice	Definition	I Would Feel Comfortable Using this Practice to Promote SEL Skills (Yes or No).	Order of Preference for Each Skill You Marked Yes in Column to the Left.
Discussion	Discussions can occur in pairs, small groups, or class.		
Didactic instruction	Teacher provides specific instructions outside of an open discussion. This might include providing definitions, teacher modeling, or imparting specific information.		
Book/story	Whole-class or small group discussion of book or story that covers specific scenarios or skills.		
Vocabulary	Activities used to teach language, words, or terms related to specific concepts.		
Handouts	Use of a tool or material to promote specific strategies, often used to help students visualize concepts in a concrete way.		
Writing	Students are asked to write about personal experiences related to a specific theme or to record the experiences of others.		
Art/creative project	Art or creative project other than drawing that can be individual projects or a collaborative project.		
Visual display	Charts, posters, or other visual displays.		
Video	Videos that demonstrate challenging situations used to prompt group discussions.		
Technology	The use of apps and computer programs that explicitly teach skills.		
Mindfulness	Activities involving students promoting mindful or contemplative awareness and focus.		
Project-based learning	Students acquire deeper knowledge through active exploration of real-world challenges and problems.		
Game-based learning	Using games to practice and promote skills and competencies.		

to learn how to calm their bodies before you begin a mindfulness lesson? And most of all, are your expectations realistic based on the time given for the task? Action steps are more than just a list. They are a changing document that must consider new information all the time. The action plan works in tandem with your diffusion of innovation to provide structure and momentum. Figure 8.6 shows an example of a plan for a single goal.

Figure 8.5 Instructional Practices Questionnaire—High School

High School Instructional Practice	Definition	I Would Feel Comfortable Using this Practice to Promote SEL Skills (Yes or No).	Order of Preference for Each Skill You Marked Yes in Column to the Left.
Discussion	Discussions can occur in pairs, small groups, or class.		
Didactic instruction	Teacher provides specific instructions outside of an open discussion. This might include providing definitions, teacher modeling, or imparting specific information.		
Book/story	Whole-class or small group discussion of book or story that covers specific scenarios or skills.		
Vocabulary	Activities used to teach language, words, or terms related to specific concepts.		
Handout	Use of a tool or material to promote specific strategies, often used to help students visualize concepts in a concrete way.		
Writing	Students are asked to write about personal experiences related to a specific theme or to record the experiences of others.		
Art/creative project	Art or creative project other than drawing that can be individual projects or a collaborative project.		
Visual display	Charts, posters, or other visual displays.		
Video	Videos that demonstrate challenging situations used to prompt group discussions.		
Technology	The use of apps and computer programs that explicitly teach skills.		
Mindfulness	Activities involving students promoting mindful or contemplative awareness and focus.		
Leadership training	Involvement in leadership tasks to reach a goal.		
Project-based learning	Students acquire deeper knowledge through active exploration of real-world challenges and problems.		
Game-based learning	Using games to practice and promote skills and competencies.		

Figure 8.6 Goal to Outcomes Action Plan Example

Goal	Steps (See Action Plan Template, Figure 8.1)	Timeline	Responsible Party	Outcome
Students and staff will learn and practice self-regulation skills.	• Freestanding lessons = mindfulness curriculum taught once a week • Teaching practices = competence building • Integration of SEL into academic practices = mindful minute before tests • Systems change to support SEL = time in day to practice strategy	Whole school year	All staff agreed to start the morning with mindfulness.	Measured by self-report and schoolwide survey

What Is Loose and What Is Tight?

One of the principals I worked with asked our team a great question, "What is loose and what is tight?" She was asking what was required by the district and what is in her control as the building principal. I thought that was a profound question that spoke to the many decision-making controls in a medium or large district. The district may mandate something, and the procedure can be very tight, a step-by-step process that must be followed. Or it can be loose, as in, Here is what the goal is, and it is up to you to get there. Leaders must identify whether the mandate is loose or tight when they are creating a plan. If your systems change is mandated, it will require extra work on the part of the change agent to convince individuals that the change is worth the time and effort. They will do it because someone above them in the hierarchy has mandated it. This is not the best position to be in for most interventions, because they won't be done intentionally or with fidelity. Lack of knowledge about whether it has been mandated will create more work for you. You should try to understand what is under your control and what is not. This will guide you to determine where you should concentrate your efforts.

Administrative Goals

Administrators or the lead systems change agent should have goals in addition to the goals set by the team. Their leadership responsibilities should be embedded in these goals, which work to complement the goals that the team is setting.
Some items that may be included on a leader's goal list include these:

- ❑ Check that all information pushed out to staff is user friendly and inclusive.
- ❑ Clarify the roles of team members and their relationship to the larger staff.
- ❑ Provide time for collaboration and sharing.
- ❑ Seek ongoing feedback throughout the year from stakeholders.
- ❑ Support staff learning through leadership or administrative means by providing materials and training for staff.
- ❑ Consistently acknowledge gains (individually, small groups, and whole staff) in a meaningful way.

Addressing Teacher Questions and Concerns

Administrators, change agents, and SEL leadership teams should take care to address teacher questions and concerns. If teachers can see what the action plan looks like, and if they know there are plans to support them during implementation, they will feel less anxious. Here is a list of things to consider addressing when discussing the action plan with teachers:

- How will teachers access help?
- How does this new process/program fit in with programs already in use?
- What is the role of the change agent?
- How do we find the balance between enthusiasm for the prospective change and the reality that change takes time?

- Have you determined a realistic timeline to guide implementation? Are all stakeholders aware of it?

- How are professional development opportunities/time determined and structured?

- How will the intervention be monitored for effectiveness?

What Do We Want? Change! When Do We Want It? Should've Happened Yesterday!

Your school-level team is critical in following through with best-practice strategies to accomplish your school goals. Action planning uses data to drive decisions included in the beginning of the plan. It guides what the teams do. Therefore, it is important to include this type of action planning for each step of the intervention. It creates a sense of responsibility and accountability for the team members.

Meeting the Needs of Your School

Even in schools where there is a lot of support and the emphasis on SEL is high, there will be some compromise to deliver SEL curriculum and supports and meet the needs of your school. One of the school staff members that I spoke to said they had to change their initial strategy after hearing that the teachers were overwhelmed trying to teach the SEL curriculum every day in their middle school. They found that teaching it during the advisory period once a week for the whole period (55 minutes) and reinforcing it the rest of the week worked best. They also include whole-school activities first thing in the morning and after lunch. The team was initially worried about how the eighth-grade students would receive the lessons, but it was discovered that they had the best outcomes.

Middle and high school staffs will especially have to do some negotiating to find the best way to integrate SEL into the school day. I have seen success in adding it to homeroom or advisory classes. Some schools have study hall, but not all students participate in it. You will need to strategize to meet the needs of your school when obstacles like the traditional schedule create a barrier for implementation.

Documents and Documenting: Creating Documents That Support Your Action Plan

When creating documents for your school, include action steps, who is responsible for completing each step, resources that are needed, deadlines, dates of completion, additional notes (which could include progress updates), reasons extensions were granted, additional questions raised, et cetera.

PBIS (Positive Behavior Interventions and Supports) recommends that school teams use the same agenda template for organization and data collection for every meeting (Todd, 2018). This is a useful strategy for your SEL teams when creating organizational documents.

Here are some additional things to consider when creating organizational documents:

- How do they reflect your culture?

- Will they be uniform across the district, or unique for each school, to reflect its needs?

- Building a flowchart: The purpose is for all personnel in the school or district to understand the process and learn the language of innovation.

- Integrate an accountability metric—this creates a sense of ownership and responsibility. It should include the following:
  o What they did
  o What went well
  o Barriers they overcame, and those they did not
  o Troubleshooting strategies they tried

It may be helpful to use a rubric. A rubric can offer systems a common set of expectations by defining different levels of completion for a task or a goal. Rubric levels can use a continuum of development or a check list to determine where you are in the process. Using a rubric to guide your change efforts will provide everyone with a central document to work with. This is helpful to communicate expectations about the intervention or change process. All stakeholders can identify where your process falls along a continuum toward a specific criterion that you plan to reach.

Using the worksheets contained in this book provides a good start at documentation of your change effort. One of the most powerful strategies is to document by keeping a list of "what works" or "good stuff" that you encounter along the way, even if it is not necessary in the moment. These are the one-off items that you may not have planned for such as increased test scores or fewer staff sick days.

Communication is another part of documentation. Your action plan should include a strategy for communicating your efforts to stakeholders. This could be a page on the school's website, e-mails, a newsletter, team communication within the school, et cetera. Let people know what you are doing, and help them feel a part of this process.

Scope and Sequence

One of the more common ways I have seen the organization of SEL competencies is through a scope and sequence document. Teachers and administrators are usually familiar with such a process, so they do not have to be introduced to a new, unfamiliar tool. Scope and sequence documents are often created at the leadership level with input from other educational staff on the appropriate content and order based on grade level. SEL curriculums are often designed with this user-friendly practice in mind. This can be another way to introduce procedural documents into your action plan.

Practitioner's Voice

Most teachers love to talk about and share ideas that have worked well for their students. Teacher teams can harness that energy by encouraging members to try new practices in their classrooms and then to share their experiences with the team. Allowing teachers to have choices and flexibility goes a long way toward creating ownership and buy-in for a new change initiative.

—Kurt Ruckman, Assistant Principal/Instructional Coach/Teacher

Resources

Printed material

- What Works Clearinghouse—Programs, Practices, and Policies in Education (http://ies.ed.gov/ncee/wwc).

- *How to Implement Social and Emotional Learning at Your School* (Elias, Leverett, Duffell, Humphrey, Stepney, & Ferrito, 2016).

- *The School Principal as Leader: Guiding Schools to Better Teaching and Learning* (Wallace Foundation, 2013).

Videos

- *Systems Thinking and Evaluation*—An example of how systems thinking can be used in program evaluation to maximize effectiveness of the program: https://youtu.be/2vojPksdbtI

- *Diffusion of Innovation Theory: The Adoption Curve:* https://youtu.be/9QnfWhtujPA

Strategies

- Work with your team to design a rubric about social and emotional skills. Learn the seven steps for creating a rubric: https://youtu.be/vfRP9HGVHGo

- Learn how to create an action plan: https://youtu.be/-_1iDN4LBqI

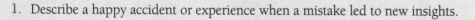

REFLECTION QUESTIONS

1. Describe a happy accident or experience when a mistake led to new insights.

2. Can you provide actionable steps toward achieving school or district goals that are accountable to the vision?

3. How are you explicitly voicing the positive changes you observe after enacting the plan? Are stakeholders aware of the positive changes?

4. How are you recording or documenting the action plan and any necessary changes that need to be made?

5. Can you elaborate how this plan connects to your why?

6. What is the best way to provide check-ins for your stakeholders? How will you use it regularly to guide your efforts?

7. What documents do you need to create to collect data in a meaningful way?

Strategy #7: Invest in Your Infrastructure

Building a culture of collaboration and shared responsibility among teachers, principals and administrators; focusing on continuous professional development for teachers; and ensuring teachers have the time, tools and trust they need to improve teaching and learning are essential ingredients to building strong public schools and a quality teaching force.

—Randi Weingarten, President, American Federation of Teachers (Gimbel & Leana, 2013, p. xiv)

What Is Infrastructure and Why Do We Need It?

Infrastructure is the organizational strategy needed for operation. In a 2016 article, Henry Doss wrote,

> We need real, meaningful, actionable science of innovation systems, and we need the infrastructure—culture engineers, organizational anthropologists, system experts and so on—that can support the shift in thinking we need to be more innovative. That shift is away from reductionist, piecemeal approaches to innovation, and toward holistic, system-based approaches. Both elements—the science and the infrastructure that supports it—are necessary if we are to make progress. (Doss, 2016, p. 4)

Interventions need a meaningful framework of action to combat the resistance to change. Fidelity is a clearly articulated essential feature of implementation, which provides the avenue for a common understanding and consistency in practices across all stakeholders. Fidelity is meaningful when the focus is on the decision-making process and implementation versus merely "adherence to the rules." In previous chapters we have elaborated upon many areas that contribute to a well-developed infrastructure. A meaningful framework for action should be developed, because there will be challenges in implementation that need to be prepared for. This will be done by creating a plan to deal with these challenges. This will require both leadership and collaboration within the system. It is important to invest time and energy in school-level teams as part of the infrastructure for any lasting change to your system.

The Strategies That Have Been Introduced Include These

- ❑ Roles/responsibilities—Chapter 6
- ❑ Rubrics—Chapter 4
- ❑ Feedback loop—Chapter 6
- ❑ Data collection—Chapter 5
- ❑ Data-driven decision making—Chapter 5

- ❏ Evidence-based practices—Chapter 4
- ❏ Problem-solving process—Chapter 4
- ❏ Progress monitoring (accountability tool)—Chapter 4

The two areas that need to be looked at are fidelity of implementation and building capacity for stakeholders, who include employees of the school district, students, and nonemployee stakeholders (parents, families, community). These are two crucial parts to allow for stakeholders to be engaged in the change process.

Fidelity of Implementation

Fidelity of implementation is an often-used term to describe implementation for a wide variety of academic and behavioral interventions. The term *fidelity* is often a charged and misunderstood term. The RTI Action Network provides a thorough description of the term and what it means in practice (Miller, 2010). These practices include having clearly articulated essential features based on evidence, a practice of measurement of implementation that considers the cost and time associated, a culture of honest evaluation and reflection, review of agreements and outcomes to be accountable to stakeholders, and being a part of the problem-solving process to determine what was and wasn't done that might have impacted the outcomes (Miller, 2010).

This is useful in our work with SEL implementation, because we must demonstrate that we are delivering the intervention practices in a thoughtful way that accentuates the active ingredients that promote positive outcomes. This focus on quality is embedded throughout the fidelity process. A caution for you as a change agent is to consider how you will address fidelity issues if you have multiple interventions at once. How are you implementing the interventions in a way that stays true to the intent of the program and focuses on the active ingredients? One method of recording implementation is to create a teacher implementation log. Daily or weekly use of the log may have to be negotiated with staff, but it is necessary to understand whether the school is implementing the intervention with fidelity. The questions in Figure 9.1 will help schools understand the dosage (or amount of implementation delivered), adherence to the program, quality of delivery, and reception of the program, which all help in assessing the fidelity with which the intervention was delivered.

Figure 9.1 Fidelity of Implementation of SEL Intervention

Fidelity of Intervention	Lesson 1	Lesson 2	Lesson 3	Lesson 4	Lesson 5	Lesson 6
Date/time lesson taught						
Did you (1) follow the lesson verbatim, (2) alter it with agreed-upon editing by team, or (3) change it due to time or other issues?						
Did you use any additional materials to support the lesson?						
How long did it take to prep the lesson?						
Did you feel prepared to deliver the lesson?						
How do you know that the students learned the material? (survey, observation, knowledge tests)						

What Is Loose and What is Tight—Intervention Addition

At Herrick Elementary School, we asked teachers to rate their experiences with the curriculum, what lessons they taught, and any additional resources they used. We started this method of fidelity checks in a very nonevaluative way. We wanted to know how the curriculum was being used and what types of successes and challenges the teachers were having with it. But a very interesting piece of information was showing itself in the data. Teachers would sometimes report that they skipped a lesson because "they didn't see how the lesson helped" or "they didn't think their kids would get anything from this lesson." And this is where the concept of what is loose and what is tight can affect the fidelity of your intervention. We had the opportunity to dig deeper with these responses and talk about the active ingredients and why teachers felt that way about specific lessons. Could the teachers use another intervention that develops the skill in place of that lesson? These are the issues that can only be identified if we are gathering data around the use of the lessons and potential outcomes.

Building Capacity

Building capacity is an important piece of investing in your infrastructure. This includes a well-developed professional development strategy that is stratified to include training for individuals new to SEL implementation, those who have been practicing, and those who can mentor or coach others. To achieve the vision and goals of your SEL implementation, you must improve the knowledge and skills of all stakeholders, including students, parents/families, and community members.

Professional Development

Professional development is crucial for all educators. The field changes, and new ideas and new strategies are becoming regular practice. Change agents need to advocate for as much SEL development as possible. This new learning is a process and requires scaffolding and development of schema. "SEL interventions need to be taught in such a way that teachers understand the purpose of each intervention core component, the psychological explanation supporting it, and the parameters for acceptable adoption" (Rimm-Kaufman & Hulleman, 2015, p. 162).

Comprehensive professional development includes training, conducting demonstration lessons and modeling competencies, guiding the pacing of the lessons, and planning for all stages of implementation. This may include supporting implementation through additional resources such as books, videos, and games. Training includes identifying strategies for teaching SEL skills and concepts through content area subjects.

Great care and consideration should be taken when thinking about professional development for SEL. This is where your understanding of your workplace and the people within it will be beneficial.

Things to Consider

Building level approach

- ❏ Common language of intervention
- ❏ Where to begin
- ❏ Tool kit—training manual
- ❏ How to invest in teachers

- ❏ Foundational principals (active ingredients)
- ❏ What is most important
- ❏ Present activities at staff meetings
- ❏ Handouts (material support)
- ❏ Information for parents/family

Break down professional development

- ❏ Date
- ❏ Training
- ❏ Delivered by
- ❏ Resources: book study, videos, online modules, articles
- ❏ Areas, departments, or grade levels at which coaches will work

Professional Development Musts

In delivering professional development to teachers, afterschool personnel, counselors, bus drivers, administrators, families, and others, I have found three nonnegotiables. Professional development needs to be meaningful, appropriate, and applicable. This is where knowing your audience is most helpful.

Edit your professional development to the best and most succinct information, so that the stakeholders can use that information. It must be meaningful to that specific group. What's in it for me? Why do I need to give you my attention and active participation?

Is it appropriate? I have been guilty of both giving too much information at one time and talking in acronyms. I learned that I need to understand what the audience already knows and scaffold the learning to educate them about the theory, principles, and details of the intervention. I need to discover what they need to know to practice the SEL strategies in the classroom. Tailor the professional development to meet the specific needs of your audience.

And finally, what is applicable? Am I giving the audience strategies and skills that they can use right away? Professional development is not meant to be a semester course like you would take in college. It is meant to disseminate key pieces of information and offer opportunities to continue to learn and grow.

Once the intervention is in full swing, professional development may change to reflect less education (sit and get) and more active participation. One strategy for brief professional development sessions is the following format: accomplishments, practice scenario, brainstorm, strategy, feedback. This allows the stakeholders to take a more active role in discussing the intervention and using the skills for their specific class. It is not just the implementation of direct teaching of social and emotional skills to students. Professional development includes implicitly giving strategies for how the language of the intervention can be included in both daily routines and academic subjects.

Professional development should be a flexible process. Feedback serves to inform the pacing of professional development. Are we going too fast? Does everyone feel supported in this work? It is up to schools to answer the questions: How would we collect feedback? What is the flow of communication? What could it look like? What is the frequency and form? Communication of how you are structuring professional development tells stakeholders that you hear them. If there is a problem of practice that seems to come up often in feedback, you address it in the next professional development session. Perhaps a flowchart will help ease communication. Building a flowchart can help illustrate these concepts or your path in a visual way for all stakeholders to understand the process and learn the same intervention language.

We must do more to enhance professional development in and out of school settings. We have learned that manuals are necessary for an SEL intervention but not sufficient. The train-the-trainer model does not provide enough support for individuals implementing this complex intervention. Workshops help to introduce concepts and increase knowledge but are not as helpful in continual implementation. Professional development should include consultation and coaching to connect the learning with practice. Allow teachers to talk to each other about their process, and if possible include a coach who can work side-by-side with the teachers or other professionals to strategize ways to implement SEL into the everyday life of their classes.

Components of professional development

- ❑ Needs assessment
- ❑ Clear targets or goals and teaching to those objectives
- ❑ Active learning strategies
- ❑ Visual techniques
- ❑ Monitoring and adjusting to the needs of the audience
- ❑ Feedback; practical applications
- ❑ Training must include scenarios to walk through the process of intervention; it helps for people to hear about real kids or cases and makes it more applicable to their own setting.

Consider creating documents to support the things that teachers learn during the professional development, for example, a cheat sheet that has key concepts, especially when trying to integrate SEL into the everyday routine of the classroom. The cheat sheet may have reminder sentences and prompts for what to look for. It could contain brief strategies or problem-solving processes. When learning any new skill, it is helpful to have reminders or cues to help educators.

Onboarding New Staff

Schools should prepare to educate staff new to the school on the work that has been previously done for SEL. Human resources and building procedures often help teachers learn all the new practices and policies when they first start at a new school. However,

The Power of Modeling

One practice that I have seen demonstrated positively is modeling SEL teaching. Teachers who are given the ability to observe another teacher complete a lesson for their students benefit in many ways. First, they learn based on observation. How to pace the lesson, address student questions, and keep the students engaged are all important lessons. They learn what the lesson should look like, which may not always be clear when just reading the lesson from a curriculum book. They can ask questions of the teacher who is modeling the lesson. Why did the teacher choose to do certain things? What did the teacher learn from teaching this lesson in the past? And teachers can also get ideas about how to incorporate SEL skills throughout the day. How is this teacher embedding SEL in everyday language? Or in everyday practices like lining up, teaching vocabulary words, or managing the classroom? Teachers who model also benefit from this practice. Teachers who can model SEL lessons are an asset for their school and among other teachers.

the more nuanced and not universally practiced (yet) SEL practices might be new to teachers even if they aren't new to teaching. Administrative leadership and change agents should consider developing a procedure for educating new staff about SEL and the curriculum or strategies that are used in the school, helping them identify what sort of prep is needed to integrate the lessons into their day, supporting them through modeling or demonstration, and providing them with other materials that they can use to augment SEL through their academic instruction.

Design Training for Stakeholders: Year Over Year

Every school experiences transition year to year. Staff members leave your building, and you receive new staff members. The years of development that it takes to integrate SEL into daily practice may be forgotten when you design onboarding programs. Development of these capacities may take years. Systems do a disservice to their work if they only offer one type of training for new staff. Learning modules alone will not be enough for the new staff to feel supported in an intervention and knowledge base that they may not have been trained for at their university or previous school. Here are some questions to ask yourself:

1. What training will the stakeholders need to implement? How will the training grow year after year? Who will be trained?

2. How will the training schedule be adapted to different stakeholders' needs? Will individuals be allowed to opt in or out of training? Can different stakeholders use an identified group of online learning modules as they find they need them?

3. Who will conduct the training? Some options include these:
    *   Coaches
    *   Change agents
    *   Principals
    *   Teams
    *   Consultants
    *   Outside learning structures—professional development

An SEL Coach

If you are fortunate enough to have a coach dedicated to helping teachers/staff integrate SEL into your classroom, there are some things that will make your work together more productive. Coaches should come to the work understanding that they must

1. Build relationships with ALL of your staff.

2. Treat individuals as experts in their field.

3. Meet your staff where they are, not where you expect them to be.

4. Reinforce that this is a process, and that your role is to support them in the process.

A coach may identify a need from the teachers and help develop solutions for all. The coach may make a video to illustrate the procedure, observe a classroom, work with the teacher's current technology to make use of interventions more seamless, create a flipchart, model a lesson, or do other things to help teachers with the implementation.

Overall, coaches are there to problem solve with their teachers, leadership, and the system. They can use the problem-solving steps identified earlier in the book, or they can use the consultation model (Myrick, 1977). In the consultation model, coaches need to

Step 1: Identify the problem

Step 2: Clarify the consultee's or educator's situation

Step 3: Identify the goal or desired outcome

Step 4: Observe and record relevant behaviors

Step 5: Develop a plan

Step 6: Initiate the plan

Step 7: Follow up

Education of Stakeholders: Not Only One Voice

Stakeholders in our educational system include students, parents/families, and community. Changing one thing in a positive way can affect the entire system. Change agents are tasked with getting everyone on the same page and using the same language *but* inviting stakeholders to determine their own personal whys. It is up to the school to provide communication that is not confusing and full of educational jargon. This includes maintaining a consistency of language in terms of roles, meeting names, resources used, evidence-based practice, materials on websites, and brochures.

Empowering Student Voice

Students are an important voice in the work of making a more positive school culture. We cannot do this work without them. Their opinions, thoughts, beliefs, and actions can inform the direction of the SEL intervention. As a system, you must decide how student voice can be included in your intervention efforts. Many times, it begins with providing students access and permission to participate meaningfully during planning, training, implementation, and evaluation of your SEL program. Students know more about the day-to-day interactions between students in the building than the adults do. That knowledge is priceless in helping you reach your goal of a positive school culture. They see the issues from their vantage point, and that can be helpful when you are designing plans for implementation.

Once you have shown an interest in their opinions and given them access to the planning process, students need a way to meaningfully have those conversations. This may require instruction on how to give feedback, how to openly ask questions, and how to interpret data and problem solve. This may require some extra work to plan these discussions, but you will give students the opportunity to meaningfully contribute to their school.

Here are some things to think about: How do you create an environment of respect and rapport? Describe what it means to advocate for a student. How are you empowering students to advocate for themselves? To be empowered is to have a sense of safety, a place where students feel unthreatened and have some control about the decisions in their lives. Students need to feel physically and psychologically safe in their environment.

Emphasis on Equity

Schools should be reflective about their current equity practices. Students can be impacted by the cultural competencies of the adults who serve them. As we braid together the threads of school culture, we want to include discussions that further our understanding of equity in our schools. SEL helps to provide us with empathy and skills for under-standing others who are different from us. SEL and equity can be braided together by developing communication skills that allow us to analyze all practices through an equity lens. Through development of social-emotional skills, students will learn about the differences between people and how to develop relationships despite differences. Teachers are encouraged to learn more about their students, their culture, and what it is like to be a student today. These positive relationships between adults and students help to provide a greater connectedness to school. As previously mentioned, students who have a trusting and positive relationship with teachers have better attendance and performance. The emphasis on evidence-based strategies is important, because they are found to be effective for students from all backgrounds.

Schools can look at the cultural backgrounds of their students to develop understanding of how culture plays out in school. It is important for the team to be aware of the cultural issues of the students they serve. This focus on universal and schoolwide practices to improve school climate and culture allows for all students to benefit. To empower students, we must ensure equitable treatment and opportunities for everyone in our system.

Inviting Students Into the Decision-Making Process

Stakeholders may want to create a youth advisory board. This group should be formed with the same care and consideration that is used in forming the teams at the school. Diverse students should participate. This is a leadership opportunity, where students can provide guidance on the wording of surveys that are going out of the school, feedback on specific lessons or practices from the chosen SEL intervention, analysis of the data that directly affects them, and solutions that they and their peers buy in to.

Adult leadership will want to decide and set expectations for the things that students will and will not have a choice in in this process. Setting expectations about the purpose of the group and what sort of decisions they will be able to make is vital. Students do not want to waste their time on this work if it is just a meaningless exercise where no real change that they suggest will be accepted. Make their work meaningful, and they will continue to be invested in the process.

Providing Opportunities for Students to Practice Social and Emotional Skills in Real-World Environments

Many prosocial behaviors, including kindness, empathy, and helpfulness, can be practiced through community-service activities. Service learning and community service offer direct practice of social-emotional skills. The purpose is to learn the skills, practice the activities, and commit to action through service to others. Community-service learning or service learning has become a more widely accepted practice for schools for academic learning (Ohn & Wade, 2009). Researchers have found that community service is learning by doing. But it was suggested by Ohn and Wade (2009) that community-service learning also should include learning how students solved social problems and made informed decisions relating to that information.

A meta-analysis of 62 studies that involved 11,837 students was conducted to determine the outcomes of using service learning in an educational context (Celio, Durlak, & Dymnicki, 2011). In comparison to controls, students who participated in service learning or community service had significant gains in five outcome areas: attitudes toward self, attitudes toward school and learning, civic engagement, social skills, and academic achievement. These studies further examined the effects of the recommended practices in the implementation of the service-learning program. Schaps (2003) suggested ways to implement community-building approaches. Four approaches were particularly beneficial. The first one was to actively cultivate respectful, supportive relationships among students,

Infusing SEL Into Community Service Projects

A few years ago, I worked with two different student groups. The group were designed to help students learn prosocial and peer relational skills. Both skills fall under the SEL competencies. The students were taught the skills using a variety of modalities—didactic, games, cooperative learning and experiential activities, and expressive arts. The students were also challenged to "help others through action." The students determined who they wanted to help, what steps they would need to do to help, and how they would accomplish their goals. The first group of students raised pennies for an animal shelter. The second group sold lollipops and the proceeds went to a local women's shelter. Students had to use their prosocial and peer relational skills to accomplish this community service project. The children and their families reported that the experience of helping others made them feel good about themselves.

teachers, and parents. Cultivating supportive relationships allowed students from diverse backgrounds to feel included and allowed for all to assume active roles in the school. The second recommendation was to emphasize common purposes and ideals. Empowering students with a strong sense of community contributed to the development of characteristics essential to good character and citizenship, such as fairness, concern for others, and personal responsibility, which became a norm. The next recommendation was to provide regular opportunities for service and cooperation. Students learned the skills of cooperation, collaboration, and communication and thus were more likely to develop richer relationships. This included the goal of learning to help others. Finally, the students should be given developmentally appropriate opportunities for autonomy and influence (Schaps, 2003).

Another way to meet students, need to practice is through peer mentoring. Providing students with individuals to meet with is mutually beneficial. Students are able to practice their social and emotional skills and strategies and increase school connectedness. The feeling of belongingness is accentuated when relationships between peers are developed.

Parent/Family Involvement

When involving parents/families in this work, you must remember to be inclusive of the different people among this population. This is especially important when designing educational opportunities for SEL competencies. Learning is contextual. It should be scaffolded so that adults with full plates won't be overwhelmed. Understanding parents' perspectives on any new initiative begins with understanding your parent population, especially those parents who are underrepresented in typical parent outreach activities, like the PTA (parent teacher association), foundations, parent nights, or curriculum nights. What are the barriers between them and the school? There are barriers in communications, misunderstanding of norms, misapprehensions resulting from their own school experience, and sometimes a misperception that the only information coming from the school must be negative. This is critical information that you will want to have to develop the relationships that will help your students practice SEL both inside and outside the school building.

Parent/Family Network: Education Through Parent Workshops

Schools can educate their parents and families about SEL. These efforts may require extra time and resources, but they will provide families with greater understanding of the skills involved with SEL. Education efforts can help to bring about greater parent involvement and understanding. It is important to include information about why SEL is good for kids, why schools find value in teaching SEL, how it can make a difference in their lives, and how families can use this information at home. Again, parents and families need to know what's in it for them.

Integrating School and Home Practice

In my experience, "drive-by SEL," where students are given a worksheet to give to their parents/families or a webpage to show them, has not been very successful. Many families do not know what it is and often think that it is required homework. In some districts, homework, specifically how much and the type, is a hot button issue. Families may be immediately turned off by having to do more homework that they do not connect to any academic subject. Before sending out a worksheet or link, make sure to understand your parent population. Is this something they are prepared for? Do they understand what it is for and how it connects to their child's education? Do they feel prepared to have these discussions with their children? How are you supporting the families in their learning of SEL competencies? Consider what you do with math curriculum. I have seen examples of cheat sheets, answer sheets, parenting workshops, and websites—all to help us figure out our children's math equations. We need that sort of integrated practice for the link between school and home practice of SEL. SEL should be introduced and intentionally integrated into the communication. Do you have SEL workshops? Is it a topic during parent-teacher conferences? Is it on your website and in your newsletters? The more intentional we are about including SEL in our work with parents and families, the more important it will be for them.

Family engagement can start with education. In my experience, parents and other caregivers want to know how to help their children. They are looking for tools and skills to use, because they may be struggling at home. Change agents can build the bridge between school and home by first providing education about SEL and then providing some strategies that can be used in the home. For example, if your school is emphasizing emotional regulation, give the families ideas about what they can do for the student to practice emotional regulation at home. Education nights or workshops provide a communication link about the SEL work. These education nights should include demonstration and practice for the families. This active participation will help to lock in those skills more effectively than having parents and families passively listening as you provide a PowerPoint presentation. SEL support for adults is as unique to the parents' environment as it is to the students' environment. Change agents may need to gather information about the needs of the families before designing their educational workshop.

Parent/Family Focus Groups

When we think about involving parents, it is often more about parent permission rather than parent participation. Parents, guardian, and families need meaningful ways to participate that allow them to feel part of the process. One way to do that is to create a family focus group that can brainstorm ways to improve social and emotional skills outside of the school. Families can provide the link between practicing these skills in the school environment and practicing them in their homes. A family focus group can also look at data and help to devise solutions for creating a robust program for their students. Communication between the family and the teacher or school about the child's social and emotional skill growth will help the family feel more connected to the work. They are learning about their own children's accomplishments and opportunities for growth, and the families can help grow those skills at home.

Families are privy to information that can be useful in designing relevant programming. Their students bring home the impacts of their school culture every day. And sometimes families are at a loss for how to bridge the divide between school and home. But like the youth advisory board, the family focus group will need to have parameters that guide their practice. Its meetings are not an opportunity to complain but a time to work together and problem solve. Expectations of participants will need to be clear and detailed prior to forming the focus group.

Building Community Understanding

To build community understanding, a team that includes community stakeholders and personnel from all schools gathers together to make recommendations about the role of SEL. Community involvement can be a very powerful thing. There are a few suggestions for increasing community buy-in.

Government Advocacy

Community members can speak with local and state legislators about the importance of SEL. Crucial points to consider when advocating to your legislators include these: who you are and how you connect with the work, and why you are requesting their support of bills that benefit schools and systems working toward the availability and implementation of SEL. Change agents who are truly looking at the whole system cannot ignore those who make the policy and create the state budgets at the government level. It may be possible to network with those individuals through your family network.

Community Stakeholders

Invite community stakeholders to visit schools and classrooms doing SEL work. This may include demonstration of a lesson or observations of classrooms, or students can produce a presentation about a service-learning project they have done or other results of using social-emotional skills.

   The use of mentors can also be especially powerful. Mentors are usually individuals in the community who want to help serve the youth in the area. Change agents can leverage these relationships to reinforce SEL. Mentors can use professional development of their own to learn about SEL and the place it plays in prevention. They can benefit from learning strategies to improve the use of skills such as cooperation, resilience, and problem-solving skills.

Programs That Serve Students Outside the School Day

Discuss SEL with outside partners that serve schools. This can include afterschool programs, mentorship programs, and local activity centers that serve youth, like the YMCA or a local recreation center. I have heard of examples where this is especially doable in small communities. Individuals in health and human services, places that employ teenagers or have youth as customers, the library, and even the convenience and local grocery stores can all be informed about the expectations and skills that the youth are

Success Stories in the Community

One valuable exercise is to collect the stories that you hear about students demonstrating their social and emotional skills in the community in a positive way. These stories can be retold in verbal or written form to promote the work that you are doing in the schools. These stories can be used to inform other teachers, parents/families, and other students. Stories that emphasize the importance and demonstration of SEL are vital for promoting understanding. A student who practices positive social, emotional, and behavioral skills helps to animate a connected and vibrant community. Local media can be a valuable resource for telling your story of positive skill development among youth.

learning. The students get to practice these skills in real situations and observe adults in the community model those skills.

Infrastructure Issues: The Leadership Merry-Go-Round

When Your Leader Leaves

Staff and leadership changes can rock the boat of your intervention, especially if your leader was also your most vocal advocate. You may have the following questions. What if the new administrator doesn't agree with the direction of the intervention? What sort of training will the new administrator have to undergo? It is up to the change agent and the leadership team to help the new administrator understand the history of the intervention. Keeping records of your decision-making process is crucial for maintaining integrity of your intervention as staff and administration changes are made from year to year. Figure 9.2 shows an example of a leadership log that you can use for this purpose.

Here are some things you should consider:

- Keep a journal for each calendar year.

- Know reports and familiarize your self with overall data.

- Ask yourself: If I were new to the building, what questions would I have?

- Capture the major milestones—what happened?

Upsetting Leadership Changes

Many times, districts set up transition plans for new administrators. But I have seen cases when principals are released from their positions or forced to transfer. There may be anger, confusion, and sadness. The staff is impacted by the loss of their leader, whether they thought it was the right decision or not. The system must rally to keep momentum of the change effort alive. There will be transition with staff as well. Sometimes staff members follow their principal. Principals can decide to disengage from the

Figure 9.2 Example Leadership Log		
August Professional development for staff	**September** Meet with SEL team Family workshop #1 Districtwide training	**October** Universal screener Meet with SEL team CASEL convention
November Meet with SEL team Meet with youth advisory board	**December** Meet with SEL team	**January** Meet with SEL team Districtwide training
February Meet with SEL team Family workshop #2	**March** Meet with SEL team	**April** Meet with SEL team SEL leadership luncheon (multidistrict)
May Meet with SEL team Districtwide training	**June** Community SEL meeting	**July** Schedule family workshops—Sept and Feb

work (and the school) or become resentful. This will undoubtedly affect the rest of the staff. Because this typically happens at the end of the year, the stress level is even higher. You as the change agents must continue to do everything you are doing. The work does not change, even if there is a change in leadership. It is time to look at your accomplishments, look at what you have done, and think about what your next steps will be. Embrace the discomfort. You may feel overwhelmed. Therefore, developing your own social and emotional capabilities is so important. Invest in your personal self-care strategies, and plan for the realities of your upcoming change.

Practitioner's Voice

I truly believe this stuff works, both individual classrooms and the synergistic effect school-wide when it is consistently practiced. I have worked with students of concern on an individual basis and seen the positive effects, but making systemic changes are powerful for both the student and the staff who work with them.

—Mari Stevens, Student Support Coach

Resources

Printed Material

- *Changing Climates of Conflict: A Social Network Experiment in 56 Schools* (Paluck, Shepherd, & Aronow, 2016). Students with influence over peers reduce school bullying by 30 percent.

- *Mikva Challenge: A Strong Advocate for Youth Voice* (Rivera & Jimenez, n.d.). An article about one example of youth empowerment through civic action. Mikva's five program areas focus on issues of juvenile justice, public health, education, civic participation, and youth training. Using a civic action framework, all the programs focus on building social and emotional skills, democratic participation, and youth empowerment.

- Guskey's *Five Critical Levels of Professional Development Evaluation.* (https://www.cdc.gov/healthyschools/professional_development/e-learning/pd101/_assets/06_FiveCriticalLevelsPDEval_508c.pdf)

Videos

- *Teaching Math as a Social Activity:* https://youtu.be/KZxNldBEU6o

- *No Teacher Is an Island.* High school teachers offer each other support and feedback for improving their work: https://youtu.be/nFCU1ThXTGk

- *The Shift From Engaging Students to Empowering Learners:* https://youtu.be/BYBJQ5rIFjA

Strategies

- Discover student engagement tips and attempt to implement them in your specific school environment: www.edutopia.org/blog/student-engagement-tips-from-student-harley-center

- Think about changing your professional development to become more inclusive and hands on: https://youtu.be/aiW0s6_83dw

REFLECTION QUESTIONS

1. How would you describe fidelity of implementation to another person?

2. How will you meet the professional development needs of all staff?

3. What are a couple of ways that you could invite students into the decision-making process around SEL?

4. What does your state legislature understand about SEL?

5. How would you invite community members to participate in learning more about SEL?

6. What parent/family education methods work for your school? How can you use this knowledge to develop programs for families that will be well attended?

7. What are the principal's responsibilities to continue progress of interventions in case the principal leaves the school?

Strategy #8: Plan for Resistance to Change

Educational change depends on what teachers do and think—it is as simple and complex as that.

—Michael Fullan (2001, p. 115)

Resistance to Change

In my work as a counselor, I have experienced resistance to growth or change with the students, parents, and clients I work with. It is a natural part of any new change. When it happens at a systemic level, the resistance manifests itself in different ways. There can be passive resistance or refusal to participate. There is active resistance or lobbying against the change. And there are many other types of behaviors that come from a place of resistance. You will have to deal with resistance. It may be passive, where no one tells you that they don't like the plan; they just don't go along with it. Or it may be aggressive, where you or members of your team are yelled at. It is important that at this stage you expect some resistance and you develop a plan for dealing with probable responses to change.

Each challenge creates another potential roadblock to effective implementation of SEL. Challenges to school-based interventions must be met with strategies that will overcome resistance to improve the mental, emotional, and behavioral health of children in the school environment.

Personal Plan—The Oxygen Mask

Most of us have experienced or seen the flight attendant give the speech that includes the guidance to put your oxygen mask on first before helping those around you. For parents, this can seem out of the natural order, as we often give to the little people in our lives before we get for ourselves. Parenthood is built upon the foundation of selflessness. Even if we don't see it in all cases, it is culturally normed that we take care of our dependents first. For those of us in education, this may be even more true. We don't have to search long for examples of teachers and school staff putting their lives on the line to save children who are not their own. For those individuals, the resistance can become personal. Change agents who understand the rationale and reasoning for implementing processes that support students' social and emotional growth may find it inconceivable that others don't see things the same way. This lack of alignment between the change agent and those who are resistant to change causes hard feelings and resentment. People who are implementing must have additional personal resources to deal with the unpredictability and stress of systems change. Self-care is a significant consideration and must be a planned event for implementers. Putting your oxygen mask on first is not selfish; it is essential.

There are three ways I have found to deal with the challenges of resistance:

1. **Develop personal resilience**: This includes learning how to care for yourself, creating boundaries for what you will and will not tolerate, and developing your skills at working with people with different leadership styles.

2. **Lean on your team:** Your team will help cheer you on or cheer you up. You all have the same goal. Perhaps they have strategies that you haven't thought of. At the very least, you have others going through it with you.

3. **Find the good.** When times are difficult, you need extra resources to keep yourself afloat. Training your mind to find the good in the day, the moment, or the person will help you shift your perspective. Keeping alert for the good things is a skill that pays to develop.

Challenge Scenarios

Systems change can be dependent on how individuals in the system perceive the intervention. It is the change agent's responsibility to identify the stakeholder's perception of SEL. You should understand your stakeholders' perspectives around time (how will this fit on their already full plates?), how isolated their practice is (do they regularly work on improving their practice, or is this brand new territory?), appreciation (do they feel their efforts are appreciated?), and effectiveness (do they perceive the intervention/innovation to be something that will work?). A plan for resistance to your framework for action

---

Challenge #1: Intervention Is Not Well Received. Change Agents Receive Regular Negative Feedback or Comments. There May Even Be Personal Attacks.

Strategies for Change Agents

1. Listen deeply.

   - Pay attention to the individuals who disagree: What is their understanding of and reaction to the intervention? Try to discover the root of the problem from their perspective.
   - Build rapport.
   - Respect how people define their own goals and self-interests. (Tap into that.)
   - Offer an action option, and encourage them to take the next step—don't force them. Give them grace.

2. Voice difficulty.

   - Acknowledge the difficulty of the change process.
   - Recognize that all processes are not the same, and that is okay.

3. Check your ego.

   - Don't let your position/title/role affect your reactions to the negativity.

4. Practice self-care.

   - Provide yourself preplanned strategies that calm you when in a stressful situation.
   - Know when you need to get supervisors involved.

5. Address teachers' questions

   - Provide a time and place that teachers can ask questions and voice concerns.
   - Determine whether there is a theme to the type of questions they ask; is there something else you can provide to meet that need?
   - Give them a realistic timeline.
   - Set the expectation that their input will be valued.

Challenge #2: Staff Is Tired of Change and Just Wants Things to Be the Same, They Just Can't Handle "One More Thing."

Strategies for Change Agents

1. Recognize that a schema is developing.

   - A schema is the pattern of thoughts or behaviors that organizes categories of information and the relationships among them.
   - It is used to organize current knowledge and provide a framework for future understanding.
   - Staff may need to hear about their developing schema and how this new information is being applied to former understandings.

2. Understand limits.

   - There are limits on individual capacity to absorb new information.
   - There is a balance between individuals' desire to hear about research and evidence-based work, and their ability to apply it.

3. Understand "initiative fatigue."

   - If teachers have experienced many initiatives, you may need to implement yours at a slower pace.
   - Make your initiative more enjoyable to learn and implement.

4. Show appreciation.

   - Give staff appreciation for the work they have already accomplished.
   - Provide them a roadmap of how the new intervention is built upon the positive things they have already done.

Challenge #3: Staff Believes This Is Just a Repackaging of Previous Innovations. They Have Already Tried This Before.

Strategies for Change Agents

1. Conduct an inventory of programs implemented previously.

   - Include program, purpose, targeted group, expected outcome, evidence of fidelity, and outcome data. (Is it working?)

2. Be curious.

   - Ask staff questions: What programs can we eliminate? What programs can we combine? What programs need to be enhanced for improved outcomes and sustained functioning?

3. Demonstrate the gap.

   - Use what they have done to discover what they haven't done.

4. Measure impact.

   - Discuss with staff any measurable impact of previous interventions and plans to measure the proposed intervention.

Challenge #4: One or More Specific Groups Do Not Support the Change Efforts.

Strategies for Change Agents

1. Promote understanding.

   - Don't talk at them without learning who they are and what they care about.
   - Conduct a role-play to better understand their perspective. Change agents can use this strategy to think through how they might resolve conflicts before engaging with people who don't support the change.
   - Understand that this could be fear based, and develop ways to discuss it.

2. Provide opportunities to observe good work.

   - Give teachers or other stakeholders the opportunity to observe the intervention in other classrooms or in other buildings.

3. Use a clear, consistent procedure.

   - Provide individuals with information about who they go to for help, how they ask for help, and what the expectations are for when they should receive help during the intervention.

Challenge #5: Change Agents Immersed in a Lead Implementation Role Face New Challenges as They Transition From Their Previous Role in Their School or District. New Responsibilities May Involve Coaching or Evaluation of Former Colleagues.

Strategies for Change Agents

1. Be transparent about your new role as a lead implementor in your school. Explain how you plan to support teachers who were previously your colleagues, and inform them if your new role may include observations, meetings, and teaming with them.

2. Train continuously to develop your own capacity.

   - Learn terms and concepts.
   - Learn strategies.
   - Identify barriers to implementation.

3. Invite teachers to provide input for your new role.

   - How can they share ideas with you or with the staff?
   - Invest them in the work by including their ideas.

Challenge #6: One Individual or Group Actively Pushes Back on Intervention.

Strategies for Change Agents

1. Prepare for pushback.

   - Reinvest in goals.
   - Ask yourself: How are we answering questions? How are we providing extra support? How are we reinforcing good work?
   - Thank stakeholders for their time and energy.
   - Give lots of appreciation.

2. Understand the odds.

   - When working with a school, you may have meaningful things in your action plan, and you hope to accomplish all of them. But in my experience, I could get three out of twelve items adopted. Another quarter of the things that districts agreed on were pushed back against by individual schools. As for the other items in the action plan, we decided to investigate why these action items seemed to have less traction. Based on that information, we were better able to strategize how to move forward. We learned that these other action items would take more time to implement. For change agents, it doesn't mean that you give up; you strategize. You talk to the stakeholders; you look at the variables; you explore possibilities. You continue to advocate and work with your stakeholders.

3. Respond to conflict as a normal process.

   - Realize that this is a normal process; not everyone will agree in any system.
   - Build a foundational understanding (rules of engagement).
   - Plan for discussion of facts, not feelings.
   - Reflect on your own reactions.
   - Change as needed.
   - Repair relationships.

Challenge #7: The Attitude From Stakeholders Is Passive Nonacceptance: "This Too Shall Pass."

Strategies for Change Agents

1. Keep a list of what works.

   - Keep a list of "what works" or "good stuff" that you encounter along the way, even if it is not necessary in the moment.

2. Reinforce the work of stakeholders.

   - Reinforce the work of stakeholders as part of the process.
   - Be specific about what they are doing, for example, the positive interventions they have made.
   - Let them know when you hear good things about them.
   - Empower them.
   - Emphasize relationships over data.

Challenge #8: Teachers Believe That This Is Just Another Tool With Which They Will Be Evaluated, Not Something That Is Meant to Support Them.

Strategies for Change Agents

1. Communicate with stakeholders.

   - Develop relationships and good communications to discover their needs and opinions about the intervention.
   - Learn about potential conflicts between commitments, and about their understandings of what is expected of them with respect to the intervention.

2. Have teachers invested in teams.

   - Managing teams means teaching teams to learn the terms and be invested in the plan and outcomes (teach a person to fish).
   - Focus on training needs, relationships, growth, and collaboration.

3. Discuss confidentiality of conversations.

   - Verbalize to staff that if they need help during implementation process, this should not affect evaluations of their teaching performance.
   - Build trust among staff.

Challenge #9: Stakeholders Say They Have Too Much on Their Plates. They Have Workload and Time Concerns.

Strategies for Change Agents

1. Discuss the braiding of initiatives. Ask them these questions:

   - What processes and procedures are you doing that look at how each initiative meets the varying needs at the school level?
   - Are new initiatives coming up that contradict, add more to, replicate, or confuse what you are already doing? If so, work toward eliminating them.
   - Can you integrate processes between PBIS (if you are currently using it) and SEL? Between the problem-solving process and behavioral expectations?

2. Allow for sharing of concerns about the initiative from the stakeholders. People often just want to be heard.

   - Principals can plan for a time for sharing concerns for the new initiative. Principals and change agents can then develop strategies to help stakeholders meet their needs.
   - Have a clear plan for how to respond to the stakeholders' concerns. Include items you are working on to resolve and items that you are unable to change due to outside factors.

3. Voice acknowledgment of and respect for positions.

   - Acknowledge work done and previous practice.

4. Capitalize on a good thing.

   - Any opportunity to move the ball down the field should be referenced.
   - Be aware of things that the stakeholders want to do or enjoy doing, and see if you can integrate that into what needs to be done for intervention.

5. Provide flexibility and time-saving strategies when possible.

- Discuss with the team how to make interventions more manageable to work with time constraints. Are there ways to simplify the interventions or break them down into smaller pieces that can be taught over several days?
- Everyone can benefit from a time-saving strategy. Share with the staff something that is easy to implement and measure.

6. Let teachers know they are not on their own.

- Provide support after professional development sessions.
- Follow through on any requests for help.
- Itemize things they are responsible for and not responsible for.

Challenge #10: The Intervention Lacks Support From Parents, Families, or the Community.

Strategies for Change Agents

1. Provide opportunities to learn.

- Introduce SEL gradually, with information that they can use and that has meaning in their everyday lives with their children.
- Accept them as partners in learning.

2. Be aware of barriers.

- Is there a lack of open communication or differences in communication styles?
- Have there been previous conflicts between school staff and parents or the community?
- Are the parents aware of how to navigate communication sources? Do they have access to e-mail, or access to the district's website? Websites can be a barrier to clear and quick communication if parents are unsure how to navigate them.
- Do parents and community members understand the acronyms used in education?

should be developed, because there will be challenges in implementation that need to be prepared for. This will be done by creating a plan to deal with these challenges. This will require both leadership and collaboration within the system. Below are some of the most common challenges (problems) and suggestions for solutions in the system.

Figure 10.1 summarizes some of the challenges change agents can encounter and lists strategies for overcoming them. It includes a column for you to add your plans to use the strategies you choose.

As you consider resistance as a natural part of the change process, focus on the big picture. Change agents will often have conversations about whether a practice, intervention, or process is working. Many teachers have procedures that they continue to use, because that is the way they were taught, that was the way their mentor teacher did it, or that is the way their first principal liked it. Ghosts of interventions past live in our classrooms even as new evidence proclaims them useless or in some cases damaging.

We will be confronted with practices that we determine arcane. But from my experience, we should focus on what works better or more efficiently, rather than demonizing a practice from the past. We should invite individuals to be curious about their practices, rather than showing them research that indicates what they have been doing for

Figure 10.1 Planning for Challenges

Challenge	Strategies for Change Agent	Planning for This Strategy
Intervention is not well received. Change agents receive regular negative feedback or comments. There may even be personal attacks.	• Listen deeply. • Voice difficulty. • Check your ego. • Practice self-care. • Address teacher questions	
Staff is tired of change and just wants things to be the same; they just can't handle one more thing.	• Recognize schema is developing. • Understand limits. • Understand initiative fatigue. • Show appreciation.	
Staff believes this is just a repackaging of previous innovations. They have already tried this before.	• Conduct an inventory. • Be curious. • Demonstrate the gap. • Measure impact.	
One or more specific groups do not support the change efforts.	• Promote understanding. • Provide opportunities to observe good work. • Provide clear, consistent procedure.	
Change agents immersed in a lead implementation role face new challenges as they transition from their previous role in their school or district. New responsibilities may involve coaching or evaluation of former colleagues.	• Be transparent. • Train continuously to develop capacity. • Invite teachers to provide input.	
One individual or group actively pushes back on intervention.	• Prepare for pushback. • Understand the odds. • Respond to conflict as a normal process.	
The attitude from stakeholders is passive nonacceptance: "This too shall pass."	• Keep a list of what works. • Reinforce work of stakeholders.	
Teachers believe that this is just another tool with which they will be evaluated, not something that is meant to support them.	• Communicate with the union. • Have teachers invested in teams. • Discuss confidentiality of conversations.	
Stakeholders say they have too much on their plates. They have workload and time concerns.	• Discuss the braiding of initiatives. • Allow for sharing of concerns • Voice acknowledgment of and respect for positions. • Capitalize on a good thing.	

	• Provide flexibility and time-saving strategies when possible.	
	• Let them know they are not on their own.	
The intervention lacks support from the parent/family/community.	• Provide opportunities to learn.	
	• Be aware of barriers.	

years is ineffective. Change agents combat resistance through inviting teachers into the conversation about evidence-based practices, learning what practices support SEL and what practices should be culled. Jim Collins speaks of the "flywheel effect," where if we slowly and methodically but consistently put our shoulders to the flywheel and push, we can get momentum. That momentum is built upon collection of tangible evidence of our plan and how it is working (Collins, 2001). This momentum is a slow build. Change does not happen overnight, so going for the long haul must be in everyone's understanding as they take on systems change.

General Strategies

If your challenge was not addressed in the scenarios above, there are a few general strategies that I would recommend:

1. **Be as transparent as possible:** Let your stakeholders know the details of the intervention, communicating the steps, who is involved, and what the plan is.

2. **The system will have growth and gains:** Celebrate the gains, and learn as you grow.

3. **Reinforce the good work of stakeholders:** This cannot and should not be a one-person journey. It is a collective experience. Let the stakeholders and those who are advocating alongside of you know how much you value their work.

4. It bears repeating. Yes, you guessed it. **SELF-CARE!!**

The End of Her Rope

A long time ago, I was taking a graduate course in classroom management. One of our assignments was to shadow an elementary teacher. She had had a challenging year, and by the time I had come to her classroom in March, she was burned out. I arrived one day, and she said that she had had enough, and she told me that she kept 10 boys in at recess and told them that she wasn't going to take any more of them disrupting the classroom. She told them that they were ruining things for the rest of the class, and that if they caused any more problems for the class, they would be asked to go outside for the remainder of the lesson.

In talking to my professor about this observation later, I said, "I don't know if it would have been my place to ask if she had considered using a more democratic classroom." My professor agreed and felt empathy for the teacher: "My heart goes out to her. I think it is wise not to say anything unless you are asked."

I learned a lot from the empathy that my professor gave this teacher. Teachers struggling or feeling burned out may resort to reactive practices—not proactive ones. While my suggestion might have been a good one, it probably wouldn't have been well received. She may have been defensive and resistant. The more important thing in the moment was to try to understand what this teacher was going through. Being sensitive to the needs of our educators is a priority if we are to be effective.

Resources

Printed Material

- *Difficult Conversations*. Learn how to achieve shared goals while remaining true to yourself, even when the stakes are high (https://cdn-media.leanin.org/wp-content/uploads/2013/10/Difficult_Conversations_RD4.pdf).

- *Listening Dyads Can Transform Your Team* (Safir, 2014).

- *Self-Care Resources—Realistic Self-Care: 8 Key Questions* (http://www.mindfulteachers.org/p/self-care-resources.html).

Videos

- *Inside Chicago Public Schools: SEL at Marcus Garvey Elementary:* https://youtu.be/d6vS0UBGSW4

- *Mindful Breathing (Stop Breathe and Think):* https://youtu.be/SEfs5TJZ6Nk

- *How to Persuade Others With the Right Questions: Jedi Mind Tricks:* https://www.youtube.com/watch? v=WAL7Pz1i1jU

Strategies

- For self-care, try implementing a tap-in/tap-out strategy: https://www.youtube.com/watch? v=qPtsP7pBobI

- Find videos to make yourself and other teachers laugh: Watch "TeachingCenter": https://youtu.be/dkHqPFbxmOU

REFLECTION QUESTIONS

1. How will you demonstrate transparency about the intervention with stakeholders?

2. How will you communicate growth and gains to stakeholders?

3. Do you think your staff will exhibit resistance to SEL? If so, in what ways?

4. Do you think your parents/families/community will exhibit resistance to SEL? If so, in what ways?

5. How will you personally prepare for encountering resistance?

6. What challenge scenario seems most realistic for your school?

7. Which strategy do you think you need to actively employ today?

Strategy #9:
Assess Your Outcomes

We do not need magic to change the world; we carry all the power we need inside ourselves already; we have the power to imagine better.

—J. K. Rowling (Harvard University Commencement Address, 2008)

Gold Standard for Change: The "Fire Drill Effect"

The overall goal for the intervention is integration and sustainability. Every school has a procedure for conducting a fire drill. This is an expectation for every building that includes procedures that are reinforced every year. If there are changes to the building—a new addition or possibly a portable placed in the schoolyard—the fire drill procedures are updated to reflect these changes. I call the gold standard the "fire drill effect." This is achieved when policies and resources are aligned within a system, systems are self-correcting and achieve positive outcomes, and leadership provides staff ongoing support. To achieve this goal standard with SEL implementation, we must prepare for a consistent need for clarification, recognition of work done, and stabilization of the system in both leadership and collaboration efforts. The outcome of a fire drill is that all individuals exit the building in a safe an efficient manner. The outcome of your SEL intervention will be more complex but still important to measure.

Big Question: Did Anything Change for the Better?

As we assess the outcomes of the SEL intervention, we must keep in mind that the program evolves. It may not be exactly as you originally conceived it. There should be respect for the resiliency of a school's culture. Any norms or beliefs may be entrenched, and there is a reason for their existence. Respecting and validating that will help to uncover that there might be a different way and to educate staff about it.

Assessing outcomes will be a continuous task throughout the life of the school, as suggested in the fire drill effect. But what things should we look at for whole-school SEL outcomes? A caution for all change agents: In the first few years, you may not see huge gains. Minimal gains should be celebrated. It will take time.

The Every Student Succeeds Act (ESSA) calls for independently verified indicators to meet its evidence standards. Robert Slavin recommends the use of MOOSES (measurable, observable, objective, social-emotional skills) (Slavin, 2017). He recommends using these measures rather than a self-assessment or behavior rating by a teacher, because these measures are objective. He recommends three types of evidence standards. The first is data from discipline referrals, suspensions, and bullying incidents as indicators of SEL. The second is behavioral observations from observers who do not know the social and emotional skills the students have been taught. The raters can observe whether the sought-after behaviors occur naturally during the school day or an activity. The third is a self-report measure given to students that asks about the behaviors or attitudes that relate to the items that they were taught (Slavin, 2017). For example, if they were explicitly taught self-regulation, how do they rate themselves at waiting their turn in the lunch line?

Change agents can assess your data in three ways. One method is to review the descriptive data about the school. The descriptive data will not likely be affected by your SEL intervention, but it can affect your intervention. For example, a change in the number of students who qualify as English language learners will mean that your SEL leadership team will need to reassess whether the needs of the current school population are being met. Or a high staff turnover may affect the amount of training that must be conducted before the school year begins. Your intervention can be measured through proximal and distal outcomes. In Chapter 2, proximal and distal outcomes were defined, and this chapter looks at how they can be measured.

Descriptive Data About Your School

Consider features of a school that impact the students regardless of the SEL intervention, such as school location, student/teacher ratio, student and teacher demographic information (age, race, gender, socioeconomic status, special programs, ability status, culture, languages spoken, etc.). Figure 11.1 gives you a way to organize these features and their implications for your SEL intervention.

Figure 11.1 School Descriptive Data Tracker

Descriptive Data Type	Longitudinal Data	Current Data	Implications
Type of school: urban, suburban, rural			
Student/teacher ratio			
Age range of students			
Racial makeup of school			
Gender distribution			
Socioeconomic status of students and families			
Number of students who qualify for free/reduced-price lunch			
Number of students eligible for Section 504 plans			
Number of students eligible for an IEP			
Cultural backgrounds in school community			
Number of students who qualify for ELL services			
Average years of experience of classroom teachers			

A Self-Report Proximal Measure

To determine if my students were able to understand and use the concept of making friends because of the social skills intervention, I asked them to please tell me what they would do for this example:

"A new student has arrived in your class. He isn't talking to anyone and by the third day you notice that he sits next to the classroom door at recess and doesn't play with any other kids. What do you think you could do?"

I then analyzed all the interviews and found that the students understood how to make friends through intentional actions. These actions reported by the students included shaking his hand, asking him questions, inviting him to play, cheering him up, helping him, or talking to him. Using concepts discussed in the program, all the students came up with different ways based on their personalities and what they felt comfortable doing. Some of the students would invite the student to play, while others would want to find out the reason for him not playing. One student went so far as to speculate why he might not be playing with others. One student came up with the creative solution of saying, "If we get [to pick] partners in something, I could choose him."

Friendship and the process of making a friend through action was a topic that was discussed many times over the 12 weeks of the intervention. And while friendship was not an unfamiliar topic with them, understanding the intentional actions that it takes to make a friend or notice someone who does not have friends was something new. The students went from a general understanding of "friends" to a more specific understanding of what a good friend looks like, how to make friends, how people support the students, and how to stand up for themselves with those who might be considered "friends" (Rogers, 2015, p. 96).

Proximal Outcome Data

Proximal outcomes demonstrate changes in the skills of students based on the intervention. These can be measured more immediately and should impact the distal outcomes. Below are examples of evidence-based strategies for measuring SEL implementation. Schools may choose to use all or some of them. They may begin with one approach and add more with time. Or they may begin with teachers understanding their own competencies and then teaching them to students (recommended approach).

Distal Outcome Data

Distal outcomes are reflected in long-range school-level data. Measures of distal outcomes show the collective impacts of interventions on the whole school. Each school and district may measure these impacts differently or not at all. Change agents are encouraged to advocate for measurement of this information, because it will more accurately represent the collective change of the SEL implementation to the whole school.

These distal measures were chosen because they are linked to the findings of the seminal meta-analysis done by Durlak, Weissberg, Dymnicki, Taylor, and Schellinger in 2011. SEL programs were found to enhance prosocial behaviors (positive social behavior), reduce conflict, improve academic performance, and reduce internalizing problems (emotional distress) (Durlak et al., 2011). The National Center on Safe Supportive Learning Environments developed three domains of school climate: engagement, safety, and environment. Engagement includes cultural and linguistic competence, relationships, and school participation. Measured under safety are emotional and physical safety, bullying/cyberbullying, substance abuse, and emergency readiness/management. And under environment, the US Department of Education School Climate Surveys (EDSCLS) model includes physical environment, instructional environment, physical health, mental health, and discipline (National Center on Safe Supportive Learning Environments, 2018). These outcomes can be measured to determine whether your prevention initiative is working.

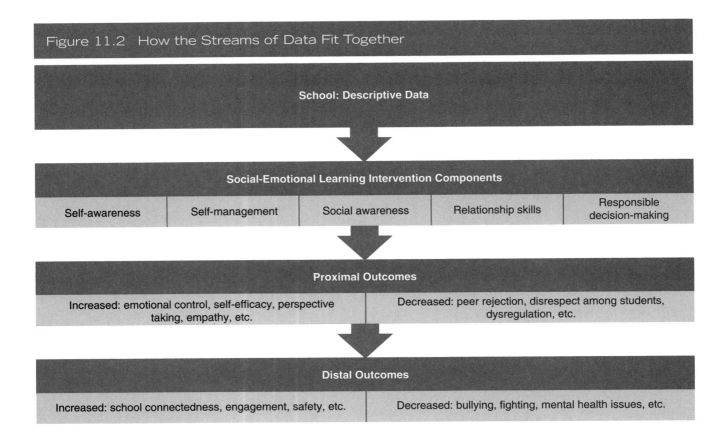

Figure 11.2 How the Streams of Data Fit Together

School: Descriptive Data

Social-Emotional Learning Intervention Components

Self-awareness	Self-management	Social awareness	Relationship skills	Responsible decision-making

Proximal Outcomes

Increased: emotional control, self-efficacy, perspective taking, empathy, etc.	Decreased: peer rejection, disrespect among students, dysregulation, etc.

Distal Outcomes

Increased: school connectedness, engagement, safety, etc.	Decreased: bullying, fighting, mental health issues, etc.

SEL Intervention Outcomes

Figure 11.2 represents how these streams of data fit together. The descriptive data informs the SEL intervention components. The intervention has the following proximal outcomes. And those proximal outcomes can determine the distal outcomes.

Measuring Your SEL Implementation

Determining how to assess your outcomes is the next step. Figure 11.3 shows an overview of this. In the left-most column are the expected outcomes of your SEL implementation. These are based in research as outcomes typical of interventions focused on improving social and emotional skills and improving school climate and culture. The second column shows how to measure the outcome directly. This is another way to determine if your current data collection methods are meeting your needs. Can you determine whether students are demonstrating conflict resolution? If not, how could you do that? You could conduct observations of students in times where conflict happens; or you could measure their conflict-resolution skills using self-reports, surveys, screeners, interviews, or other methods. The third column shows the indirect assessments. Indirect assessments make sensible connections (correlation, not causation) between your SEL intervention and the outcome. For example, if there are fewer referrals to counseling, then students may be experiencing a reduction in emotional distress. Just make sure to take these indirect assessments with a grain of salt and look for other "confounding variables" that could be causing the decrease in counseling referrals in this example.

Figure 11.3 Measuring Your SEL Implementation

Outcome	Direct Assessment	Indirect Assessment	Major Finding
Positive social behavior	Evidence of positive peer relationships at school, conflict resolution, working well with others, teaming	Attendance School climate survey	
Decreased conduct problems	Evidence of a decrease in aggressive and disruptive behavior, restorative discipline practices	Referrals Suspensions Detentions	
Decreased emotional distress	Evidence of decreases in depressive symptoms, anxiety, social withdrawal, school refusal behavior, internalizing and externalizing behaviors	Counseling Crisis Attendance	
Increased engagement	Evidence of school participation, school pride	Cultural competence Equity School climate/culture Attendance	
Improved academic performance	Evidence of perseverance, grit, growth mindset	Grades Test scores Graduation rates	
Increased perception of safety	Evidence of emergency readiness and management, safety protocols, bullying and harassment training and procedures	Fighting/Assault Harassment Bullying Substance abuse	

Figure 11.4 School Outcomes and Implications of Change

School Outcomes	Historical Data	Current Findings	Implications of Change
Academic performance			
Social behavior			
Conduct problems			
Emotional distress			
Engagement			
Safety			
Environment			

Figure 11.4 puts it all together. Your SEL leadership team can determine, based on your historical data and your current findings, what the implications of change can be. For example,

In the past 10 years, our school has seen an increase in students reporting depression and anxiety. We have also seen an increase in absences and school refusal. In the past two years, we have implemented a whole-school SEL intervention. Recently, the students took a screener that showed our internalizing behaviors have decreased, and our attendance has improved by 5 percent.

Be Sensitive to Outcome Overload

Before becoming too overwhelmed by the amount of data collection necessary to identify the outcomes of your intervention, take a moment. Remember that this is a process, one that will not be accomplished in a year or two. This process involves new learning, adoption of new systems, and, as previously discussed, *change*. Reflect on your why. This is important, and it is possible. It will just take change agents who see the long road ahead and think the journey will be worth it—for the students *and* for you!

If you are feeling overwhelmed, imagine some of your colleagues who aren't as invested in the work. That is why it is vital to take the temperature of the systems change endeavor. Are we moving too fast? I used to say that I am lovingly pushing my change agents into new growth. I support and help them and provide them a shoulder to cry on and ideas to work with. But along with that I have the confidence that they can do it and the determination that we need to keep moving forward, finding the balance between feeling sure about the mission but unsure about the path. You know what you want for your school, and you have an idea about the direction and what equipment you need. But you are open to receive the information that the path is giving you to slow down, speed up, change direction, revisit a plan, or best of all have a party to celebrate your achievements.

Overall Goal of Assessing Outcomes: Improve Systemic Integration and Sustainability

The purpose of assessing your outcomes is to improve systemic integration and sustainability of whole-school SEL. The purpose is *not* to use the outcomes to punish individuals and schools that are not reaching a specific benchmark by a specific date. It will be up to school leaders to decide whether the school is making progress based on its unique culture and expectations for the change effort.

Schools should use this data to look at their current decision-making structure. They can use it to guide improvements to the system, determine whether policies and resources are aligned within the system, and change them if need be. Schools can use the information to help leadership provide staff support. These things will help your school sustain implementation of SEL.

Illustrating Protective Factors as Outcomes

As emphasized in this book, we want to tell the story of our SEL intervention. Meaning making through the voices of the educators and students is very powerful. Protective factors are skills or strategies that help to reduce the impact of risk factors in a student's life. Our goal in prevention is to increase protective factors for youth. Figure 11.5 illustrates one way to connect protective factors to practices and gives an example.

Figure 11.5 Connecting Protective Factors to Practices

Protective Factor	SEL Implementation	Example at Our School
Strong, prosocial peer relationships	1. Four lessons per semester from SEL curriculum on positive relationship skills 2. Students intentionally paired with students they could build a relationship with for science project 3. Teacher uses cooperative learning practice during instruction 4. Students encouraged to play games that strengthen their team-building skill at recess. 5. Workshops for parents/families on SEL to reinforce relationship skills.	Recess was a typically trying time for our elementary students. The educational assistants who were on duty reported that they spent most of their time managing groups of students who were arguing about the playground equipment. Soon after implementation, Ms. S reported that she saw two of the students who regularly argued over who got the "good" basketball. She walked over to them expecting to have to break them up. Instead, she was happy to report, they were actually negotiating on a game and agreed that they would play HORSE together.

This is one way to connect what you want (protective factors) with what you are doing (SEL intervention) and provide meaningful examples of what it looks like at your school.

Practitioner's Voice

Be a listener, stay calm, and be there to help. Stay humble and share your own growth and challenges when needed. You will hear things that make you cringe. Just listen, build trust, and deepen those relationships. This is incremental in order to learn alongside your staff and is what will slowly break down mindsets and beliefs over time.

—Lacey Borgen, Teacher

Resources

Printed Material

- *Measuring Student Engagement in Upper Elementary Through High School: A Description of 21 Instruments* (https://ies.ed.gov/ncee/edlabs/regions/southeast/pdf/REL_2011098.pdf)

- *To Reduce Student Suspensions, Teachers Should Try Being More Empathetic* (Underwood, 2016).

- *How Long Do the Benefits of SEL Programs Last?* (Flynn, 2017).

(Continued)

(Continued)

- *Three Principles to Improve Outcomes for Children and Families* (https://developingchild .harvard.edu/resources/three-early-childhood-development-principles-improve-child-family-outcomes/)

Videos

- *Recent Research on Science Behind Social Emotional Learning:* https://youtu.be/FOL-Rn0QtEw

- *Health, Education, and Child Welfare: Measuring Outcomes Across Systems:* https://youtu .be/L5yqtzFBQG8

Strategies

- Build sustainability of outcomes by securing funding and financing of resources by looking at the road map to financial sustainability: http://financialsustainability.casel.org/

- Identify early learning centers to include them in your SEL work. Learn about policies to leverage outcomes when students are in early childhood by reading *A Science-Based Framework for Early Childhood Policy*: https://46y5eh11fhgw3ve3ytpwxt9r-wpengine .netdna-ssl.com/wp-content/uploads/2016/02/Policy_Framework.pdf

REFLECTION QUESTIONS

1. Looking at all you have done, what is your general impression of the work?

2. What is your plan for sustainability?

3. Are there policies and procedures that need to be changed to be aligned to your SEL work?

4. How do you plan to communicate what you learned about implementation to your stakeholders?

5. Did any of the outcomes surprise you? If so, why?

6. How will you continue the momentum you have built?

7. How will you address any of the negative outcomes that have developed because of the implementation?

Strategy #10: Fill in the Gaps of Your Foundation

Change is a journey, not a blueprint.

—**Michael Fullan (1993, p. 24)**

Filling in Gaps

Once you have looked at the outcomes of your systems change work, you can ask yourself, What needs to be done differently? For some of the work, the answer will be to continue, to maintain the status quo, or to get more information. But for other parts, where you are not progressing as you would like to or expect to, you will need to investigate features of the systems change model that you chose to guide your intervention. Regardless of which model you chose for implementation, you need to know three things—what you did, what data you collected to inform you, and what you know now. These are crucial pieces of information to understand your overall outcomes. Did your model of systems change serve your needs? What needs to be changed and what needs to be reinforced? These details help to sustain interventions in your environment.

Prepare for pushback and to reinvest in goals to stabilize the system and move forward. In a system, it is vital to process the ups and downs of your change effort. Continue to build the schema and capacity of all the stakeholders in the system. And for those in leadership roles, always keep an eye on how different parts of the implementation affect the system. Integrate new learning *as needed*. Do not be the "next best thing," or you will lose credibility from those who have seen all the next best things come and go. The power is in the process, and that is not always easily followed using only a flowchart and a five-step strategy. *Always keep an eye on the effect to the system. Ask yourself, How will this impact the system if we adopt this idea/book/curriculum?*

The Importance of Looking Back

At North Star Middle School, I recently spoke with an individual who has been implementing SEL for three years. She told me that the staff is just beginning to see the importance of understanding their "why." When the staff first talked about their understandings and beliefs about the change process for schoolwide SEL, they had little buy-in. They reported that they would have answered differently on some of the questions if they knew the surveys were important. The process of taking SEL to scale in their building has been a roller coaster. The leadership team encountered resistance—"this isn't us"—when the staff heard the results of surveys or information that had been collected by the team. They had a rotating set of assistant principals, all of whom were enthusiastic but had different goals and directions for SEL. They spent a lot of time on data collection but found that they couldn't do much with the information. Outside of the leadership team, there was little commitment from the teachers to try new strategies. Despite all of this, they had done some really great work. But they realized that they had to fill in the gaps of their foundation; the "why" wasn't universally understood by all stakeholders. Unfortunately, while the leadership team was clear with their reasons for adopting SEL, the rest of the staff wasn't there yet. This does not mean that all their work was for nothing. They learned a lot from this experience. They just realized that they needed to check for buy-in and understanding. This is part of the process. We learn, we do, we evaluate, we revisit, we try it again. SEL is systems change.

Revisiting the Past:
How Is Your Framework Meeting Your Needs?

Look at the framework to continue building fidelity for the process. Once an intervention is live in the actual school environment, it can take a different form than was intended. New things that are not evidence based can get added, et cetera. Revisiting the framework provides change agents a guide for development or getting it back on track.

You as a leader should try to keep all details in order, so you can pinpoint your journey and what the ingredients for success might be for your specific culture. Some ideas to keep in mind can be to journal for the first calendar year, to know the content of reports on the implementation, and to familiarize yourself with overall data. For the second year, you can refer to their journals for larger-scale changes, and ask yourself, What questions do I have? What is not making sense? What happened—capture the major milestones. Try to understand the status quo and take the temperature of your school community. Institutional memory is important. Form relationships in different departments and navigate politically. Who are your allies? Competition happens—what happens when you are no longer the new innovation in town? Who are your naysayers? Have a personal vision, mission, and goals to keep accountable.

Another question to ask your team is, How did we link our SEL practices to other parts of the system? Were we successful at braiding things together, such as rewards with expectations, the discipline process, and parent/family communications? SEL practices can be linked to all these items and more. Does your framework address these linkages? Did you use a tiered fidelity inventory (modified for your culture)? What is it telling you about the gaps that need to be addressed? You can summarize your answers to these questions using the chart in Figure 12.1.

Your Feedback Loop

A feedback loop is often used to make changes. When you can provide educators with information about a topic in real time, they can act on the information. A feedback loop

Figure 12.1 Systems Change Model

Systems Change Model	What Did You Do?	What Data Did You Collect?	What Do You Know?	Next Steps?
Why				
Framework				
Data collection				
Vision				
Political Understanding				
Action plan				
Infrastructure				
Plan for resistance				
Assess outcomes				

3, 2, 1 Exit Slip

When I work with coaches, I continually ask for feedback on the process, procedures, and use of SEL; on their individual processes of their work; and on what I can do to provide more to help them in their work. But at the end of the year, I ask them to reflect on their experiences, and I ask them to present to their colleagues a 3, 2, 1 Exit Slip. They share with their colleagues the three things that they did that *"rocked,"* the two things that they want to improve for the next year, and the one thing that they want to reflect on. This process has been very successful in our work, because it has provided the staff and me an understanding of their successes and challenges. But it also provided us a concrete feedback loop. The information can be used to help others who might be working on a similar challenge, and it can be encouraging that someone else saw success. The information can be used to provide support for the things the staff wants to improve. And if there were trends in the information—where they were all finding success or all finding challenges, we could use that information to target our resources.

is very helpful in understanding the gaps in your foundation. When determining the needs of your SEL intervention, you begin the feedback loop. What are the principal's understandings, needs, and actions that affect the changes you want to make? How does that inform the SEL leadership team's understandings, needs, and actions that affect SEL implementation? And how does that information affect the committees that are working on SEL? And how does that information affect the professional development that is created and delivered? And how does that information affect the staff? And how does that affect the students? Their families? Then how does each individual and process in this loop react to this information? You must continually get feedback from each of the stakeholders to understand what the needs are for your system. At the end of a feedback cycle, you hope to get reflections and recommendations that guide the next iteration of your plan, which starts the next round of feedback.

Generate and End-of-Year Report

Once you have identified your process, stakeholders must understand what you have done, what you have learned, and what the next steps are. While it may take time and effort to put together a report that gathers all you have done year over year, it is beneficial for many reasons. It provides an easy-to-read summary of the work. It can be used for groups outside of the everyday SEL work that your staff is doing, such as school board members, parent-teacher associations, or community members. It is valuable for stakeholders inside and outside of the school to understand your process. This way others do not have to reinvent the wheel if you have something that can be replicated by other schools or districts.

One of the ways an end-of-year report can be done is through an evaluative framework. Qualitative evaluation is the examination of your SEL program effectiveness conducted systematically and empirically. This type of report is helpful for individuals looking through a researcher's lens. The evaluation would include an executive summary, an introduction of the report with the purpose, any needed disclaimers or limitations, and an overview of the contents. Next the report should describe the focus of the evaluation and an overview of the evaluation procedures. Conclusions and recommendations should include as many stakeholders' inputs as possible, including dissenting views and recommendations. Include both positive and negative aspects of the program as it was implemented and the subsequent outcomes. The report should conclude with any responses to it. This report should also include appendices, including the detailed evaluation plan, copies of instruments, and detailed analyses. This is a more complex analysis that can be used.

For a more user-friendly version, I used a template with the following sections. Much of the initial work that you have done can be included in this report. The first section is acknowledgments and partnerships; this will include anyone who has directly or indirectly shaped your SEL program. The vision statement is one of the first things you would have worked on, according to this book. There should be an introduction to SEL, because you want the readers to place SEL in the context of education. In the history of the intervention section, you will likely include only the major milestones of the innovation. While this will be helpful to some, most will not want to hear how many meetings you had to have to get something accomplished. The intervention implementation plan is a shortened version of your action plan. Terms and definitions are helpful, especially since education is very acronym heavy. You want to make this report as reader friendly and not non–audience-specific as possible. The fidelity of implementation section should be brief and discuss the checks for fidelity that you have in place. A sustainability section might refer to the budget and staffing attached to your SEL initiative. And the evaluation section will show how you have determined the outcomes. In the first few years, it may be more about collecting data on the processes and procedures as you are getting these things set up. The key findings section will hopefully be your strongest section in this report, what have you learned after implementation of SEL. This section is used to make meaning of all the work that you have done in an empirical way. This is not based on opinions but instead on outcomes. Finally, the recommendation section can be used to provide your next steps. I have used it to provide recommendations from different stakeholders in the system. Change agents need to be aware of all the various invested stakeholder groups' recommendations and take them into account.

This is a list of the sections discussed above:

- ❑ Acknowledgments and partnerships
- ❑ Vision statement
- ❑ What is SEL?
- ❑ History of the intervention
- ❑ Intervention implementation plan
- ❑ Terms and definitions
- ❑ Fidelity of implementation
- ❑ Using data to guide direction
- ❑ Sustainability and evaluation
- ❑ Key findings
- ❑ Recommendations

Tell Your Story

While the report is valuable, the most paramount idea is to connect the dots for the stakeholders. Graphs and charts are impressive, but the best value of the report is to tell the reader these things: This was our need; here's what we did first, and then we did this. We learned this, which made us do this. We are doing this because the information will give us good data to give us next steps to do this. Telling the story of the innovation, making it live, is a crucial task for a leader and advocate. People want to know that what

Figure 12.2 What Is Your Story?

This was our need: _____. Here's what we did:
first _____, and
then _____.
We learned about our SEL program implementation:
To train the staff, we used this professional development: _____
The most impactful practice was _____.
Teachers need time to plan and recommended _____ to plan for
SEL lessons.
Teachers found these lessons most useful _____.
Teachers found these lessons least useful _____.
Staff uses these materials to supplement the SEL program _____.
Teachers integrated SEL into academic subjects in the following ways _____.
We gathered feedback by _____, which made us do

_____.
The data showed that _____
and our outcomes were _____.
In the future, we plan to _____.

they are doing makes a difference in the lives of children. Help them understand how they did that. You can use the form in Figure 12.2 to help you tell your story.

Celebration Time! Okay, Now Back to Work

At this stage, going into the next year of implementation, it is essential to stabilize the system to move forward. It is your responsibility as the change agent to make sure all stakeholders can get their needs met while continuing the course. This includes a continued cultivation of the system's "why." Reaffirm your message about why you are going down this path, the successes you've already seen, and the goals for the future. As you determine your long-term planning, your process will continually be evolving. It will be modified as things change, events happen, and new data is collected. But while the process and goals may be altered, the vision should remain consistent.

First, determine goals for the second year. This includes continuing and expand training for different stakeholder groups. Foster underlying whys—What are the staff's beliefs? Have they changed? Have you added additional staff? Get commitments and agreements on goals to provide continuity with the implementation even if the staff has changed.

Also, continue to invest in building schema. Building schema to understand concepts and places to store new information makes the information more acceptable. Districtwide training can provide the link to continuity for year-over-year implementation. Continue to build on schema while providing more sophisticated and mature trainings, tools, and interventions. How do they fit in the whole? What identified need do they meet?

Capitalize on successes from the first year, and add to make them grow in the second year. But don't assume that everyone is on the same page. Understand key components of interventions that are necessary, and which can be altered for the needs/wants of administration. Things that you perceive as givens may not be. Individuals may require more information or education about how your intervention/program is linked to better behavioral, social, emotional, or mental health outcomes.

Evaluate the action plan. Action planning should reflect how to maintain momentum and energize people. Get feedback from all stakeholders. This can include gathering feedback in personal conversations, in exit slips after professional development or other learning sessions, in meetings with staff, using a survey or assessment, or using other formalized means.

Revise and Resubmit: The Evolution of Your Intervention

As you, your leadership team, and your staff discover the outcomes and findings of your first year of implementation, you will discover that certain aspects require transformation. This can include staffing needs, additional interventions, work preferences, and training needs.

Look at staffing needs for the upcoming year. How many people will need to be retrained due to transition, resignation, or promotion? Embedding new staff into an intervention is an important consideration. New staff may need to know the details of your SEL interventions. You can help them with daily planning, collecting data, learning specific skills and strategies related to the intervention, and general teaching strategies. If you provide good support, teachers will use it. Institute a plan for follow-up. For example, if modeling an SEL lesson, make sure the teacher stays to watch, and schedule a meeting to discuss and ask questions.

Retain a list of resources. This can be a cumbersome endeavor, so a team member or the change agent should be responsible for collection and archiving of this information, so it is accessible to others. These resources are gold, because they help save time and energy searching for a graphic or video to embed in a training presentation, or for an article that you may want to use with your staff but also use next year with families.

Select and implement additional interventions to complement your current work. In the process of looking over your data, you may discover unforeseen gaps. Are there other interventions that complement what you are already doing that can provide a bridge for that gap?

Keep discussions about intervention on the radar. Make sure that discussions are not minimized or put in the category of last year's intervention. In one case, SEL collaboration was decreased by 30 minutes per meeting. The staff had to advocate for more time and more regular meetings. Every year, you will have a more sophisticated understanding of how the staff and administrators like to work. Take advantage of their preferences in work style to get the most out of your time with them. In many cases, you may only have one shot at good feelings about implementation. Being thoughtful should help you avoid some of the pitfalls.

Stakeholders will require specific and sometimes differentiated supports to meet their individual needs. Principals may want concrete ways that the change agent can help or assist them. A checklist can provide individuals a quick way to see how the change agent can help them with the implementation.

Here is an example of some of the things I have used to build a checklist:

Knowing what I know now, the following are how I can best support my staff for the next year of our SEL intervention:

❑ Teacher professional development

❑ Staff professional development (certificated, classified)

- ❑ Help with survey administration and results
- ❑ Support SEL curriculum through resources
- ❑ Manage universal screener data and analysis
- ❑ Assess needs for an electronic data-collection system
- ❑ Self-care strategies
- ❑ Designing a flow chart
- ❑ Setting agendas
- ❑ Staff development of decision-making process
- ❑ Data collection
- ❑ Assist in development of action plans
- ❑ Develop team member roles
- ❑ Other

Manualize Implementation (Make It Yours)

While SEL curriculums often have a manual for implementation, you may need to think about manualizing procedures that are specific to your building and context. This could include specific ways that you train staff to embed SEL in academic or classroom management procedures.

As a change agent, you should consider, What does this intervention/program/process look like in my school or district? Create a document that reflects the practices that serve your implementation. As previously discussed, context is vital in determining how the intervention will work. A manual that explains the process to anyone who is new to the system will be one of the quickest ways to bring new people on board. A manual is a great introduction to the intervention for all stakeholders, especially those who are new to your building or culture. Begin by asking yourself, What is our process? How do we go about our SEL instruction? What procedures can be manualized so that new teachers do not have to reinvent the wheel?

Include information about innovative procedures used during implementation. Some examples could include:

- ❑ Monthly themes
- ❑ Educational assistant/paraprofessional-specific trainings
- ❑ Teachable moments
- ❑ Application in the dean's or principal's office
- ❑ Problem solving for recess attendants
- ❑ Training for classified staff: bus drivers, secretaries, lunch room staff
- ❑ Books used to stimulate discussion of social and emotional skills
- ❑ Videos created or used during implementation
- ❑ Tier 2 or 3 (small group or individual) use of SEL

Time: Making and Managing This Precious Resource

In my experience, not having enough time is the most often stated roadblock to implementing SEL. As change agent, you will have the dual responsibility of advocating for more time to do this work *and* helping stakeholders to strategize to make best use of the time they have to do this work. You need to think about aspects of the work that can be lessened, eliminated, or combined. The hope is that with a collection of evidence of the impacts of your efforts, you will demonstrate that this *should* take a bigger piece of the "time pie." One strategy to help chunk the material is to create a yearly month-at-a-glance document that outlines the main or highlighted tasks that are expected for each month. With each task, estimate about how much time the teacher or staff member would need to complete it. This will help you understand whether your expectations are unrealistic due to the number of hours available for SEL work. The eventual goal is that SEL will become so seamless that the practices are integrated in the everyday skills, knowledge, language, and practice of the staff, so that time no longer is a consideration. But until that day, you will need to think about time, what it means to you and your staff, and how you can make the most of it. And the time will be spent, either on the front end through prevention and support or on the back end through remediation and repair.

Impact

Those of you who have been in the classroom know that there are moments that your classroom lessons fly and moments when they flounder. Sometimes, despite your best preparation and planning, the lesson is not as impactful as you had hoped. Yet other lessons feel like you really "hit one out of the park." I have learned to try to milk those really good ones. Once, I was working with a group, and for a month we seemed to have hit a wall, where no progress was being made, and they didn't seem to grasp the concepts we were working on. Then the next lesson something changed. And with that, I changed the plan for the next day to keep learning about this. They taught me what they needed, and I made time to enhance their progress.

Practitioner's Voice

It cannot be overstated how important it is [to] engage in a self-assessment of the school community to determine what is already in place to support the social, emotional, and behavioral needs of staff, students, and families. This allows the system to create logical next steps with stakeholders that builds on the foundation, regardless of scale, that is already established. The evolution of a system, when resources are precious, must be done with efficacy and efficiency with a laser focus on the short and long-term goals to keep moving the needle in this critical work. When we meet people where they are, honor the work they have done and create a shared vision for the future where everyone has a role, our ability to create lasting change is greatly increased.

—Tanya Fredrich, PhD, Director of Student Services

Resources

Printed Material

- "Get Happy: Four Well-Being Workouts" (Scelfo, 2017).

- "A New Model of School Reform" (Zakrzewski, 2014).

- *Creating Healthy Schools: Ten Key Ideas for Social Emotional Learning and School Climate Community* (https://www.air.org/sites/default/files/downloads/report/Ten-Key-Ideas-for-Social-Emotional-Learning-School-Climate-Occtober-2016.pdf).

Videos

- *The Happy Secret to Better Work:* https://youtu.be/fLJsdqxnZb0

- *Get Comfortable With Being Uncomfortable:* https://youtu.be/QijH4UAqGD8

- *A Teacher Can Change a Student, a School, a Community:* https://youtu.be/Sgo6jxBtPS0

Strategies

- Play "Tipping the Scales, the Resilience Game" to learn how the choices we make can help children become more resilient: https://developingchild.harvard.edu/resources/resilience-game/

- Create supportive activities for school staff that everyone can participate in out of school to build stronger connections and relationships.

  o Trivia night
  o Sports team—kickball, softball, darts, bowling, et cetera
  o Community service project for teachers and their families
  o Book club
  o Noncurriculum learning—how to cook, how to build a robot, painting, et cetera
  o Foreign language practice and travel club

REFLECTION QUESTIONS

1. Preparing for the final reports as soon as possible will save time; what is your plan to prepare?

2. What is the "feeling" of your intervention? How can you capture this feeling and discuss it?

3. What will staff changes mean to your organization and to the implementation?

4. What were your personal goals for this implementation? Were you able to achieve them? If not, will they continue to be goals for the next year?

5. Were there any key turning points during SEL implementation? If so, what are they?

6. What was the most difficult or challenging part of implementation? What did you do to deal with these challenges?

7. What was the most rewarding thing about implementing SEL?

Conclusion

Success is to be measured not so much by the position one has reached in life as by the obstacles which he has overcome while trying to succeed.

—Booker T. Washington

Your SEL intervention is a process that is informed by research that has been going on for over 20 years, but it is unique to your context. We know that negative school culture contributes to poor student outcomes and teacher dissatisfaction, which can cause educators to leave the profession. Integration of whole-school SEL will help to improve the skills and strategies that students and staff use. Any whole-school change will require us to look at it from a systems perspective. Systems change is a movement that school districts use to change school climate and culture. Individuals and leaders that we call change agents can assume leadership roles within the schools to promote better well-being and overall positive school climate. To effect change, schools can promote an environment that practices SEL and demonstrates positive relationships. Change agents can use their expertise and leadership abilities to help teachers learn social-emotional competencies that will support them and the students they teach, which will impact school culture and student outcomes positively.

The goal is to improve school environments, so students and staff feel safe and connected to the school and to each other. The purpose for these kinds of social, emotional, and behavioral interventions is to reach this goal. Social-emotional learning and practice have multiple layers. We can see these evidenced in the curriculum and the decisions that leaders make for the betterment of the school. We can see it in the culture and the way we feel when we are at school, based on our feelings of safety, engagement, and connectedness to the school. We can see it in ourselves as we make decisions about how we interact with our students and the other adults around us and how we react to stressful situations and difficult times.

This book was designed to offer strategies for individuals who are thinking about, beginning, or immersed in changing their schools to include SEL. The strategies here are based on my work and the work of others who have been involved in making change for educators and the students they serve.

The first two chapters provide an overview of the why and what of SEL. In Chapter 1 (pages 7–18), we discuss the current need for SEL and what we are seeing in our schools and classrooms that impacts us. In Chapter 2 (pages 19–31), there is a review of whole-school SEL tailored to provide evidence for different audiences.

The remaining chapters are dedicated to the ten strategies that will help change agents move their whole-school SEL interventions forward. We begin the strategies with Chapter 3, Identify Your Why (pages 33–41). We learn to tie in what staff already believes to create momentum and buy-in for our SEL intervention. We include strategies to understand and motivate our staff and create a personal goal for the work. The next strategy is in Chapter 4, Adopt a Framework (pages 43–51). This chapter emphasizes the importance of choosing a framework that meets the needs of our school or district. It describes the distinctions between a framework, a model, and an intervention and when and how we can best use these items. Strategy #3 is Do Your Detective Work—Data Collection and Data Analysis in Chapter 5 (pages 53–71). This chapter looks at the data we currently collect and the data we need to collect to provide us the most complete picture of our SEL needs. Readers are encouraged to be thoughtful about their data collection to understand what can be done with the data. The fourth strategy—Work With Others to Develop a Vision to Guide Change—is in Chapter 6 (pages 73–83). It discusses the importance of working with others to develop a vision that embeds social and emotional skill development as a priority in our school or district. This chapter discusses strategies for investing in your leadership for the SEL intervention. Understand the Politics of Your Workplace is the fifth strategy (Chapter 7, pages 85–98). This chapter considers how social networks, power, history of interventions, and norms of collaboration can all affect the acceptance and use of SEL. The importance of teams and recommendations for individuals on the team and making teaming work are focused on here.

In Chapter 8 (pages 99–112), Strategy #6, Develop an Action Plan for Implementation, is the topic. This chapter looks at various ways to embed SEL in the everyday processes and language of the school. It includes ways to make the SEL rollout help teachers feel supported and less anxious about another item on their plates. Strategy #7 is Invest in Your Infrastructure (Chapter 9, pages 113–126). This chapter focuses on the fidelity of implementation and building the capacity of various stakeholders. The education of stakeholders is broken down for students, parents/families, and the community. In Chapter 10, Strategy #8 is Plan for Resistance to Change (pages 127–137). It lists ten challenges to your SEL intervention that can occur and suggestions for how to meet those challenges. Barriers are typical of any intervention, and having strategies to mediate some of these issues can help alleviate some of the stress of your change effort. Strategy #9 is Assess Your Outcomes (Chapter 11, pages 139–146). Change agents are given ideas for using data to assess outcomes, including the use of descriptive, proximal, and distal data. Connecting the outcomes to protective factors can help to provide stakeholder investment in SEL. Finally, Strategy #10 is Fill in the Gaps of Your Foundation (Chapter 12, pages 147–156). This strategy helps us to be reflective about our practices and consider ways to tell their story. There is discussion of the evolution of our SEL intervention and how feedback can improve our procedures and processes.

Making Room for Everyone

This final note is for individuals in power positions. I was recently at a conference where I heard someone speaking about SEL efforts. I was sitting next to some paraeducators who came from a rural district to hear more about SEL. While I was listening to the speaker, I couldn't help but feel that this information was creating a barrier. I spoke with the paraeducators afterward, and they stated that this presentation made them feel like they were already behind. As leaders and change agents we must be sensitive to meeting others where they are in this work. Are we inviting people into our process, or are we creating barriers through terminology, "good versus bad," unrealistic expectations, and confusing information? I advocate for making room for those not yet on the path. Take advantage of the momentum that researchers, practitioners, and advocates have been working on for years, but don't let the wave of momentum crush those who are interested but not yet able to take part in the movement. Schools and individuals must be given the grace to own their process. Other schools/districts/states may appear to be further along in implementation of SEL. The emphasis must be on understanding and living your own practice. Focus on the growth that your system is making, and invite others along the path to learn and grow with you.

A Final Message for You: The Agent of Change

If we want to have real lasting success in leadership or advocacy, we must prove ourselves invaluable in the process of creating a better school environment. This will happen when we recognize the need for our skill sets and the use of our expertise to help others navigate the sea changes that schools are undergoing. Change agents will become more successful in their efforts when relationships with stakeholders are established. Relationships that include trust and respect will allow for our leadership efforts to be received and valued as a part of the collaborative environment of the school.

> You can improve your leadership efforts and outcomes by improving your style of leadership, by incrementally increasing your goals in reach and scope as you gain experience and credibility, by matching your needs with the needs of your followers and by understanding various leadership models. (Dollarhide, 2013, p. 18)

Patience, Persistence, and Grit

There are three characteristics that embody a change agent:

1. **Patience:** the capacity to accept or tolerate delay, trouble, or suffering without getting angry or upset

2. **Persistence:** firm or obstinate continuance in a course of action despite difficulty or opposition

3. **Grit:** courage and resolve, strength of character

Implementing SEL will require these characteristics and more of you as a change agent. Therefore, it is important to be clear about *why you believe this work is so important.* One strategy is to write a mission statement for your advocacy.

For example,

- I believe that children who learn social-emotional skills in school are better prepared for life.

- I work to create an environment that is positive.

- I want my school to be a place where kids want to be.

- I want to develop opportunities for children to be successful.

- I strive to be open and collaborative with my coworkers.

Developing a personal mission statement for your work can help when you hit a road bump. It reminds you of the purpose for your work, the big picture. This process of taking interventions to scale is difficult. It may require a grassroots movement, where early adopters must be the change that they want to see to influence others to join them. You just may be the beginning of the movement to make things better for the people in your school environment. Or you may be several years into this work and looking to revamp your strategies. Wherever you are, know that your work is valuable.

Remember that, for many in the school, this is a change of perspective. Social-emotional competencies can improve academic learning. Students who can self-regulate are better able to concentrate on math. Students who can problem solve will ask the teacher for help even if they are intimidated. Students who have strong relationship skills can assert themselves to not be pressured into cutting class. The central point here is learning. Social and emotional skills can be taught just like academic skills. You will need to accentuate this point. And when students make mistakes in their social or personal skills, which they will, you reteach. Reteaching social skills and behavioral expectations can become a norm in your school, just as remediation is provided for other subjects. When we punish students when they have made a mistake, without learning whether the mistake was due to a skill deficit, we lose. We lose that opportunity to help them learn to make better choices and different decisions. This is especially true for the students who have made many mistakes in the past. We may unintentionally set the bar lower for those kids. I advocate to keep the expectations high and build the system to teach them. Teach them how to accomplish their goals. Teach them to be successful by starting with improved social and emotional competencies. This is the calling of the change agent.

Systems change is challenging but valuable work. People who choose to dive into this work should be recognized for their bravery and leadership, but sadly they often are not. This said, I would like to take this opportunity to express my gratitude for those of you who are making things better one child, one family, one classroom, one department, one school, one district, one community at a time. Your efforts, although not always recognized, are not wasted. I have had the privilege to work with change agents who put their blood, sweat, and tears into their work, for the betterment of children who are not their own.

I see you, I acknowledge your work, and I appreciate you.

Appendix 1

SEL and System Change Strategies Rubric

Changing schoolwide systems and sustaining this change require key strategies. Change requires an examination and transformation of the infrastructure, norms, and policies within the school environment. School staff must view their current and prevalent beliefs, norms, and procedures with a new lens. This rubric is designed for change agents and stakeholders to assess their school or district on the use of these strategies.

Strategies for Systems Change	Specific Objectives of Each Strategy	We have completed 0–2 objectives for this strategy. Score = 1	We have completed 3–4 objectives for this strategy. Score = 2	We have completed 5–6 objectives for this strategy. Score = 3
Strategy #1: Identify your why.	• Identify your personal connection to SEL. • Determine the perspectives of your school climate/ school culture. • Understand current social, emotional, and behavioral issues that impact your school and district. • Find a source of positive motivation among staff. • Determine how to understand staff beliefs. • Engage in discussions about belief barriers with stakeholders.			
Strategy #2: Adopt a framework.	• Investigate frameworks that fit your culture. • Check frameworks for reasonable requirements for ability and effort. • Identify a framework that is compatible with potential SEL interventions. • Provide stakeholders with learning opportunities to understand central components of the framework. • Scan your school for current evidence-based practices that contain the active ingredients of SEL.			
Strategy #3: Do your detective work— data collection an data analysis.	• Understand local context—what has proven successful in the past and what hasn't been successful. • Identify your current data sources and needs. • Develop team training on data collection and analysis. • Begin creating or adopting a problem-solving process to use SEL data. • Conduct a needs assessment to determine your school's strengths and weaknesses. • Develop or modify your own accountability tool.			

(Continued)

(Continued)

Strategy #4: Work with others to develop a vision to guide change.	• Develop a vision statement, and get staff consensus. • Maintain standards for the vision that are braided to the school or district vision. • Create statements for stakeholders about the why and how of SEL. • Determine the principal's level of interest in, comfort with, and perceived need for the change. • Build a team of motivated individuals to guide the change process. • Embed the vision in the decision-making/problem-solving process, and reinforce actions that fall in line with the vision.			
Strategy #5: Understand the politics of your workplace.	• Analyze sources of political power and social influence in your school and district. • Discover the impact of previous intervention implementations. • Use your understanding of the school social network to develop an SEL leadership team for systems change work. • Identify what your SEL team needs, and determine what skill sets members have, to maximize use of talents. • Model good working relationships, conflict resolution skills, and a growth mindset. • Determine whether outside experts or trainers are needed to consult.			
Strategy #6: Develop an action plan for implementation.	• Perform an evaluation of what is currently happening in the system to determine whether SEL practices are SAFE. • The plan should include the goal, action steps, phases or timeline, responsible parties, and expected outcome. • Survey staff on preferred instructional practices. • Create or collect resources that support your action plan. • Check in formally and informally to get an understanding of how the plan is going, and document changes in the implementation over time, including unanticipated positive outcomes. • Address stakeholder concerns and questions.			
Strategy #7: Invest in your infrastructure.	• Develop a process to check fidelity of implementation. • Schedule professional development that meets the needs of all the staff, including yearly onboarding of new staff. • Empower student voice in your change efforts—include students' feedback, and invite them into the decision-making process for any changes that will impact them directly.			

	• Build community understanding through meetings, presentations, and communications. • Provide parents and families with a role in the systems change implementation. • Prepare for changes in leadership year over year, so the process is not derailed by turnover of administration.			
Strategy #8: Plan for resistance to change.	• Be transparent about the potential difficulty of the change process. • Highlight growth and gains in the process. • Plan for prospective challenges to SEL implementation. • Create support networks. • Reinforce the good work of stakeholders. • Provide resources and training on communication, difficult conversations, and self-care.			
Strategy #9: Assess your outcomes.	• Evaluate outcomes according to your plan, using descriptive, proximal, and distal data • Determine whether policies and resources are aligned within your system. • Plan for a consistent need for communication and clarification. • Discuss the positives and negatives of the change process with stakeholders through direct and indirect assessment. • Illustrate protective factors as outcomes of SEL interventions. • Create a plan for sustainability after assessment.			
Strategy #10: Fill in the gaps of your foundation.	• Based on your outcomes, identify next steps. • Invest in a formal feedback loop. • Review your framework, and determine whether it is meeting your needs. • Use your accountability tool to gauge progress year over year. • Generate an end-of-year report and determine the evolution of your intervention. • Understand stakeholders' experience from narratives, and determine whether you should manualize implementation.			

Rubric Score

Strategies	0–15 points Exploring and Planning	16–24 points Developing	25–30 points Leading
Total Score			

Appendix 2

Professional Development Exit Ticket

Name _____

Date _____

School _____

Professional development workshop title _____

What do we KNOW after this professional development workshop?

_____

_____

_____

_____

_____

What do we WANT to know that has not been answered today?

_____

_____

_____

_____

_____

What have we LEARNED from this presentation?

_____

_____

_____

_____

_____

How will this information BENEFIT me?

_____

_____

_____

_____

_____

Contact email (optional): _____

Appendix 3

List of Figures and Graphics

Figure 1.1   Reflections on Your Practice: Self-care

- What are my favorite things about teaching or counseling or administration? Have they changed since my first year?

- Am I being challenged at an optimal level—new learning feels invigorating versus overwhelming?

- Are the relationships that I have with my colleagues affirming? Do I seek them out to share good or bad news?

- Do my actions reflect my beliefs about students?

- What is the mindset that I go into staff meetings with?

- What things am I currently doing that I could remove or cut down and still meet the demands of my role?

- Do I have a good understanding of my priorities and make time to eliminate what is not a priority from my day?

- In what ways am I focusing on my own mental, emotional, and physical health every day?

- Am I excited to go to work today? What motivates me?

- Are my students excited to see me?

Figure 2.1 Evidence for Teachers

1. Students who participated in quality SEL instruction demonstrated improved attitudes and behaviors (Durlak J., Weissberg, Dymnicki, Taylor, & Schellinger, 2011). Students showed greater motivation to learn, deeper commitment to school, increased time devoted to schoolwork, and better classroom behavior.

2. The lead teacher is the best provider of direct instruction of social skills to students (Pelco & Reed-Victor, 2007). The lead teacher is the adult who is most often available throughout the school day to provide the students with the ongoing practice they need before they can independently demonstrate the learning-related social skills that they have learned during explicit lessons. This practice can include modeling, role-playing, and acknowledging examples of positive student behavior.

3. Students will learn best from interventions if they are done in the classroom environment (Lynch, Geller, & Schmidt, 2004). Classrooms are particularly appropriate for the implementation of prevention programs for young children, because the structured, supportive environment creates a protective factor.

4. Teacher implementation of SEL curriculum can lead to the experience of less stress, greater teaching efficacy, and greater job satisfaction (Collie, Shapka, & Perry, 2012). This study investigated whether and how teachers' perceptions of SEL and climate in their schools influenced three things—teachers' sense of stress (workload and student behavior stress), teaching efficacy, and job satisfaction. It was found that SEL has an important impact not only on students but on teachers. "In the short-term, learning new skills for SEL appears to be stressful; however, in the long term—once teachers' confidence for implementing SEL increases—they are likely to experience less stress, greater teaching efficacy, and greater job satisfaction" (p. 1198).

5. Social skills can be generalized by embedding them in lessons (McIntosh & Mackay, 2008). To create an efficiency of efforts, attention should be paid to lesson design and delivery so that multimodal prevention (behavior management, social skills, and learning strategies) is intentionally embedded within the lesson delivery of classroom teachers, paraprofessionals, and tutors.

6. Students need opportunities to practice and apply SEL skills in actual situations (Lane, Menzies, Barton-Atwood, Doukas, & Munton, 2005). To increase their mastery of social skills, students need to be provided skill instruction, and they need sufficient opportunities to master the skills that they learn, become fluent in their use, and adapt the use of these skills to a wide variety of social settings. Students are more likely to generalize the social skills they are taught if the social skills instruction focuses on targeted social behaviors that are valued and likely to be reinforced in students' natural settings. Generalization is enhanced when the social skill instruction is provided across persons and settings that the student is likely to encounter daily.

Figure 2.2 Evidence for Administrators

1. Students who participate in quality SEL instruction demonstrated fewer negative behaviors (Durlak J., Weissberg, Dymnicki, Taylor, & Schellinger, 2011). This included decreases in disruptive class behavior, noncompliance, aggression, delinquent acts, and disciplinary referrals.

2. Learning and behavior are interconnected, and schools that systemically address both academic learning and SEL have shown increased student achievement (Elliott & Kushner, 2007). Schools that use a proactive, systematic process for identifying and addressing student needs through universal and early screening across both academic and social/behavioral areas are better able to provide supports and promote skill development in the key areas before many students develop a more serious or prolonged problem that requires intensive, formalized, and expensive supports.

3. SEL enhances students' knowledge about empathy, anger management, impulse control, and bullying prevention (Edwards, Hunt, Meyers, Grogg, & Jarrett, 2005).

4. SEL programs return eleven dollars on every dollar spent (Belfield et al., 2015). This cost-benefit analysis included the reductions in aggression, substance abuse, delinquency, depression, and anxiety, and their resulting costs to the education system.

5. School environments high in connectedness promote a sense of security (Blum, 2005). A report supported by a grant from the US Department of Defense demonstrated the importance of a school environment that promotes a feeling of security through connectedness (Blum, 2005). A sense of belonging and relationships with other students and teachers were important in feeling connected to school, and nonacademic aspects of school were a significant contributor to those feelings. This report revealed seven qualities that influence students' positive attachment to school: had a sense of belonging, liked school, perceived that teachers were supportive and caring, had good friends within the school, were engaged in their current and future academic progress, believed discipline was fair and effective, and participated in extracurricular activities.

Figure 2.3   Evidence for Parents/Families

1. Students who participate in quality SEL instruction perform better academically (Durlak Weissberg, Dymnicki, Taylor, & Schellinger, 2011). Their achievement scores are an average of 11 percentile points higher than those of students who have not received SEL instruction.

2. Classrooms high in emotional support may be particularly helpful for children whose temperamental characteristics are not well matched with the demands of the classroom (Rudasill, Gallagher, & White, 2010). Highly supportive classroom climates (teacher is in tune with the needs of the students and readily responsive to them) may buffer children from lower academic achievement associated with poor attention, and children's temperamental attention and classroom emotional support work together to predict academic achievement.

3. SEL is a good return on investment (Belfield et al., 2015). The overall goal is for children to identify and understand their emotional state and to manage and communicate their emotions appropriately and so increase social competence and reduce aggressive and delinquent behaviors. The overall result suggests a good return on an SEL investment under a variety of assumptions.

4. Programs that promote academics, social skills, and school connectedness have long-term positive outcomes (Lonszak, Abbott, Hawkins, Kosterman, & Catalano, 2002). Longitudinal gains from theory-based programs that promote academic success, social competence, and bonding during elementary school can prevent risky sexual behavior and adverse health consequences in early adulthood.

5. Social competence in kindergarten predicts future wellness (Jones, Greenberg, & Crowley, 2015). A longitudinal study that followed students for 20 years determined that those rated high in social competence in kindergarten were more likely to graduate from high school, attain a college degree, and have a full-time job at the age of 25.

6. SEL competencies of middle school students predict current and future grades and test scores (Fleming et al., 2005). Results of this study indicated that higher levels of school connectedness and better social, emotional, and decision-making skills were related to higher test scores and higher grades.

Figure 2.4   Evidence for College/Career Readiness

1. Kindergarteners' social-emotional skills are a significant predictor of their future education, employment, and criminal activity (Jones, Greenberg, & Crowley, 2015). Kindergarten teachers were surveyed on their students' social competence. Researchers used that data and compared it to follow-up data collected 19 years later, when these same students were approximately 25 years old. It was found that students rated as having higher social competence in kindergarten were more likely to have graduated from college, to be gainfully employed, and to not have been arrested than students rated as having lower social skills.

2. SEL can improve the factors known to help students through college (Taylor, Oberle, Durlack, & Weissberg, 2017). This study analyzed results from 82 different programs involving more than 97,000 students from kindergarten through middle school in the US, Europe, and the UK. The effects were assessed at least six months after the programs completed. The researchers found that SEL continued to have positive effects in the classroom but was also connected to longer-term positive outcomes. Students who participated in programs graduated from college at a rate 11 percent higher than peers who did not. Their high school graduation rate was 6 percent higher. Drug use and behavior problems were 6 percent lower for program participants, arrest rates 19 percent lower, and diagnoses of mental health disorders 13.5 percent lower.

3. The top five attributes that employers seek in their applicants include leadership, ability to work in a team, communication skills (written), problem-solving skills, and communication skills (verbal) (National Association of Colleges and Employers, 2016). Four of these attributes are intentionally taught through SEL.

4. The US Department of Education has an "Employability Skills Framework" that includes effective relationships though interpersonal skills and personal qualities, critical thinking skills, and communication skills (Office of Career, Technical, and Adult Education, 2018). These skills are improved using SEL practices.

5. Students with high self-efficacy or self-awareness appear to adapt more successfully to college than students without these attributes (Ramos-Sanchez & Nichols, 2011). This study found that learning to be self-aware and self-sufficient before entering college helped students to adjust to the first year of college.

Figure 2.5   Evidence for Mental Health Practitioners

1. Students who participate in quality SEL instruction have fewer emotional distress and conduct problems than students who have not participated (Durlak, Weissberg, Dymnicki, Taylor, & Schellinger, 2011). This meta-analysis found fewer reports of student depression, anxiety, stress, and social withdrawal. Students who participated in SEL programs implemented by their teachers showed these gains in diverse communities across K–12 grade levels and locations.

2. Integrated approaches of PBIS (positive behavior interventions and supports) and SEL produced greater improvements in overall mental health than either approach alone (Cook, Frye, Slemrod, Lyon, & Renshaw, 2015). Findings from this study speak to the power of implementing a more comprehensive structure of universal supports by integrating PBIS and SEL interventions together using a blended approach both theoretically and practically speaking. This combined approach produced additive effects on mental health outcomes, including internalizing and externalizing behavior problems, beyond changes that occurred when implementing only one intervention.

3. SEL is an effective component in bullying prevention (Smith & Low, 2013). Skills taught in SEL programs contribute to the prevention of bullying at school.

4. The school environment offers an ideal setting in which to work with child survivors of trauma, as all students have accessibility to school mental health resources (Thompson & Trice-Black, 2012). Children exposed to the trauma of domestic violence tend to experience difficulties with internalized and externalized behavior problems, which can include deficits in social skills and academic functioning. Domestic violence can be a hidden issue that the school may not be aware of, so school staff cannot provide individual support to students who are living through this trauma. Whole-school SEL approaches can support those students who are experiencing trauma at home that the school and mental health practitioners are not privy to.

5. Students with disabilities can benefit from small group social instruction (Ledford & Wolery, 2013). Small group instruction provides multiple opportunities to observe social and other behaviors performed by peers, which may increase the ability to understand and perform the social skills that are reinforced at the school.

6. Nurturing environments promote well-being and reduce the impact of mental and emotional disorders (Biglan, Flay, Embry, & Sandler, 2012). Environments that are nurturing have impacts in the following ways: They minimize biologically and psychologically toxic events; teach, promote, and richly reinforce prosocial behavior, including self-regulatory behaviors; monitor and limit opportunities for problem behavior; and foster psychological flexibility— the ability to be mindful of one's thoughts and feelings and to act in the service of one's values even when one's thoughts and feelings discourage taking valued action.

Figure 2.6 Student Inclusion

What do your students need to know about SEL?	
How do you get students to buy in to learning social skills?	
What expectations need to be set for students when discussing SEL?	
How can you make these concepts relatable to students?	

Figure 2.7 Perspectives on Your School

Looking at My School as a Newcomer	What Is the School Climate?	How Does That Impact the School Culture?
From the outside the school seems. . . .		
On the Great Schools website and other websites, people are saying. . . .		
When I enter the front office, I experience. . . .		
Communication between parents who come to the school is. . . .		
When there is an emergency on the campus, the staff is. . . .		
Families who are new to the area experience. . . .		
Teachers collaborate with. . . .		
Students resolve their difficulties by. . . .		
During holidays or special occasions, we. . . .		
Staff receive appreciation when. . . .		
The pressure to succeed academically at this school feels. . . .		
The staff room is. . . .		
Certificated staff feel. . . .		
One special tradition at our school is. . . .		
Our school is known for. . . .		
Our afterschool programming promotes. . . .		
Teachers say _____ about the professional development offered.		
Administration helps teachers to. . . .		
The feeling in the lunchroom is. . . .		
The best thing about our school is. . . .		
The most challenging thing about our school is. . . .		
Community members think _____ about our school.		

Figure 4.1　Adopting a Framework

How User Friendly is it?	How Much New Learning Will We Have to Do?	How Much Effort Will It Require?	What Is the Estimated Timeline to Integrate the Framework?

Figure 5.4 Accountability Tool

Category	Expectations/ Agenda Items	Action Steps	Data Sources Documentation	Scoring Criteria	Score
Vision	Goal 1				
	Goal 2				
	Goal 3				
	Goal 4				
Teaming	Tier 1 team				
	Tier 2 team				
	District team				
Professional Staff Development	Administration				
	Teams				

Certificated staff				
Classified staff				
Out-of-school-time (OST) staff				
Whole-School SEL Competencies	Self-awareness			
	Self-management			
	Social awareness			
	Relationship skills			
	Responsible decision making			
Staff SEL Practices	Social teaching practices			
	Instructional interactions			
	Adult SEL competencies			

(Continued)

(Continued)

Data	Needs assessment				
	Universal screener				
	Surveys				
Communication	Internal				
	In district				
	External				
Outreach	Students				
	Family engagement				
	Community				

Figure 6.1 Braiding Example

Vision: (District/School or Initiative) Vision Statement Here
Goal 1:
Goal 2:
Goal 3:

Initiative, Project, or Committee	Purpose	Aligns With Which Goal	Target Group	Staff Involved	Outcomes
SEL curriculum	Teachers will deliver the selected SEL curriculum to increase their students' social and emotional competencies.	Goal 1	All students	All staff	This school year all students received 20 SEL lessons. Competencies were measured through teacher reports.
Growth mindset book study					
Bullying education					
School improvement plans					
PBIS (positive behavior interventions and supports)					
Academic curriculum					
School-based mental health services					
Afterschool programming					
MTSS/RTI					
College and career readiness					
Discipline practices					

Administrative	• Principal • Vice or assistant principals • Deans
Certified	• Teachers (grade levels represented) • Counselors • Psychologists
Classified	• Paraprofessionals or educational assistant • Secretary • Nurse
Students	
Parents/Families	

Figure 6.2 Sound Bite Examples

Question	SoundBite
What is my role in this systems change effort?	I am advocating for whole-school SEL at our school. Would you like to learn more?
Where do I practice my role?	I use SEL in my classroom and I am working with school leadership to form a team. Would you like to join the team?
When do we practice?	Team meetings will be monthly, but I practice weekly in my classroom. Would you like to drop by and watch?
How do I support this change effort?	You can support the change effort by participating in the training and advocating for SEL with me. Would you be interested in participating in a training?

Figure 6.3 Identify Change Agents

Who are your proponents for change in your school?	
Are your change agents able to collaborate across grade levels and job roles?	
Do your change agents have the trust of the staff?	
What skills do your change agents possess to advocate for change?	

Figure 6.4 Principal Checklist

Need Procedures for _____

	Steps:
A checklist	
Timeline	
Professional development	
Resources	
How can they support?	
How do they evaluate?	
How do they communicate?	

Graphic 7.1   Sociogram Table Example

Teacher	Help	Strategies	Admire	Friends
Smith	Washington	Wilson	Wilson	Ortega
Washington	Taniq	Adams	Salazar	Hamilton
Ortega	Salazar	Adams	Jefferson	Hamilton
Lincoln	Jefferson	Wilson	Jefferson	Jefferson
Adams	Washington	Taniq	Salazar	Salazar
Wilson	Ortega	Ortega	Washington	Adams
Salazar	Ortega	Hamilton	Jefferson	Adams
Taniq	Salazar	Adams	Jefferson	Adams
Jefferson	Franklin	Lincoln	Hamilton	Lincoln
Franklin	Washington	Adams	Wilson	Wilson
Williams	Taniq	Taniq	Taniq	Taniq
Hamilton	Adams	Adams	Washington	Washington
Total	Washington = 3	Adams = 5	Jefferson = 4	Adams = 3

Strategies

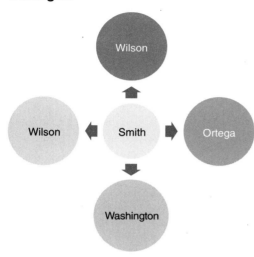

For each category:

1. Who is represented the most? Is it the same person in every category?

2. Is there anyone who was not chosen by anyone?

3. Are most of the choices mutual or one-way, where the choice is not reciprocated?

4. Do you see groupings of individuals who only choose each other?

5. Determine if you can find patterns to discover which teacher might have the most social capital to be on your team?

Figure 7.1 An Introductory Conversation About Previous Interventions

Intervention	Pros	Cons	Suggestions
Introduction to intervention			
Education of staff about intervention			
Training for intervention			
Continuing discussion of intervention			
Discussion of outcomes of intervention			
Revision of intervention as new information is learned			

Action Plan

1. Goals
2. Steps
3. Timeline
4. Person/s responsible
5. Outcome

Diffusion of Innovation

1. Elaboration on benefits
2. Compatibility to culture
3. Usability
4. Impact

Figure 8.1 Action Plan Template

Action Steps	Who Is Responsible	Resources Needed	Leadership Check	Due Date	Notes
Step 1					
Step 2					
Step 3					
Step 4					

Figure 8.2 SAFE Implementation

How Can We Implement SEL in Our School or District?	Ideas	Are They Sequenced, Active, Focused, and Explicit? (SAFE)
Freestanding lessons		
Teaching practices		
Integration of SEL into academic practices		
Systems change to support SEL		

Figure 8.3   Instructional Practices Questionnaire—Elementary

Elementary Instructional Practice as Defined in Jones et al., 2017	Definition	I Would Feel Comfortable Using this Practice to Promote SEL Skills (Yes or No).	Order of Preference for Each Skill You Marked Yes in Column to the Left.
Discussion	Discussions can occur in pairs, small groups, or class.		
Didactic instruction	Teacher provides specific instructions outside of an open discussion. This might include providing definitions, teacher modeling, or imparting specific information.		
Book/story	Teacher reads aloud a book or short story that may or may not include pictures.		
Vocabulary	Activities used to teach language, words, or terms related to specific concepts.		
Handouts	Use of a tool or material to promote specific strategies, often used to help students visualize concepts in a concrete way.		
Writing	Students are asked to write about personal experiences related to a specific theme or to record the experiences of others.		
Drawing	Drawing activity with a goal other than depicting an event or experience. The focus is on the artistic expression.		
Art/creative project	Art or creative project other than drawing that can be individual projects or a collaborative project.		
Visual display	Charts, posters, or other visual displays.		
Video	Videos that demonstrate challenging situations used to prompt group discussions.		
Song	Songs and music videos or chants used to reinforce skills; these often involve dances, hand movements, and/or strategy practice.		
Skill practice	Students actively practice skills or strategies outside of a game or role-play scenario.		
Role-play	Teacher role-plays, entire class role-plays in pairs, or two students perform in front of the class.		
Game	Can be used to reinforce themes, build community, practice specific skills, or transition students into/out of a lesson, et cetera.		
Kinesthetic	Activities involving student movement and physical activity.		
Teacher choice	Teachers are instructed to choose their own activities from a range of options, such as choosing from a selection of different games and songs based on class preferences.		

Figure 8.4 Instructional Practices Questionnaire—Middle School

Middle School Instructional Practice	Definition	I Would Feel Comfortable Using This Practice to Promote SEL Skills (Yes or No).	Order of Preference for Each Skill You Marked Yes in Column to the Left.
Discussion	Discussions can occur in pairs, small groups, or class.		
Didactic instruction	Teacher provides specific instructions outside of an open discussion. This might include providing definitions, teacher modeling, or imparting specific information.		
Book/story	Whole-class or small group discussion of book or story that covers specific scenarios or skills.		
Vocabulary	Activities used to teach language, words, or terms related to specific concepts.		
Handouts	Use of a tool or material to promote specific strategies, often used to help students visualize concepts in a concrete way.		
Writing	Students are asked to write about personal experiences related to a specific theme or to record the experiences of others.		
Art/creative project	Art or creative project other than drawing that can be individual projects or a collaborative project.		
Visual display	Charts, posters, or other visual displays.		
Video	Videos that demonstrate challenging situations used to prompt group discussions.		
Technology	The use of apps and computer programs that explicitly teach skills.		
Mindfulness	Activities involving students promoting mindful or contemplative awareness and focus.		
Project-based learning	Students acquire deeper knowledge through active exploration of real-world challenges and problems.		
Game-based learning	Using games to practice and promote skills and competencies.		

Figure 8.5 Instructional Practices Questionnaire—High School

High School Instructional Practice	Definition	I Would Feel Comfortable Using This Practice to Promote SEL Skills (Yes or No).	Order of Preference for Each Skill You Marked Yes in Column to the Left.
Discussion	Discussions can occur in pairs, small groups, or class.		
Didactic instruction	Teacher provides specific instructions outside of an open discussion. This might include providing definitions, teacher modeling, or imparting specific information.		
Book/story	Whole-class or small group discussion of book or story that covers specific scenarios or skills.		
Vocabulary	Activities used to teach language, words, or terms related to specific concepts.		
Handout	Use of a tool or material to promote specific strategies, often used to help students visualize concepts in a concrete way.		
Writing	Students are asked to write about personal experiences related to a specific theme or to record the experiences of others.		
Art/creative project	Art or creative project other than drawing that can be individual projects or a collaborative project.		
Visual display	Charts, posters, or other visual displays.		
Video	Videos that demonstrate challenging situations used to prompt group discussions.		
Technology	The use of apps and computer programs that explicitly teach skills.		
Mindfulness	Activities involving students promoting mindful or contemplative awareness and focus.		
Leadership training	Involvement in leadership tasks to reach a goal.		
Project-based learning	Students acquire deeper knowledge through active exploration of real-world challenges and problems.		
Game-based learning	Using games to practice and promote skills and competencies.		

Figure 8.6 Goal to Outcomes Action Plan Example

Goal	Steps (See Action Plan Template, Figure 8.1)	Timeline	Responsible Party	Outcome
Students and staff will learn and practice self-regulation skills.	• Freestanding lessons = mindfulness curriculum taught once a week • Teaching practices = competence building • Integration of SEL into academic practices = mindful minute before tests • Systems change to support SEL = time in day to practice strategy	Whole school year	All staff agreed to start the morning with mindfulness.	Measured by self-report and schoolwide survey

Figure 9.1 Fidelity of Implementation of SEL Intervention

Fidelity of Intervention	Lesson 1	Lesson 2	Lesson 3	Lesson 4	Lesson 5	Lesson 6
Date/time lesson taught						
Did you (1) follow the lesson verbatim, (2) alter it with agreed-upon editing by team, or (3) change it due to time or other issues?						
Did you use any additional materials to support the lesson?						
How long did it take to prep the lesson?						
Did you feel prepared to deliver the lesson?						
How do you know that the students learned the material (survey, observation, knowledge tests)?						

Figure 9.2 Example Leadership Log

August Professional development for staff	**September** Meet with SEL team Family workshop #1 Districtwide training	**October** Universal screener Meet with SEL team CASEL convention
November Meet with SEL team Meet with youth advisory board	**December** Meet with SEL team	**January** Meet with SEL team Districtwide training
February Meet with SEL team Family workshop #2	**March** Meet with SEL team	**April** Meet with SEL team SEL leadership luncheon (multidistrict)
May Meet with SEL team Districtwide training	**June** Community SEL meeting	**July** Schedule family workshops—Sept. and Feb.

Figure 10.1 Planning for Challenges

Challenge	Strategies for Change Agent	Planning for This Strategy
Intervention is not well received. Change agents receive regular negative feedback or comments. There may even be personal attacks.	• Listen deeply. • Voice difficulty. • Check your ego. • Practice self-care. • Address teacher questions.	
Staff is tired of change and just wants things to be the same; they just can't handle one more thing.	• Recognize schema is developing. • Understand limits. • Understand initiative fatigue. • Show appreciation.	
Staff believes this is just a repackaging of previous innovations. They have already tried this before.	• Conduct an inventory. • Be curious. • Demonstrate the gap. • Measure impact.	
One or more specific groups do not support the change efforts.	• Promote understanding. • Provide opportunities to observe good work. • Provide clear, consistent procedure.	
Change agents immersed in a lead implementation role face new challenges as they transition from their previous role in their school or district. New responsibilities may involve coaching or evaluation of former colleagues.	• Be transparent. • Train continuously to develop capacity. • Invite teachers to provide input.	

One individual or group actively pushes back on intervention.	• Prepare for pushback. • Understand the odds. • Respond to conflict as a normal process.	
The attitude from stakeholders is passive nonacceptance: "This too shall pass."	• Keep a list of what works. • Reinforce work of stakeholders.	
Teachers believe that this is just another tool with which they will be evaluated, not something that is meant to support them.	• Communicate with the union. • Have teachers invested in teams. • Discuss confidentiality of conversations.	
Stakeholders say they have too much on their plates. They have workload and time concerns.	• Discuss the braiding of initiatives. • Allow for sharing of concerns. • Voice acknowledgment of and respect for positions. • Capitalize on a good thing.	
	• Provide flexibility and time-saving strategies when possible. • Let them know they are not on their own.	
The intervention lacks support from the parent/family/community.	• Provide opportunities to learn. • Be aware of barriers.	

Figure 11.1 School Descriptive Data Tracker

Descriptive Data Type	Longitudinal Data	Current Data	Implications
Type of school: urban, suburban, rural			
Student/teacher ratio			
Age range of students			
Racial makeup of school			
Gender distribution			
Socioeconomic status of students and families			
Number of students who qualify for free/reduced-price lunch			
Number of students eligible for Section 504 plans			
Number of students eligible for an IEP			
Cultural backgrounds in school community			
Number of students who qualify for ELL services			
Average years of experience of classroom teachers			

Figure 11.2 How the Streams of Data Fit Together

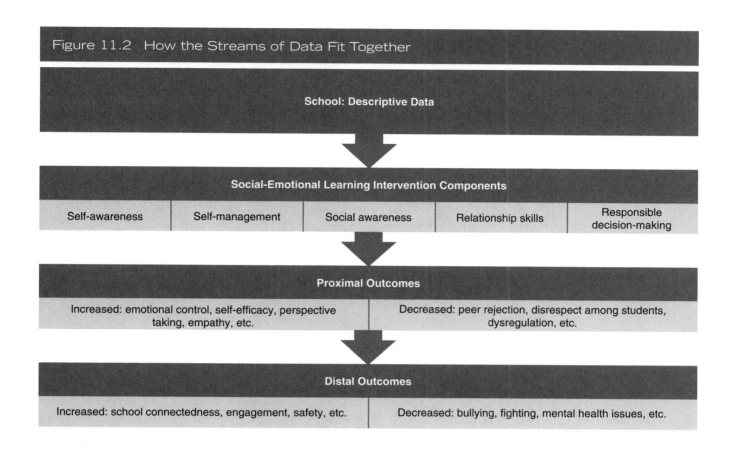

School: Descriptive Data

Social-Emotional Learning Intervention Components

| Self-awareness | Self-management | Social awareness | Relationship skills | Responsible decision-making |

Proximal Outcomes

Increased: emotional control, self-efficacy, perspective taking, empathy, etc.

Decreased: peer rejection, disrespect among students, dysregulation, etc.

Distal Outcomes

Increased: school connectedness, engagement, safety, etc.

Decreased: bullying, fighting, mental health issues, etc.

Figure 11.3   Measuring Your SEL Implementation

Outcome	Direct Assessment	Indirect Assessment	Major Finding
Positive social behavior	Evidence of positive peer relationships at school, conflict resolution, working well with others, teaming	Attendance School climate survey	
Decreased conduct problems	Evidence of a decrease in aggressive and disruptive behavior, restorative discipline practices	Referrals Suspensions Detentions	
Decreased emotional distress	Evidence of decreases in depressive symptoms, anxiety, social withdrawal, school refusal behavior, internalizing and externalizing behaviors	Counseling Crisis Attendance	
Increased engagement	Evidence of school participation, school pride	Cultural competence Equity School climate/culture Attendance	
Improved academic performance	Evidence of perseverance, grit, growth mindset	Grades Test scores Graduation rates	
Increased perception of safety	Evidence of emergency readiness and management, safety protocols, bullying and harassment training and procedures	Fighting/Assault Harassment Bullying Substance abuse	

Figure 11.4 School Outcomes and Implications of Change

School Outcomes	Historical Data	Current Findings	Implications of Change
Academic performance			
Social behavior			
Conduct problems			
Emotional distress			
Engagement			
Safety			
Environment			

Figure 11.5 Connecting Protective Factors to Practices

Protective Factor	SEL Implementation	Example at Our School
Strong, prosocial peer relationships	1. Four lessons per semester from SEL curriculum on positive relationship skills 2. Students intentionally paired with students they could build a relationship with for science project 3. Teacher uses cooperative learning practice during instruction 4. Students encouraged to play games that strengthen their team-building skill at recess 5. Workshops for parents/families on SEL to reinforce relationship skills	Recess was a typically trying time for our elementary students. The educational assistants who were on duty reported that they spent most of their time managing groups of students who were arguing about the playground equipment. Soon after implementation, Ms. S reported that she saw two of the students who regularly argued over who got the "good" basketball. She walked over to them expecting to have to break them up. Instead, she was happy to report, they were actually negotiating on a game and agreed that they would play HORSE together.

Figure 12.1 Systems Change Model

Systems Change Model	What Did You Do?	What Data Did You Collect?	What Do You Know?	Next Steps?
Why				
Framework				
Data collection				
Vision				
Political understanding				
Action plan				
Infrastructure				
Plan for resistance				
Assess outcomes				

Figure 12.2   What Is Your Story?

This was our need: _____. Here's what we did:

first _____, and

then _____.

We learned about our SEL program implementation:

To train the staff, we used this professional development: _____.

The most impactful practice was _____.

Teachers need time to plan and recommended _____ to plan for SEL lessons.

Teachers found these lessons most useful _____.

Teachers found these lessons least useful _____.

Staff uses these materials to supplement the SEL program _____.

Teachers integrated SEL into academic subjects in the following ways _____.

We gathered feedback by _____, which made us do

_____.

The data showed that _____

and our outcomes were _____.

In the future, we plan to _____.

References

Aber, L., Brown, J., Jones, S., Berg, J., & Torrente, C. (2011). School-based strategies to prevent violence, trauma, and psychopathology: The challenges of going to scale. *Development and Psychopathology, 23,* 411–421. doi:10.1017/S09554579411000149

Adelman, H., & Taylor, L. (n.d.). *Frameworks for systemic transformation of student and learning supports.* Los Angeles: Center for Mental Health at Schools in UCLA. https://blog.apastyle.org/apastyle/2010/11/how-to-cite-something-you-found-on-a-website-in-apa-style.html

Aguilar, E. (2018, May 25). *Building teams that stay.* Retrieved from https://www.edutopia.org/article/building-teams-stay

Belfield, C., Bowden, B., Klapp, A., Levin, H., Shand, R., & Zander, S. (2015). *The economic value of social and emotional learning.* New York, NY: Center for Benefit-Cost Studies in Education.

Berg, J., Osher, D., Moroney, D., & Yoder, N. (2017). *The intersection of school climate and social and emotional development.* Washington, DC: American Institutes of Research.

Berg, J., Osher, D., Same, M., Nolan, E., Benson, D., & Jacobs, N. (2017). *Identifying, defining, and measuring social and emotional competencies.* Washington, DC: American Institutes for Research.

Berman, S., Chaffee, S., & Sarmiento, J. (2018, March 12). *The practice base for how we learn: Supporting students' social, emotional, and academic development.* Aspen, CO: The Aspen Institute.

Biglan, A., Flay, B., Embry, D., & Sandler, N. (2012). The critical role of nurturing environments for promoting well-being. *American Psychologist, 67*(4), 257–271.

Blum, R. (2005). *School connectedness: Improving the lives of students.* Baltimore, MD: Johns Hopkins Bloomberg School of Public Health.

Bolman, L., & Deal, T. (2003). *Reframing organizations: Artistry, choice, and leadership* (3rd ed.). New York, NY: Jossey-Bass.

Busch, B. (2018, January 4). *Research every teacher should know: Growth mindset.* Retrieved from https://www.edutopia.org/article/building-teams-stay

Carr, P., & Walton, G. (2014). Cues of working together fuel intrinsic motivation. *Journal of Experimental Social Psychology, 53,* 169–184.

Celio, C., Durlak, J., & Dymnicki. (2011). A meta-analysis of the impacts of service-learning on students. *Journal of Experiential Education, 34*(2), 164–181.

Center on the Developing Child, Harvard University. (2018). *Our innovative approach.* http://www.developingchild.harvard.edu

Centers for Disease Control and Prevention. (2018). *About adverse childhood experiences.* Retrieved from https://www.cdc.gov/violenceprevention/acestudy/about_ace.html

Clarke, A., & Dawson, R. (1999). *Evaluation research: An introduction to principles, methods and practice.* London, UK: SAGE.

Collaborative for Academic, Social, and Emotional Learning (CASEL). (2012). *2013 CASEL guide: Effective social and emotional learning programs* (Preschool and elementary school ed.). Chicago, IL: Author.

Collaborative for Academic, Social, and Emotional Learning. (CASEL). (2017). *Sample teaching activities to support core competencies of social and emotional learning.* Chicago, IL: Author.

Collaborative for Academic, Social, and Emotional Learning. (CASEL). (2018). *History.* Retrieved from https://casel.org/history/

Collie, R., Shapka, J., & Perry, N. (2012). School climate and social-emotional learning: Predicting teacher stress, job satisfaction, and teaching efficacy. *Journal of Educational Psychology, 104*(4), 1189–1204.

Collins, J. (2001, October). *Good to great.* Retrieved from http://www.jimcollins.com/article_topics/articles/good-to-great.html

Colvin, G., & Sprick, R. (1999). Providing administrative leadership for effective behavior support: Ten strategies for principals. *Effective School Practices, 4,* 65–71.

Cook, C. R., Frye, M., Slemrod, T., Lyon, A., & Renshaw, T. Z. (2015). An integrated approach to universal prevention: Independent and combined effects of PBIS and SEL on youths' mental health. *School Psychology Quarterly, 30*(2), 166–180.

Cook, C. R., Volpe, R., & Livanis, A. (2010). Constructing a roadmap for future universal screening research beyond academics. *Assessment for Effective Intervention, 35*(4), 197–205.

DeGraff, J. (2009). How you innovate is what you innovate. In *The 2009 Pfeiffer annual: Leadership development* (pp. 188–200). Retrieved from https://www.innovatrium.org/wp-content/uploads/2013/12/How-you-innovate-article-2009.pdf

Depaoli, J., Atwell, M., & Bridgeland, J. (n.d.). *Ready to lead: A national principal survey on how social and emotional learning can prepare children and transform schools.* report for CASEL. Washington, DC: Civic Enterprises with Hart Research Associates.

Dollarhide, C. (2013, July/August). The messy process of school counselor leadership. *ASCA School Counselor,* 10–18.

Doss, H. (2016, June 1). It's time to build a national innovation infrastructure. *Forbes.* Retrieved from https://www.forbes.com/sites/henrydoss/2016/06/01/its-time-to-build-a-national-innovation-infrastructure/#6ce49ca01dfd

Dotterer, A., & Lowe, K. (2011). Classroom context, school engagement, and academic achievement in early adolescence. *Journal of Youth Adolescence,* 1649–1660. doi:10.1007/s10964-011-9647-5

Durlak, J. (2015). What everyone should know about implementation. In J. A. Durlak, C. E. Domitrovich, R. P. Weissberg, & T. P. Gullotta (Eds.), *Handbook of Social and Emotional Learning* (pp. 395–405). New York, NY: Guilford Press.

Durlak, J., Domitrovich, C., Weissberg, R., & Gullotta, T. (Eds.). (2015). *Handbook of Social and Emotional Learning: Research and Practice.* New York, NY: Guilford Press.

Durlak, J., Weissberg, R., Dymnicki, A., Taylor, R., & Schellinger, K. (2011). The impact of enhancing students' social and emotional learning: A meta-analysis of school-based universal interventions. *Child Development, 82*(1), 405–432.

Durlak, J., Weissberg, R., & Pachan, M. (2010). A meta-analysis of after-school programs that seek to promote personal and social skills in children and adolescents. *American Journal of Community Psychology, 45,* 294–309.

Durlak, J., & Wells, A. (1997). Primary prevention mental health programs for children and adolescents: A meta-analytic review. *American Journal of Community Psychology, 25,* 115–152.

Edwards, D., Hunt, M., Meyers, J., Grogg, K., & Jarrett, O. (2005). Acceptability and student outcomes of a violence prevention curriculum. *Journal of Primary Prevention, 26*(5), 401–418.

Elias, M., Leverett, L., Duffell, J. C., Humphrey, N., Stepney, C., & Ferrito, J. (2016, March 24). *How to implement social and emotional learning at your school.* Retrieved from https://www.edutopia.org/blog/implement-sel-at-your-school-elias-leverett-duffell-humphrey-stepney-ferrito

Elias, M., Zins, J., Graczyk, P., & Weissberg, R. (2003). Implementation, sustainability, and scaling up of social-emotional and academic innovations in public schools. *School Psychology Review, 32*(3), 303–319.

Elliott, J., & Kushner, S. (2007). The need for a manifesto for educational programme evaluation. *Cambridge Journal of Education, 37*(3), 321–336. doi:10.1080/03057640701546649

Every Student Succeeds Act (ESSA). (2015). 20 U.S.C. ch. 28 § 1001 et seq. 20 U.S.C. ch. 70

Felitti, V., Anda, R., Nordenberg, D., Williamson, D., Splitz, A., Edwards, V., . . . & Marks, J. (1998). Relationship of childhood abuse and household dysfunction to many of the leading causes of death in adults. *American Journal of Preventative Medicine, 14*(4), 245–258.

Fixsen, D., Naoom, S., Blase, K., Friedman, R., & Wallace, F. (2005). *Implementation research: A synthesis of the literature.* Tampa: University of South Florida, Louis de la Parte Florida Mental Health Institute, National Implementation Research Network.

Fleming, C. B., Haggerty, K., Catalano, R., Harachi, T., Mazza, J., & Gruman, D. (2005). Do social and behavioral characteristics targeted by preventive interventions predict standardized test scores and grades? *Journal of School Health, 75,* 342–349.

Florida Department of Education. (2017). *MTSS implementation guide.* Tallahassee, FL: Author.

Flynn, M. (2017, August 30). How long do the benefits of SEL programs last? *Greater Good magazine.* Retrieved from https://greatergood.berkeley.edu/article/item/how_long_do_the_benefits_of_sel_programs_last

Fullan, M. (1993). *Change forces: Probing the depths of educational reform.* London, UK: Falmer Press.

Fullan, M. (2001). *The new meaning of educational change.* New York, NY: Teachers College Press.

Fullan, M. (2003). *The moral imperative of school leadership.* Thousand Oaks, CA: Corwin Press.

Gimbel, P., & Leana, L. (2013). *Healthy Schools: The Hidden Component of Teaching and Learning.* New York, NY: Rowman & Littlefield Education.

Greenberg, M., Brown, J., & Abenavoli, R. (2016). *Teacher stress and health effects on teachers, students and schools.* University Park: Edna Bennett Pierce Prevention Research Center, Pennsylvania State University.

Gruenert, S. (2008, March/April). School culture, school climate: They are not the same thing. *Principal,* 87(4), 56–59.

Harter, J., & Blacksmith, N. (2012, February 7). *Engaged workers immune to stress from long commutes.* Retrieved from https://news.gallup.com/poll/152501/engaged-workers-immune-stress-long-commutes.aspx

Hattie, J., & Timperley, H. (2007). The power of feedback. *Review of Educational Research, 77*(1), 81–112.

Individuals With Disabilities Education Act (IDEA). (2004). 20 U.S.C. § 1400 et seq.

Ingersoll, R., Merrill, L., & Stuckey, D. (2014). *Seven trends: the transformation of the teaching force.* Philadelphia, PA: Consortium for Policy Research in Education.

Jakes, D. (2013, March 5). *How to learn.* https://www.howtolearn.com/2013/03/how-to-change-school-climate-to-improve-school-culture/

Jones, D., Greenberg, M., & Crowley, M. (2015). Early social-emotional functioning and public health: The relationship between kindergarten social comptence and future wellness. *American Journal of Public Health, 105*(11), 2285–2290. doi:10.2105/AJPH.2015.302630

Jones, S., Brush, K., Bailey, R., Brion-Meisels, G., McIntyre, J., Kahn, J., . . . & Stickle, L. (2017). *Navigating SEL from the inside out.* Cambridge, MA: Harvard Graduate School of Education.

Kane, T. (2014). *Shooting bottle rockets at the moon: Overcoming the legacy of incremental educational reform.* Retrieved from https://www.brookings.edu/research/shooting-bottle-rockets-at-the-moon-overcoming-the-legacy-of-incremental-education-reform/

Keller, M., Chang, M., Becker, E., Goetz, T., & Frenzel, A. (2014). Teachers' emotional experiences and exhaustion as predictors of emotional labor in the classroom: An experience sampling study. *Frontiers in Psychology, 5*(1442).

Kendziora, K., & Yoder, N. (2016). *When districts support and integrate social and emotional learning (SEL)*. Washington, DC: American Institutes for Research.

Ladd, G., & Burgess, K. (2001). Do relational risks and protective factors moderate the linkages between childhood aggression and early psychological and school adjustment? *Child Development, 72,* 1579–1601.

Lane, K., Menzies, H., Barton-Atwood, S., Doukas, G., & Munton, S. (2005). Designing, implementing, and evaluating social skills interventions. *Preventing School Failure, 49*(2), 18–26.

Ledford, J., & Wolery, M. (2013). Peer modeling of academic and social behaviors during small-group direct instruction. *Exceptional Children, 79*(4), 439–458.

Lee, C., & Walz, G. (Eds.). (1998). *Social action: A mandate for counselors*. Alexandria, VA: American Counseling Association and Educational Resources Information Center Counseling and Student Services Clearinghouse.

Lewis, C., Battistich, V., & Schaps, E. (1990). School-based primary prevention: What is an effective program? *New Directions for Child and Adolescent Development, 50,* 35–59.

Lewis, J., Arnold, M., House, R., & Toporek, R. (2003). *Advocacy competencies*. Retrieved from https://www.counseling.org/Resources/Competencies/Advocacy_Competencies.pdf

Litvinov, A., Alvarez, B., Long, C., & Walker, T. (2018, August 3). 10 challenges facing public education today. *NEA today.* http://neatoday.org/2018/08/03/10-challenges-facing-public-education-today/

Lonszak, H., Abbott, R., Hawkins, D., Kosterman, R., & Catalano, R. (2002). Effects of the Seattle social development project on sexual behavior, pregnancy, birth, and sexually transmitted disease outcomes by age 21 years. *Pediatrics & Adolescents Medicine, 156,* 438–447.

Lopez, S., & Sidhu, P. (2013, March 28). *U.S. teachers love their lives, but struggle in the workplace*. Retrieved from https://news.gallup.com/poll/161516/teachers-love-lives-struggle-workplace.aspx

Lynch, K., Geller, S., & Schmidt, M. (2004). Multi-year evaluation of the effectiveness of a resilience-based prevention program for young children. *Journal of Primary Prevention, 24*(3), 335–353.

McClelland, D. C., Atkinson, J., Clark, R., & Lowell, E. (1953). *The achievement motive*. New York, NY: Appleton-Century-Crofts.

McIntosh, K., & Mackay, L. (2008). Enhancing generalization of social skills: Making social skills curricula effective after the lesson. *Beyond Behavior, 18*(1), 18–25.

Miller, D. (2010, October 12). Defining "fidelity of implementation" in the context of RTI implementation [Web log post]. Retrieved from http://www.rtinetwork.org/rti-blog/entry/1/107

Moolenaar, N. (2012). A social network perspective on teacher collaboration in schools: Theory, methodology, and applications. *American Journal of Education, 119,* 7–39.

Moroney, D., & McGarrah, M. (2015). *Are you ready to assess social and emotional development?* Washington, DC: SEL Solutions at American Institutes for Research.

Myrick, R. (1977). *Consultation as a counselor intervention*. Washington, DC: American School Counselor Association.

National Alliance on Mental Illness (NAMI). (2016, September 21). *Mental health facts children and teens*. Retrieved from https://www.nami.org/NAMI/media/NAMI-Media/Infographics/Children-MH-Facts-NAMI.pdf

National Alliance on Mental Illness (NAMI). (2017, May 7). *NAMI celebrates mental health month* [Press release]. Retrieved from https://www.nami.org/Press-Media/Press-Releases/2017/NAMI-Celebrates-Mental-Health-Month

National Association of Colleges and Employers. (2015, November). *Job Outlook 2016*. Bethlehem, PA: Author.

National Center on Safe Supportive Learning Environments. (2018). *ED school climate surveys (EDSCLS)*. Retrieved from Safe Supportive Learning: https://safesupportivelearning.ed.gov/edscls/measures

National Child Traumatic Stress Network. (2018). *Secondary traumatic stress*. Retrieved from https://www.nctsn.org/trauma-informed-care/secondary-traumatic-stress

National Institute for Urban School Improvement. (2018). *Systemic change framework rubrics assessment handbook*. Retrieved from http://ea.niusileadscape.org/docs/FINAL_PRODUCTS/LearningCarousel/rubrics_assessment_handbook.pdf

Oberle, E., & Schonert-Reichl, K. (2016). Stress contagion in the classroom? The link between classroom teacher burnout and morning cortisol in elementary school students. *Social Science & Medicine, 159,* 30–37.

Office of Career, Technical, and Adult Education. (2018). *Employability skills framework handout*. Washington, DC: U.S. Department of Education.

Ohn, J., & Wade, R. (2009). Community service-learning as a group inquiry project: Elementary and middle school CiviConnections teachers' practices of integrating historical inquiry in community service-learning. *Social Studies, 100*(5), 200–211.

Paluck, E. L., Shepherd, H., & Aronow, P. M. (2016, January). *Changing climates of conflict: A social network experiment in 56 schools*. Retrieved from wws.princeton.edu/faculty-research/research/item/changing-climates-conflict-social-network-experiment-56-schools

Patton, M. (2003). *Qualitative evaluation checklist*. Retrieved from https://wmich.edu/sites/default/files/attachments/u350/2018/qual-eval-patton.pdf

Pausch, R. (2008). *The last lecture*. New York, NY: Hyperion.

Pelco, L., & Reed-Victor, E. (2007). Self-regulation and learning-related social skills: Intervention ideas for elementary school students. *Preventing School Failure, 51*(3), 36–42.

Pianta, R., & Walsh, D. (2013). *High-risk children in schools: Constructing sustaining relationships.* New York, NY: Routledge.

Pietarinen, J., Pyhalto, K., Soini, T., & Salmela-Aro, K. (2013). Reducing teacher burnout: A socio-cultural approach. *Teaching and Teacher Education, 35,* 62–72.

Pink, D. (2006). *A whole new mind: Why right-brainers will rule the future.* New York, NY: Penguin.

Pink, D. (2012). *To sell is human: The surprising truth about moving others.* New York, NY: Riverhead Books.

Ramos-Sanchez, L., & Nichols, L. (2011). Self-efficacy of first-generation and non-first-generation college students: The relationship with academic performance and college adjustment. *Journal of College Counseling, 10*(1), 6–18.

Rathvon, N. (2008). *Effective school interventions.* New York, NY: Guilford Press.

Ratts, M., & Chen-Hayes, S. (2007). The ACA advocacy competencies: A social justice advocacy framework for professional school counselors. *Professional School Counselor, 11*(2), 90–97. doi:10.5330/PSC.n.2010-11.90

Rimm-Kaufman, S., & Hulleman, C. (2015). SEL in elementary school settings: Identifying mechanisms that matter. In J. Durlak, C. Domitrovich, R. Weissberg, & T. Gullotta (Eds.), *Handbook of social and emotional learning: Research and practice* (pp. 151–166). New York, NY: Guilford Press.

Rivera, R., & Jimenez, Y. (n.d.). *Mikva challenge: A strong advocate for youth voice.* Retrieved from https://casel.org/mikva-challenge/

Rogers, J. (2015). *A before-school counselor intervention that promotes peer relational skills and influences prosocial behavior.* UNM Digital Repository. Retrieved from https://digitalrepository.unm.edu/educ_ifce_etds/8/

Rowling, J. K. (2008, June 5). *Harvard University commencement address.* Cambridge, MA.

Roysircar, G. (2009). The big picture of advocacy: Counselor, heal society and thyself. *Journal of Counseling and Development, 87,* 288–294.

Rudasill, K., Gallagher, K., & White, J. (2010). Temperamental attention and activity, classroom emotional support, and academic achievement in third grade. *Journal of School Psychology, 48,* 113–134.

Safir, S. (2014). *Listening dyads can transform your team.* Retrieved from https://www.edutopia.org/blog/listening-dyads-transform-team-shane-safir

Savin-Baden, M., & Howell Major, C. (2013). *Qualitative research: The essential guide to theory and practice.* London, UK: Routledge.

Scelfo, J. (2017, April 5). Get happy: Four well-being workouts. *New York Times.* Retrieved from https://www.nytimes.com/2017/04/05/education/edlife/get-happy-four-well-being-workouts.html

Schaps, E. (2003). Creating a school community. *Creating Caring Schools, 60*(6), 31–33.

Shapiro, E. (2014). *Tiered instruction and intervention in a Response-to-Intervention model.* RTI Action Network, 381. Retrieved from http://rtinetwork.org

Shechtman, Z., & Mor, M. (2010). Groups for children and adolescents with trauma-related symptoms: Outcomes and processes. *International Journal of Group Psychotherapy, 60*(2), 221–244.

Shenk, D. (2010). *The genius in all of us: Why everything you've been told about genetics, talent and IQ is wrong.* New York, NY: Doubleday.

Slavin, R. (2008). What works? Issues in synthesizing educational program effectiveness. *Educational Researcher, 37*(1), 5–14.

Slavin, R. (2017, May 25). Reviewing social and emotional learning for ESSA: MOOSES, not parrots [Web log post]. Retrieved from https://robertslavinsblog.wordpress.com/category/social-and-emotional-learning

Smith, B., & Low, S. (2013). The role of social-emotional learning in bullying prevention efforts. *Theory into practice, 52*(4), 280–287.

Snyder, T. D., & Dillow, S. A. (2015, November). *Digest of education statistics 2013.* Washington, DC: U.S. Department of Education, National Center for Education Statistics. https://nces.ed.gov/pubs2015/2015011.pdf

Substance Abuse and Mental Health Services Administration. (2018). *Adverse childhood experiences.* Retrieved from https://www.samhsa.gov/capt/practicing-effective-prevention/prevention-behavioral-health/adverse-childhood-experiences

Swartz, R., & McElwain, N. (2012). Preservice teachers' emotion-related regulation and cognition: Associations with teachers' responses to children's emotions in early childhood classrooms. *Early Education and Development, 23*(2), 202–226.

Tatar, M. (2009). Teachers turning for help to school counsellors and colleagues: Toward a mapping of relevant predictors. *British Journal of Guidance & Counseling, 37*(2), 107–127.

Taylor, R., Oberle, E., Durlack, J., & Weissberg, R. (2017). Promoting positive youth development through school-based social and emotional learning interventions: A meta-analysis of follow-up effects. *Child Development, 4,* 11–56. doi:10.1111/cdev.12864

Technical Assistance Center on Positive Behavioral Interventions and Supports. (2010). *Implementation blueprint and self-assessment.* Washington, DC: U.S. Department of Education, Office of Special Education Programs. Retrieved from https://www.pbis.org/common/cms/files/pbisresources/SWPBS_ImplementationBlueprint_vSep_23_2010.pdf

Thompson, E., & Trice-Black, S. (2012). School-based group interventions for children exposed to domestic violence. *Journal of Family Violence, 27,* 233–241. doi:10.1007/s10896-012-9416-6

Todd, A. (2018, November 19). *PBISApps.* Retrieved from https://www.pbisapps.org/community/Pages/Top-5-TIPS-Tips-for-Teams

Underwood, E. (2016, April 25). To reduce student suspensions, teachers should try being more empathetic. *Science.* Retrieved from http://www.sciencemag.org/news/2016/04/reduce-student-suspensions-teachers-should-try-being-more-empathetic

US Department of Health and Human Services, Centers for Disease Control and Prevention. (2009, July). *Fostering school connectedness.* Retrieved from https://www.cdc.gov/healthyyouth/protective/pdf/connectedness_administrators.pdf

Van Der Kolk, B. (2014). *The body keeps the score: Brain, mind, and body in the healing of trauma.* New York, NY: Penguin Books.

Vare, P., & Scott, W. (2007). Learning for a change: Exploring the relationship between education and sustainable development. *Journal of Education for Sustainable Development, 1*(2), 191–198.

Walker, J. (1997). The relationship between social support and professional burnout among public secondary school teachers in northeast Tennessee [Doctoral dissertation]. Retrieved from Electronic Theses and Dissertations, Paper 2988. http://dc.etsu.edu/etd/2988

Wallace Foundation. (2013). *The School Principal as Leader: Guiding Schools to Better Teaching and Learning.* Retrieved from http://www.wallacefoundation.org/knowledge-center/Documents/The-School-Principal-as-Leader-Guiding-Schools-to-Better-Teaching-and-Learning-2nd-Ed.pdf

Weisskopf, V. (1998). *The privilege of being a physicist.* New York, NY: W. H. Freeman.

Wilson, D. (2015, July 22). *Transform teaching with the diffusion of innovation.* Retrieved from https://www.edutopia.org/blog/transform-teaching-diffusion-of-innovation-donna-wilson-marcus-conyers

Wooden, J., & Jamison, S. (1997). *A lifetime of observations and reflections on and off the court.* New York, NY: McGraw Hill.

Woolf, S., & Johnson, R. (2005, Nov.). The break-even point: When medical advances are less important than improving the fidelity with which they are delivered. *Annals of Family Medicine, 3*(6), 545–552.

Yeager, D. S., & Walton, G. (2011). Social-psychological interventions in education: They're not magic. *Review of Educational Research, 81*(2), 267–301. doi:10.3102/003465431140599A9

Zakrzewski, V. (2014, May 21). A new model of school reform. *Greater Good Magazine.* Retrieved from https://greatergood.berkeley.edu/article/item/a_new_model_of_school_reform

Zins, J., Weissberg, R., Wang, M., & Walberg, H. (Eds.). (2004). *Building academic success on social and emotional learning: What does the research say?* New York, NY: Teachers College Press.

Index

A SAGE Publishing Company

Helping educators make the greatest impact

CORWIN HAS ONE MISSION: to enhance education through intentional professional learning.

We build long-term relationships with our authors, educators, clients, and associations who partner with us to develop and continuously improve the best evidence-based practices that establish and support lifelong learning.

Solutions YOU WANT | Experts YOU TRUST | Results YOU NEED

EVENTS

>>> **INSTITUTES**

Corwin Institutes provide large regional events where educators collaborate with peers and learn from industry experts. Prepare to be recharged and motivated!

corwin.com/institutes

ON-SITE PD

>>> **ON-SITE PROFESSIONAL LEARNING**

Corwin on-site PD is delivered through high-energy keynotes, practical workshops, and custom coaching services designed to support knowledge development and implementation.

corwin.com/pd

>>> **PROFESSIONAL DEVELOPMENT RESOURCE CENTER**

The PD Resource Center provides school and district PD facilitators with the tools and resources needed to deliver effective PD.

corwin.com/pdrc

ONLINE

>>> **ADVANCE**

Designed for K–12 teachers, Advance offers a range of online learning options that can qualify for graduate-level credit and apply toward license renewal.

corwin.com/advance

Contact a PD Advisor at (800) 831-6640 or visit www.corwin.com for more information